SECOND EDITION

Handling of
Radiation Accident Patients
by Paramedical and Hospital Personnel

Thomas A. Carder

CRC Press
Boca Raton   Ann Arbor   London   Tokyo

The logo for this publication, designed and drawn by the author, was investigated between 1977 and 1981 for use as the logo for the 1981 edition of this publication. No use of the logo by any organization or firm was revealed. The logo is, therefore, claimed by the copyright owner. The logo is intended to portray a professional union between the medical and field emergency medical services who, together, provide quality care to victims of radiation accidents. Although the logo is claimed by the copyright owner, organizations and service providers who wish to display the logo may do so while providing for the handling of radiation accident patients.

Library of Congress Cataloging-in-Publication Data

Catalog record is available from the Library of Congress.

International Standard Book Number 0-8493-8696-9

Printed in the United States of America   1 2 3 4 5 6 7 8 9 0

Printed on acid-free paper

ABOUT THE AUTHOR

In twelve years of emergency medical service, Mr. Carder has come to believe that additional education on the handling of radiation accident patients should be provided for those persons charged with the responsibility for the care of victims of accidents. Mr. Carder has served as a Radiation Safety Officer for a US Nuclear Regulatory Commission (NRC) ^{60}Co license and has received training and education in the field of Radiological Health Physics as well as experience in handling radioactive materials. His education and experience in radiological health physics and emergency medical service provide him with the background to write this book. This book should provide much information and education for any interested individual or agency, emergency services or otherwise, thereby replacing most common fears with respect for and knowledge of the possible hazards surrounding radiological incidents involving patients. This should enable the student to provide an adequate service through knowledge.

However comprehensive or extensive this text may be, it is written in such a manner that the reader does not need to have previous education or experience in radiological science. All readers should have no trouble understanding the material within.

H. S. Stocks

Since Mr. Stocks provided comments for the 1981 publication, Mr. Carder has become a professional Nuclear Emergency Planner at nuclear power utilities as a consultant, as a utility staff member, and as a member of the plant emergency response organization.

The Publisher

ACKNOWLEDGEMENTS

Thanks go to the following who have provided valuable information and assistance in ensuring the accuracy of particular points within this text:

Anita M. Barnette, B.S.-Radiological Health Science, Health Physicist
Debra A. Bookser , Senior Policy Specialist
Russell N. Bookser, Technological Hazards Specialist, with experience as an E.M.T, a police officer, and a firefighter
Henry C. Briggs, Ph.D.-Engineering, C.H.P.
Jeff B. Burnett, M.S.-Nuclear Engineering, Health Physicist
Gilbert H. Cosnett, E.M.T, M.I.C.P.
W. K. Evans, M.S.-Physics
Shirley A. Fry, M.B., B. Ch., M.P.H.
James F. Hefner , M.D.
Russell A. Jones, M.D.
Douglas C. Kay, M.S.-Nuclear Engineering, Health Physicist
Perry D. Knowles, M.D.
Roger E. Linnemann, M.D.
Tom Linnemann, B.S.-Nuclear Medicine Technology
Jose A. Luna, Radiation Protection Technician
James A. McGehee, E.M.T.I.
Z. L. Olkowski, M.D., Ph.D.-Radiation Biology
Michel S. Pawlowski , M.S.-Biochemistry
Kedar N. Prasad, Ph.D.-Radiation Biology
Coy M. Rice, Senior Reactor Operator
James M. Stavely, Jr., B.S.-, M.S.-Nuclear Engineering
Hal S. Stocks, Radiological Health Chief
Donald W. Waddell, B.S.-Physics

Special thanks to Mr. Rice, Dr. Hefner, Dr. Briggs, Dr. Fry, and Dr. Prasad for their patience with my impatience. Special thanks go also to Debra and Russell Bookser for their level of detail in proof reading the manuscript.

Mr. Danney R. Rodgers deserves special notice due to his patience in helping me learn how to use Macintosh computers and software.

NOTE

This text is a comprehensive "manual" for persons involved in emergency medical service to radiation accident patients. Although the material is not highly technical, there are numerous points of parascientific nature and as such would be difficult to absorb as a good novel. It is suggested that this text be made readily available to responding personnel to enable periodic and timely review of the information within.

With this information and suggested guidelines at your disposal, you should be better prepared for entering the relatively new field of emergency services, the

HANDLING OF RADIATION ACCIDENT PATIENTS
BY PARAMEDICAL AND HOSPITAL PERSONNEL

-TC-

PREFACE

Nuclear radiation and radioactive materials of varying potency and amounts are used in many ways by many types of industry, research, and commerce. Although under tight controls, radiation and radioactive materials may be encountered almost anywhere at any time. For example, some food providers have used radiation to increase the shelf-life of packaged meats. The reason for this is, as presented in Chapter 1, that nuclear radiation can destroy the living bacteria that causes the meat to spoil, but the radiation will not harm the non-living meat. Since radiation can destroy bacteria, packaged bandages can be sterilized by exposure to radiation. Some industries use radiation to measure thickness in metals. Radiation can be used to study the condition of or treat particular organs or areas of the human body. An internal "picture" of the human body can be taken without surgery by using radiation. Energy is produced utilizing radioactive materials.

The previous paragraph names only a few ways radiation and radioactive materials are used in everyday life. With so many uses for radiation and radioactive materials and many other ways not named, there are bound to be adverse incidents in the handling or use or abuse of the radiation or radioactive materials, possibly creating a hazard whether by accident or intent. Either way, special precautions and consideration may be indicated when responding to such an incident. A victim of such an incident may have received an exposure to radiation as well as possible external and internal contamination with the radioactive materials.

A point worth special notation is that the patient may be a victim of all three conditions, *external exposure*, *external contamination*, or *internal contamination*. In any case, you must assume all three conditions are indicated until a thorough survey can be performed by other professionals equipped with special instrumentation and training. Although the patient may be contaminated with radioactive materials or may have been exposed to nuclear radiation, your attention to medical emergencies must be foremost. Do not let this statement alarm you. The remainder of this text will provide greater understanding into the matters of cross-contamination and self-exposure.

COMMENT

My intent in preparing this material is to amplify the training in the 120-hour Emergency Medical Technician-A (EMT-A) training course and the "first responder" training courses. I feel the subject coverage in these courses is not adequate to provide for the radiological education of responding personnel. Further, I have learned that some emergency department physicians have not had the opportunity to obtain what they feel to be adequate training in handling radiation accident patients. This material should provide each discipline with an insight and perspective regarding the handling of radiation accident patients beyond what they may already have and should provide a good foundation to build upon.

Many sources and much training were called upon to compile this material in a manner that is understandable and straight-forward. Many of the texts and books I've seen covering this subject seemed to have been written for health physicists and scientists: this text is not. This text is written for you as field and hospital personnel. I have a great deal of respect for the health physicists and scientists and envy their perseverance in learning their expertise. However, I have more respect for the field and hospital people who must implement the guidance provided by the physicists and scientists, i.e., EMTs, Paramedics, Fire-fighters, First Aiders, Police, and volunteers who must get their boots muddy rescuing victims of accidents, radiological or otherwise. The same respect goes to the good doctor in the emergency department who must make the most sense of the nonsense of trauma.

I did not intend to plagiarize anyone's work and I feel I have not. I believe I've given credit where credit is due. Most of the materials obtained to perform research were handouts and individual pages of publications given to me over the years that did not indicate the publication's name, author, or publisher.

A great number of experts became personally invloved in this project and I cannot thank them enough. Each of them is listed on the Acknowledgements page. I tried to list them in order of their level of support, but each was so personable and willing to help me ensure the accuracy of particular points within this text that I was forced to list them alphabetically. Thanks go also to those professionals who are not listed on the Acknowledgements page and who were not personally involved but who prepared the source matieral for some of this project: the References and Suggested Reading lists most of them.

This material includes suggested procedures and guidelines for handling and decontaminating the radiologically contaminated patient, for performing radiological surveys, for using protective clothing, and for other activities, each with a common goal of helping the EMT, medic, first aider, emergency physician, nurse, police officer, firefighter, industrial safety officer...the list goes on....provide quality medical care to the patient—the victim of a radiation accident. The suggested procedures and techniques are not necessarily to be performed in the order shown—modification of each procedure and technique may be necessary to compensate for the case-specific and facility-specific needs.

Once again I offer my salute to emergency personnel in the field and the hospital. Often the work of these people is thankless and unrewarded. A special salute to the volunteers—they are not getting paid when the wrecked vehicle or smoldering structure they are crawling into bursts ablaze. I have an idea of what most of them must deal with because in my own small way I have been there. Finally, let us not forget the voice on the radio—the dispatcher helps save lives, too! Thank you—all of you. And may God bless you.

Thomas A. Carder

CHAPTER THREE (cont'd)

CHAPTER FOUR
RADIATION DETECTION

CHAPTER FIVE
RECOGNITION OF RADIOACTIVE MATERIALS

CHAPTER SIX
EXTRICATION AND TREATMENT

CHAPTER SIX (cont'd)

CHAPTER SEVEN
DISROBING THE RADIOACTIVELY CONTAMINATED
PATIENT AND RADIOLOGICAL SURVEY TECHNIQUES

FIGURES

FIGURES (cont'd)

TABLES

TABLES (cont'd)

TEXT PREPARATION

The text files were prepared using an Apple® Macintosh™ computer with 4 megabytes of RAM. An Everex®6, 20 megabyte hard drive was used for file management and storage. Software used to prepare the text was FullWrite Professional™ by Ashton-Tate®. The HRAP book logo and graphics were prepared using Canvas™ by Deneba® Software, Inc. Proof pages of the book were printed using an Apple Personal LaserWriter™ LS printer. Projected for 1994 is a HRAP Training Program mated to this book. The exam question bank for the HRAP Training Program will use LXR•TEST™ by Logic eXtension Resources®. Canvas will be used to prepare the figures and graphics for the exam question bank. FullWrite Professional will be used to prepare the text files.

- TC -

SECOND EDITION

Handling of Radiation Accident Patients
by Paramedical and Hospital Personnel

Chapter 1

BASIC RADIOLOGICAL SCIENCE

PREVIEW

NUCLEAR RADIATION!!?? What is it!!?? Will it make you glow at night!!?? Will it make you invisible!!?? Will it turn you into a zombie!!??

NO

The images of science fiction and dramatic sensationalism have affected the minds of rational people. In this Chapter, you should be able to decide for yourself just what is nuclear radiation. Topics include:

- The composition of matter
- An example of how nuclear radiation can be produced
- How nuclear radiation may cause damage to living tissue
- A comparison of the relative penetration of nuclear radiation into matter
- Non-nuclear radiation
- What happens when nuclear radiation is stopped

This Chapter is the most "technical" of all and may seem to provide the least practical information about handling of radiation accident patients. However, those who have a basic understanding of the nature and properties of nuclear radiation and radioactive material appear to have the best mixture of confidence and respect; confidence from knowing the boundaries of the possible hazards of radiation and radioactivity, but enough respect to prevent hotdog heroism. Therefore, I will present what I know about the "physics" of radiation and radioactive material.

Section 1. Introduction to Radiological Science

As stated in the Preview of this Chapter, nuclear radiation cannot make anyone glow at night. Radioactive materials such as radium on luminous, glow-in-the-dark watch and clock dials might glow, but not people. Although some may want to be invisible, nuclear radiation cannot make you so. It is not possible for nuclear radiation to turn you into something that does not exist, i.e., a zombie.

Radiation comes in many types. Webster defines radiation as "to proceed in divergent lines from any central point or surface." Examples of radiation include:

- Heat
- Visible, Infrared, and Ultraviolet light
- Microwave
- Radio and Television signals
- X-ray
- Nuclear

So, "radiation" is not so bad after all. Our very existence depends on radiation, specifically, heat and light radiation. Our dependence on plant life is thankful for ultraviolet radiation. Without visible light, you would not be able to see what is in front of you. However, in excessive amounts each of the above examples of radiation may be harmful to living organisms. Too much heat will burn you. Too much light may blind you. Strong, concentrated microwaves may be unhealthy. Nuclear radiation may also be harmful.[1]

In order to understand the properties of nuclear radiation and radioactivity, it is necessary to understand the basic structure of matter. An understanding of the basic structure of matter is necessary since nuclear radiation comes from matter, specifically, radioactive matter. Although an understanding of the basic physical properties of nuclear radiation and radioactivity is important to the objectives of this text, the vast minute details of atomic structure, radiation, and radioactivity are not important and are outside the scope of this text. Some of the material of this Chapter is conceptual simplistic condensation and interpretation of scientific findings. Applicability and technical accuracy of the material in this Chapter regarding the objectives are not lost due to the interpretations and condensations.

---

1.   The term *nuclear radiation* refers to a set of radiations from a larger set called *ionizing radiation*. Ionizing radiation will be explained in detail as you proceed.

Section 2. Matter

Everything that has weight and occupies space is called *matter*. This book is matter. The print on this page is matter. The shoes on your feet are matter. The ground you walk on is matter. The water you drink is matter. The air you breathe is matter. Hidden in the above examples is that matter has three *states of existence;* solid, liquid, and gas. Regardless of the state of existence, matter has basic building blocks called *elements*. In order to form the myriad of substances in the universe, elements combine to form *compounds*. Several examples of elements and compounds are displayed in Table 1.1.

TABLE 1.1
Examples of Elements and Compounds

Element, Symbol	Physical State	Compound, Formula	Physical State
Silver, Ag	Solid	Silver Nitrate, $AgNO_3$	Solid
Oxygen, O	Gas	Carbon Dioxide, CO_2	Gas
Sulphur, S	Solid	Sulphur Dioxide, SO_2	Gas
Hydrogen, H	Gas	Water, H_2O	Liquid
Calcium, Ca	Solid	Calcium Carbonate, $CaCO_3$	Solid
Sodium, Na	Solid	Sodium Peroxide, Na_2O_2	Solid
Nitrogen, N	Gas	Ammonia, NH_3	Gas
Chlorine, Cl	Gas	Hydrocholric Acid, HCl	Liquid
Mercury, Hg	Liquid	Mercuric Chloride, $HgCl_2$	Solid

An element may be described as a substance that cannot be chemically reduced into a simpler substance. For example, if you were to dissolve the element silver in nitric acid (a chemical reaction), the result would be silver nitrate—the silver would still be silver but dissolved as a chemical part of the silver nitrate. The silver could be removed from the silver nitrate by other chemical reactions.

In a less abstract sense, if you were to cut a block of silver into a thousand pieces, the pieces would still be silver. Even the saw shavings would be silver. If you kept separating the silver shavings into smaller and smaller pieces until you reached the smallest possible particle and still be silver, the particle would be an *atom* of silver. The atom is best described as *the smallest particle an element can be divided into and still be that element.*

A *compound* is two or more elements chemically combined. If you were to leave silver (an element) exposed to oxygen (another element) in the air long enough, the silver and oxygen would chemically combine to form the familiar black tarnish silver oxide. Silver oxide is a compound. Silver and oxygen combining happens in the same way that iron rusts when wet.[2] Rust is the compound iron oxide.

If you were to separate the silver oxide, the iron oxide, or any other compound into the smallest particle the compound could be divided into and still be that compound, the particle would be a *molecule*. The molecule is best described as *the smallest particle a compound can be divided into and still be that compound*. If you were to separate the silver oxide into silver and oxygen, the result would be two separate elements, not a compound. Figure 1.1 provides a simplified drawing of atoms as separate units and combined as compounds.

FIGURE 1.1
Atoms & Molecules

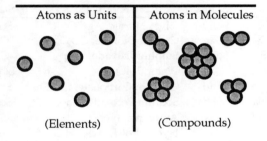

Remember:

- *Elements* combine to form *compounds*
- The smallest particle of an element is an *atom*
- The smallest particle of a compound is a *molecule*

A good understanding of the basic composition of an atom is important to understanding the nature and origin of nuclear radiation since nuclear radiation comes from radioactive atoms. A good understanding of the general structure of a molecule is necessary to understand the effects of nuclear radiation on living tissue since living tissue is comprised of a multitude of molecules.

---

2.   It is not so much the water that makes iron rust, it's the oxygen dissolved in the water. While iron is wet, the oxygen in the water (or moisture) is held in more intimate contact with the iron than when the iron is merely exposed to the oxygen in the air.

The atom of any element can be further divided into smaller particles called *subatomic particles*. However, if an atom were so divided, the particles would no longer exhibit the properties of the element. Similarly, if you were to disassemble a bicycle wheel into its component parts, it would no longer be a bicycle wheel and would not function as a bicycle wheel—merely a pile of bicycle wheel parts. Now, let's take an atom apart to study the subatomic particles.

Figure 1.2 illustrates the structure of an atom as it is known today. Figure 1.2 uses helium to illustrate atomic structure. An atom is structured with a central nucleus with particles surrounding the nucleus at specific distances and in constant motion.

FIGURE 1.2
Atomic Structure

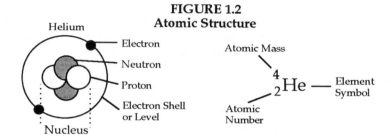

Interesting...
If all the "empty" space of all our body atoms was reduced to nothing, you or I would be less than the size of a beebee and still weigh the same. The average radius of a nucleus is about 1/10,000 the radius of the whole atom. If a nucleus was the size of a ping-pong ball, electrons would be about 600 feet away. Nuclear density is about 100,000,000 tons per cubic centimeter, or 200,000,000,000 pounds per cubic centimeter

The center of the atom is called the *nucleus*. The nucleus contains *neutrons* (n) and *protons* (p). The nucleus is orbited by *electrons* (e) in particular energy shells or levels. The nucleus of any atom contains neutrons and protons except for the nucleus of normal hydrogen which contains only one proton and no neutrons.[3] From Figure 1.2 remember that:

- *subatomic particles* are *neutrons* (n), *protons* (p), *electrons* (e)
- The *nucleus* contains *neutrons* and *protons*
- *electrons* surround the nucleus

---

3.   Henceforth in this text, when the nucleus is discussed, it is assumed the subject nucleus contains both neutrons and protons unless otherwise noted.

Other information illustrated in Figure 1.2 includes the notation of the

- *element symbol,* the
- *atomic weight* or *atomic mass number,*[4] and
- the *atomic number.*

The element symbol is one or two letters of the name of the element. For example, the symbol for cobalt is Co. The symbol for iodine is I. The symbol for uranium is U. The symbol for cesium is Cs. The symbol for zinc is Zn. The symbol for chlorine is Cl. Some element symbols may seem odd because the symbol is taken from the latin name of the element, e.g., the latin name for sodium is naturium so the symbol for sodium is Na.

The atomic mass number (or just atomic mass) of the element is the sum of the masses of particles in the nucleus in an atom of the element, specifically, the total mass of the protons and neutrons in the nucleus. The unit for measuring the mass of any subatomic particle is the *atomic mass unit (amu).* The notation of atomic mass is shown in the upper left corner of the element symbol. Helium has a mass of 4 atomic mass units since it has 2 neutrons and 2 protons.[5]

The atomic number of an element is the number of protons in the nucleus of an atom of the element. Notation of the atomic number of an element is shown in the lower left corner of the element symbol. The atomic number for helium is 2. Other examples of element notation follow.

Carbon (6n, 6p) $^{12}_{6}C$

Lawrencium (154n, 103p) $^{257}_{103}Lw$

Oxygen (8n, 8p) $^{16}_{8}O$

The *neutron* is a subatomic particle found in the nucleus. The total of neutrons in the nucleus contributes to approximately half of the mass of the atom. The mass of the neutron is approximately 1 amu. Also, the neutron has no electrical charge. The concept of electrical charge on subatomic particles will make more sense as you study the proton and electron.

---

4. The term *mass* relates weight with volume. For example, a six-inch cork ball weighs less than a six-inch steel ball because the cork has less mass.

5. Actually, the mass of helium is 4.003 amu, but that is an example of the "minute details" beyond the scope of this text.

The *proton* is the other subatomic particle found in the nucleus and also has a mass of approximately 1 amu. The total number of protons in the nucleus also contributes to almost half the mass of the atom. Where the neutron has no electrical charge, the proton has a positive electrical charge. Many things have electrical charge. Household current has electrical charge. You may build up a static electric charge when you walk across a carpet in dry humidity. Lightning is electrical charge. Just as the volt is used to express electricity, the electrical charge on the proton is expressed in *electrostatic units* (esu).[6] One esu is equivalent to 299.8 volts. The esu charge on the proton is equivalent to 0.000000144 volt, or 0.144 millionths of one volt. It takes the charge of 2,082,000,000 protons or electrons to equal one esu.

Orbiting the nucleus of the atom are *electrons*. Each electron has approximately $1/1845$ amu, so the electrons contribute very little to the total mass of an atom. The electrons orbiting the nucleus and their configuration around the nucleus determines the *chemical properties* of the parent element. How the electrons determine the chemical properties of the parent atom will be explained further as you proceed through this text. The electron has a negative electrical charge. The negative charge of the electron is exactly equal to the magnitude or strength of the positive charge on the proton but is exactly opposite in polarity. The magnitude of the charge of the electron and the proton are so exactly equal that *if they were combined, their charges would completely cancel and become neutral*. A proton and an electron combined as one unit would have an over-all charge of zero. Table 1.2 summarizes the properties of neutrons,of protons, and of electrons.

TABLE 1.2
Neutron, Proton, Electron

Neutron	Zero Charge	Approx 1 AMU
Proton	Positive 1 Charge[a]	Approx 1 AMU
Electron	Negative 1 Charge[a]	$1/1845$ AMU

[a] The proton and electron have equal and opposite charges. The charge on the proton or electron is not a volt or an esu but is a relative value.

A factor which may not yet be obvious in Figure 1.2 is that the helium atom is *neutral*. In a neutral atom, the number of protons and

---

6.   More recent terms for expressing the charge on subatomic particles is the stat volt and the stat coulomb. Generally, the esu is no longer used but provides a more easily understood concept than the stat volt and stat coulomb.

electrons are equal. The helium atom has 2 positively charged protons and 2 negatively charged electrons. The atom therefore has an equal number of opposite charges. When an atom is viewed as a single unit rather than a collection of particles, and when the unit possesses an equal number of opposite charges, the over-all effect is zero charge, or neutral. When the helium atom is considered as a single unit rather than a collection of subatomic particles, it has a zero over-all charge since it has equal number of opposite charges; algebraically stated, $(+2) + (-2) = 0$.

If one of the negatively charged electrons was removed from the parent helium atom, there would remain 2 protons (two positive charges) but only one electron (one negative charge). The atom would no longer be neutral. In effect, the one negative charge will neutralize one of the two positive charges and resultant effect would be one positive 1 charge; algebraically stated, $(+2) + (-1) = +1$. After the helium atom loses one of its electrons, it becomes positively charged since it now has one more positive proton than negative electrons. The concept of losing one or more electrons provides a basis for *ionization*, which will be presented in more detail later in this Section. Ionization is the means for detection of nuclear radiation and for causing damage to living tissues.

To further explain the concept of opposite electrical charges on subatomic particles, consider a common car battery. The battery has two oppositely charged electrical terminals, a positively charged (+) terminal and a negatively charged (-) terminal. An object which conducts electricity will conduct the opposite electrical charges. Proof in conduction of electrical charges is observed if a carelessly placed metal object, such as a wrench, is placed between the positive and negative terminals of the battery. The electrical charges will flow through the metal—violently. The charges in the negative terminal flow to the charges in the positive terminal due to the *Coulombic Law of Charges* which states that opposite charges attract and like charges repel. The flow of negative electrical charges is what makes the fireball when the wrench connects both battery terminals. If the electrical charges are on objects, the objects will be subject to the same forces of attraction or repulsion. For example, a proton and an electron close together will attract each other but two electrons will repel each other and two protons will repel each other. Figure 1.3 illustrates the Coulombic Law of Charges using electrically (statically) charged ping-pong balls hanging from a non-conducting support. Imagine the positively charged balls as protons and the negatively charged balls as electrons.

FIGURE 1.3
Coulombic Law of Charges

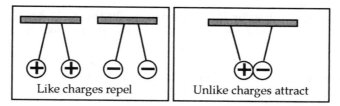

Like charges repel   Unlike charges attract

The electrically charged electrons are also responsible for the chemical properties of an element. Molecules of compounds are formed when electrons of an atom of one element bond their parent atom with the electron shell of an atom of another element. The electrical charge on electrons is what holds atoms together to form compounds. The attraction of the negative charge of the electrons of one atom to the positive charge of the protons in another atom is the force which provides the bonding between two or more atoms to form a molecule; the "glue" which holds the two atoms together, the two atoms "share" an electron. This sharing of an electron or of electrons between two or more atoms is a chemical bonding provided by the electrons. This is why the electrons and their configuration about the nucleus determine the chemical properties of an element.

Figure 1.4 graphically displays a simplified arrangement for electrons to occupy space in shells or levels of orbit around the nucleus.

FIGURE 1.4
Electron Shells/Levels

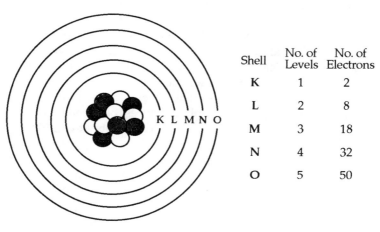

Shell	No. of Levels	No. of Electrons
K	1	2
L	2	8
M	3	18
N	4	32
O	5	50

Figure 1.4 shows that electrons occupy space in orbital shells in a particular manner. Think of electrons traveling in pairs, i.e., a shell of an atom holds electrons in *pairs*. There are five possible shells in which electrons may be located, specifically the K, L, M, N, and O shells. The number of occupied electron shells in an atom depends on the number of electrons in the atom.

The first and innermost electron shell, the K shell, has a capacity of 2 electrons. The second shell, the L shell, consists of 2 subshells although shown as one shell in Figure 1.4. The first subshell of the L shell has a capacity of 2 electrons, the second L subshell has a capacity of 6, therefore the L shell has a total capacity of 8 electrons. Note that the *capacity of an electron shell* is always a factor of 2. The third shell, the M shell, consists of three subshells, the first has a capacity of 2 electrons, the second has a capacity of 6, and the third has a capacity of 10, giving the M shell a total capacity of 18 electrons. The fourth shell, the N shell consists of 4 subshells and has a total capacity of 32 electrons. The fifth shell, the O shell, consists of 5 subshells and has a total capacity of 50 electrons. For the purposes of this text, the L, M, N, and O shells shall each be considered as one shell, rather than each consisting of multiple subshells. For example, the L shell shall be considered as one shell with the capacity of 8 electrons rather than consisting of 2 subshells having the capacity of 2 and 6 electrons. Each of the specific shells have a specific *capacity* of electrons it can hold, but that does not say the shells cannot *contain* fewer electrons.

In describing electron travel about the nucleus, I have previously used the term "orbital." However, the term orbital is at best a loose description of electron travel about the nucleus. To more closely envision the travel of an electron about its nucleus, consider the electron shells as perfectly round balloons. The five possible electron shells may be thought of as five balloons inflated inside each other not touching and all with a common center. Electrons traveling about a nucleus may be compared to pairs of shrews zipping about on the surfaces of the balloons at a meteoric pace without ever stopping or pausing, not in a neat and symmetric orbital fashion, but rather in a seemingly random fashion. Also, the shrews could never occupy space between balloon surfaces. The shrews could jump from one balloon surface to another, but could never rest between balloons.

Focus for a moment on what I said earlier about combining the negative charge of the electron and the positive charge of the proton. In fact, the positive proton can combine with the negative electron by attraction of unlike (opposite) charges to form a new particle. *The new particle can be considered a neutron.* The proton and electron held together by attraction of opposite charges satisfy the properties of a neutron (review the subatomic particle properties in Table 1.2). The combined masses are approximately 1 amu which is the mass of a neutron; algebraically stated,

$$\approx 1 \text{ amu (proton)} + {}^{1}/_{1845} \text{ amu (electron)} = \approx 1 \text{ amu} \qquad (1\text{-}1)$$

The positive charge of the proton and the negative charge of the electron combine to yield a net charge of zero, which is the charge of a neutron:

$$[+1 \text{ charge (proton)}] + [-1 \text{ charge (electron)}] = 0 \qquad (1\text{-}2)$$

A neutron is technically not the simultaneous existence of a proton and an electron, but while combined the proton and electron elements of a neutron maintain individuality of charge and mass with the net result or overall effect being neutrality and unity—one neutron.. However, a neutron can change into a proton and an electron by *neutron decay* (neutron transformation). Therefore, a neutron can be considered a proton and electron held together by the Coulombic law of charges that states unlike charges attract.. The law of charges will make more sense when you study Section 3 regarding the production of nuclear radiation when conditions are right to cause the neutron to decay (break apart) into its components; a proton, an electron, and the energy of attraction. Recall the discussion regarding an electron of an atom being held in chemical bonding by the attraction of the electron to the positive protons of another atom. The electrons of one atom which are responsible for chemical bonding to a second atom do not meet the protons of the second atom to form a neutron. The actual process of neutron formation is beyond the scope of this text.

Earlier, reference was made to ionization. To refresh your memory, while neutral an atom has an equal number of protons and electrons. For example, the element lithium in Figure 1.5 by nature has 3 neutrons, 3 protons, and 3 electrons. Since the lithium atom has 3 protons and 3 electrons, the lithium atom has 3 positive charges and 3 negative charges. When an atom possesses an equal number of opposite charges, the net result or over-all effect is zero charge, or neutral. Remove one of the electrons which balance the overall electrical charge of the atom and the resultant atom will no longer be neutral. Removal of an electron from the parent atom is called *ionization.*

Various forces can cause ionization in some elements and compounds. Example forces include a chemical reaction, electricity, and *nuclear radiation*. The ability of nuclear radiation to knock off an electron from its parent atom is why it is sometimes referred to as *ionizing nuclear radiation*, or more often just *ionizing radiation*. Ionization due to nuclear radiation is the basis for damage to living tissue and the basis for detection of nuclear radiation: both will be presented in this Chapter.

FIGURE 1.5
Ionization

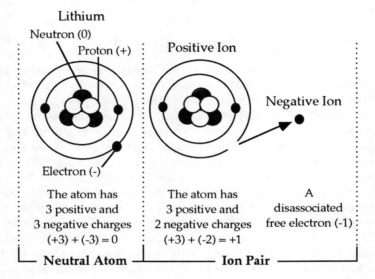

On the left side of Figure 1.5, the lithium atom has 3 positive charges and 3 negative charges combined since there are 3 protons in its nucleus and 3 electrons orbiting the nucleus. Combine an equal number of opposite charges and the result is zero: (+3) + (-3) = 0. The lithium atom on the left side of Figure 1.5 has an overall charge of zero and is neutral.

Now, suppose one of the electrons is removed from the neutral parent lithium atom as shown in the middle of Figure 1.5. The parent lithium atom now has 3 positive charges but only 2 negative charges. The parent lithium atom now has one more positive charge than negative charges resulting in an extra positive charge: (+3) + (-2) = +1. The atom is no longer neutral—it has an overall charge of positive one. Further, the electron shown on the right side of Figure 1.5 which was removed from of its orbit around the parent atom is now a disassociated free electron and is a separate entity with a negative 1 charge. The process shown in Figure 1.5 is called *ionization*. Ionization results in the production of *ion pairs*, one member of the ion pair being positive and the other member of the pair being negative. The parent atom less one of its electrons is the positive member of the ion pair. The disassociated free electron is the negative member of the ion pair. If ionization occurs in living tissue, damage to the tissue can occur. Section 4 and Chapter 3 will explain how ionizing radiation can cause damage in living tissue. Chapter 4 will explain how ionization also provides a mechanism of detecting radiation.

One subatomic particle of an atom is identical to the same type of subatomic particle of another atom. Specifically, the electron from a hydrogen atom is identical to an electron from a uranium atom, a fluorine atom, a silver atom, or any other atom. The same is true for protons and neutrons. A proton in oxygen is identical to a proton in uranium. A neutron in carbon is identical to a neutron in plutonium. The difference in the characteristics or the identity of an element lies in the *total number of protons in the nucleus of the element.* Think of the number of protons in the nucleus as the fingerprint or the identification code of the element. For example, carbon (a solid) has 6 protons in its nucleus. Nitrogen (a gas) has 7 protons in its nucleus. When the number of protons in the nucleus changes, a drastic change in physical properties can occur. Add one proton to the nucleus of carbon and you have a nucleus of nitrogen. The new element generated by adding protons to the nucleus may have totally different properties such as the obvious differences between carbon and nitrogen, or may have similar properties such as the less obvious differences between lead and tin. Yes, it is possible to change lead into gold, but the cost of doing so is astronomical. *Remember that as the number of protons in the nucleus of an element determines the characteristics or the identity of the element, the number of and configuration of electrons about the nucleus determine the chemical properties of the element.* Chemical properties include such factors as how fast the material will burn, how fast it will dissolve, in what liquids it will dissolve, how easily it corrodes, and the color of the element.

Section 3. Radiation Production

Remember that a neutron could be considered a proton, an electron, and the binding energy holding the two particles together. With that information and a basic understanding of matter, you have the basics for understanding how radiation may be produced when a neutron breaks apart. Figure 1.6 displays the components of a neutron. In Figure 1.6 the neutron is drawn as two particles intimately combined.

FIGURE 1.6
Neutron

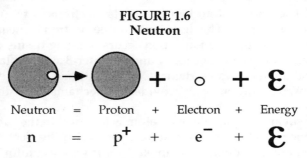

Neutron   =   Proton   +   Electron   +   Energy

$$n \quad = \quad p^{+} \quad + \quad e^{-} \quad + \quad \varepsilon$$

Under the right conditions, *a neutron can decay, or break up, into its components; a proton, an electron, and the energy of attraction holding the proton and electron together.* In elements with a high number of neutrons relative to the number of protons where the neutrons significantly out-number the protons, intranuclear forces can be strong enough to excite the nucleus and cause instability in the nucleus. The unstable and excited state may promote *neutron decay* and cause the nucleus to be radioactive and emit nuclear radiation. The number of neutrons relative to the number of protons in the nucleus, specifically, the *neutron-to-proton ratio* (n:p ratio) in the nucleus, may contribute to whether the nucleus is radioactive. In elements with a relatively low neutron-to-proton ratio, especially when the number of neutrons and protons are equal or near equal in number, nuclear stability is best and neutron decay should be least likely. All naturally occurring elements with an atomic number of greater than 83 are radioactive. Atomic number 83 is bismuth with 83 protons and 126 neutrons which represents a ratio of approximately 1.5 neutrons to every proton. The lighter element oxygen with an atomic number of 8 (8p, 8n) has a neutron-to-proton ratio of one neutron to every proton (1:1 n:p ratio). Somewhat heavier than oxygen but lighter than bismuth is sodium with 12 neutrons and 11 protons which has a n:p ratio of 1.1:1. There are additional factors which determine whether an element is radioactive, but the above examples provide a basic understanding of why some elements are radioactive.

In Figure 1.7, carbon is used to explain neutron decay producing nuclear radiation. On the left side of Figure 1.7 carbon-12 is shown. The "-12" in carbon-12 indicates the mass of carbon is 12 amu. Carbon-12 is the naturally occurring, non-radioactive carbon found in charcoal, a burnt match stick, or fireplace chimneys. Carbon-12 has 6 protons (6 amu) and 6 neutrons (6 more amu). Within the scope of this text, orbital electrons do not support or inhibit neutron decay and are not shown in Figure 1.7.[7] The carbon-12 on the left side of Figure 1.7 is described as stable since it is not radioactive, i.e., the nucleus is not in an excited state and has a one-to-one neutron-to-proton ratio (1:1 n:p ratio).

FIGURE 1.7
Neutron Decay

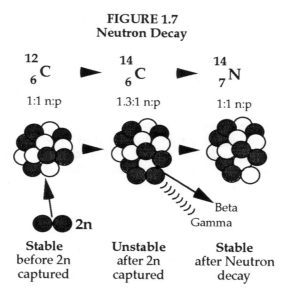

12	14	14
$_6$C	$_6$C	$_7$N
1:1 n:p	1.3:1 n:p	1:1 n:p

2n

Beta
Gamma

Stable	Unstable	Stable
before 2n	after 2n	after Neutron
captured	captured	decay

When an additional two neutrons are caused to combine with the 6 protons and 6 neutrons in the nucleus of carbon-12 as shown in the middle of Figure 1.7, the nucleus becomes carbon-14 with 8 neutrons and 6 protons (approximately 1.3:1 n:p ratio). The nucleus then becomes excited and extra-energetic due to a neutron-to-proton ratio that is *not* stable for carbon.

Carbon-14 is still carbon since it has 6 protons, but as the nucleus captures the 2 neutrons, the carbon becomes an *isotope*. When two atoms of the same element have the same number of protons (the same atomic number) but have a different number of neutrons (have different atomic masses), they are said to be isotopes. Both atoms of carbon in Figure 1.7 have the same number of protons but a different number of neutrons. Some elements have more than one isotope. This may be a little confusing—if an atom has no isotope, it is just that: an atom. However, if an atom has an isotope, both atoms are

7.   Although orbital electrons do not support or inhibit neutron decay, let me sneak in a reminder that if the nucleus of a neutral atom has 6 protons, there are 6 electrons in orbit. Electrons can be made to produce radiation, but not nuclear radiation (to be described in Section 6).

isotopes. An isotope may be unstable due to the change from the stable neutron-to-proton ratio for the element and may be radioactive.

All isotopes of an element will react chemically identical. Carbon-14 will react with other elements the same as carbon-12. Carbon-14 will combine with oxygen in fire to form carbon dioxide and carbon monoxide just as will carbon-12. Since the nucleus of carbon-14 still has 6 protons, it will have 6 electrons but remember that the orbital electrons do not support or inhibit neutron decay. As you now know, the orbital electrons are responsible for the chemical properties of the element, which is why the isotope will react chemically the same as the original form of the element since all isotopes of an element have the same number of electrons. Since carbon-12 and carbon-14 both have the same number of electrons, they have the same chemical properties.

In God's universe, matter tends to move toward stability and equilibrium. Being unstable, carbon-14 will strive to become stable. In doing so, one of the extra neutrons in carbon-14 will break apart (transform) forming a proton, an electron, and the binding energy holding them together as a neutron. Each of the components of a neutron will be accounted for in the following paragraphs which describe neutron decay.

As a nucleus strives to become stable, a neutron may decay (transform) and eject the electron component of the decaying neutron from the nucleus. The ejected electron is now a particle of *beta radiation* (β). Beta radiation is an example of particulate radiation (a particle of matter as opposed to a bundle of energy). The beta particle is therefore a high-speed free electron. The main difference between a beta particle and a free electron is the origin of the particle. The beta particle comes from the nucleus of a radioactive atom. The free electron comes from the electron shells as in the case of the disassociated electron resulting from ionization described in Section 2 and Figure 1.5. A beta particle and an electron are so similar that a beta particle may be captured as an electron by an atom that needs another electron. However, the beta particle has more more *kinetic energy* (energy of motion) than the electron since the beta particle is a projectile from a nucleus of radioactive material. Ejection of a beta particle from the neutron decay (neutron transformation) accounts for the electron component of the neutron.

Now the binding energy holding the proton and the electron together as a neutron must be accounted for as a factor of neutron decay. As the neutron decays, the binding energy that held the neutron together as a unit is emitted as a ray of *gamma radiation* (γ). Gamma radiation is an example of *electromagnetic radiation* (a bundle of energy as opposed to a particle of matter).

The electron component and the binding energy of attraction component of a neutron have now been accounted for in neutron decay. The final step to be described in neutron decay is the disposition of the proton component of the neutron. Once the beta particle and the binding energy of attraction have been emitted, all that remains of the decayed neutron is the proton component. The proton component remains in the nucleus, adding to the total number of protons in the nucleus. The number of protons in the carbon nucleus then changes from 6 to 7.

When the number of protons in the nucleus changes, the nucleus changes to a different element. As shown on the right side of Figure 1.7, the carbon-14 (6 protons) changes to nitrogen-14 (7 protons)—from a solid to a gas! Note that the second of the extra neutrons is not altered and remains in the nucleus. The resulting nucleus now has 7 protons and 7 neutrons—a one-to-one neutron-to-proton ratio! The nitrogen shown on the right side of Figure 1.7 resulting from neutron decay is stable because 7 neutrons and 7 protons (1:1 n:p ratio) is stable for nitrogen. The resulting nitrogen nucleus is the same as the nuclei in nitrogen atoms in the air, in fertilizers, and in any other common nitrogen source.

Regarding the electrons, the original carbon with 6 electrons is now nitrogen with 6 electrons, i.e., a positively charged nitrogen ion $(+7) + (-6) = +1$. The nitrogen ion can capture a free electron, which is readily available everywhere, and become a nitrogen atom. The resulting nitrogen atom is chemically the same as the nitrogen atoms in the same nitrogen sources described above. All these steps happen in a tiny fraction of a second. Other intricate actions occur as gamma and beta radiations are emitted but the details are outside the scope of this text.

Now you have a concept of how gamma and beta radiations may be produced in a radioactive material. Understand that a great deal other actions and reactions occur during and as the result of neutron decay, and that forces other than opposite electrical charges are involved (e.g., the "near" force), but those events and forces are beyond the scope of this text and are far more complicated than can be presented within this text. You should, however, understand now that radioactivity and radiation are *not* the same thing. Radioactivity is a process which results in radiation. Radioactivity is the act of one of the extra neutrons breaking apart (transforming), i.e., a process. The beta and gamma emitted are the product of the radioactivity, i.e., radiation.

A third type of nuclear radiation, *alpha radiation* ($\propto$), may be produced in heavier radioactive elements such as plutonium with an atomic mass of 242 (148 neutrons and 94 protons, 1.6:1

neutron-to-proton ratio). Alpha radiation, like beta radiation, is an example of particulate radiation. The alpha particle shown in Figure 1.8 is composed of 2 neutrons and 2 protons bundled together that have been ejected from the nucleus of a heavy radioactive element in an attempt to reduce the neutron-proton ratio closer to a stable one-to-one ratio. Ridding itself of 2 neutrons and 2 protons at the same instant provides the nucleus with a quicker reduction of the neutron-proton ratio than would neutron decay alone. The alpha particle, when slowed down, can capture two free electrons and become a helium atom. Recall the helium atom in Figure 1.2. The helium atom has the same number of neutrons (2) and protons (2) as the alpha particle in Figure 1.8.

FIGURE 1.8
Alpha Particle

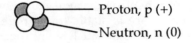

Proton, p (+)
Neutron, n (0)

Section 4. Biological Effects of Ionizing Nuclear Radiation

With all the things covered so far about nuclear radiation, there is another topic to be understood, i.e., the damage to living tissue due to radiation-induced ionization of the tissue.

Living cells depend on a natural arrangement of elements and compounds in chemical harmony. Disruption of the natural order of the chemistry of a living cell may result in cell dysfunction or death. If dysfunction or death happens in enough cells, general or local injury may occur. A great quantity of the human body is water, either as a separate compound or in chemical combination with other compounds. Living chemistry depends heavily on the chemistry of the compound water. The effects of ionizing nuclear radiation on living tissue will be centered around the effects of ionizing nuclear radiation on water as a component of living chemistry.

As explained in Sections 2 and 3, electrons and their configuration around the nucleus of the parent atom are responsible for the *chemical properties* of elements. The configuration of electrons also determines the chemistry of a compound or of compounds. The living cells within the human body depend on specific and exact chemical relationships between elements and compounds. Compound molecules depend on *chemical bonding* between element atoms to form molecular units. The bonding between the atoms of a molecule is provided by atoms *sharing* electrons in the outermost shells. The electrons shared by atoms to form a molecule are called *valence electrons*. Loss of one or more of the valence electrons can alter the chemistry of the molecule.

As shown in Section A of Figure 1.9, the water molecule, H_2O, is composed of two hydrogen atoms and one oxygen atom. The electron of each hydrogen atom is shared with the oxygen atom to make one unit (equation 1-3). Nuclear radiation (ionizing radiation) can ionize the valence electrons of a water molecule and thus create unwanted ion pairs and chemical changes in the irradiated water. Chemical changes in the water due to irradiation by ionizing radiation is called *radiolysis of water*. Ionizing radiation can also cause the creation of *free radicals* from the water molecule. The combinations of ion pairs and free radicals created by ionizing radiation can create a chemically poisonous environment for the cell or tissue that originally used the normal water molecule. Radiolysis of water and free radicals are explained below.

As early as the turn of this century, Pierre Curie found that free hydrogen and oxygen were liberated from aqueous solutions of radium salts which was later attributed to the action of alpha particles from the radium on water molecules. Also discovered was that the volumetric ratio of hydrogen to oxygen was not the 2:1 as would be expected from two atoms of hydrogen and one atom of oxygen in each water molecule: that the ratio was somewhat higher than 2:1. The higher than 2:1 ratio of hydrogen to oxygen was explained when it was discovered that *hydrogen peroxide* was present in the irradiated water. Thus, instead of being released as gas, some of the oxygen would oxidize other water molecules and create hydrogen peroxide. Apart from the generation of free hydrogen and oxygen, the irradiated water seemed to be highly reactive since it could easily induce chemical changes in other compounds dissolved in it. Thus, the irradiated water was termed *activated water*.

Other scientists saw that X-irradiated air-free water did not develop free hydrogen or oxygen gas or hydrogen peroxide but the irradiated water still became "activated"; that ionizing radiation creates in water a highly reactive chemical species with the properties of ions and/or free radicals as primary or secondary products, that both the primary and secondary products can become involved in mutual reactions, in reactions with other water molecules, or with water solutes.

A *free radical* is an atom or molecule which has extra energy and an unpaired or odd electron. Remember from Section 2 that electrons like to travel in pairs. An unpaired electron is not conducive to the overall electronic balance of the atom or molecule. As orbital

electrons travel about the nucleus, they each spin on their own axis
much the same as the Earth spins on its North-South axis while the
Earth orbits the Sun. However, while the Earth spins only one
direction about its axis (West to East), one member of an electron pair
will spin clockwise while the other member of the pair spins
counterclockwise.

FIGURE 1.9
Radiolysis of Water

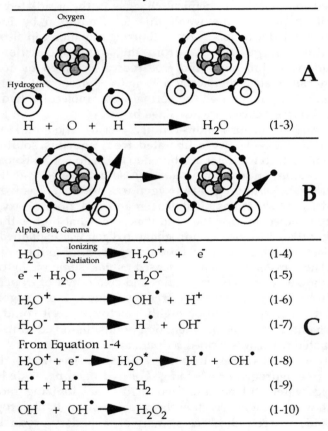

$$H + O + H \longrightarrow H_2O \qquad (1\text{-}3)$$

$$H_2O \xrightarrow[\text{Radiation}]{\text{Ionizing}} H_2O^+ + e^- \qquad (1\text{-}4)$$

$$e^- + H_2O \longrightarrow H_2O^- \qquad (1\text{-}5)$$

$$H_2O^+ \longrightarrow OH^\bullet + H^+ \qquad (1\text{-}6)$$

$$H_2O^- \longrightarrow H^\bullet + OH^- \qquad (1\text{-}7)$$

From Equation 1-4

$$H_2O^+ + e^- \longrightarrow H_2O^* \longrightarrow H^\bullet + OH^\bullet \qquad (1\text{-}8)$$

$$H^\bullet + H^\bullet \longrightarrow H_2 \qquad (1\text{-}9)$$

$$OH^\bullet + OH^\bullet \longrightarrow H_2O_2 \qquad (1\text{-}10)$$

In an atom or molecule with an even number of electrons, the
opposite spins are in balance. This state of balance of electron spins is
cause for a very stable chemical state of the atom or molecule whether
the atom or molecule is neutral or charged. An atom or molecule
with an odd and unpaired electron gives cause for the atom or
molecule to be very reactive with other substances whether the atom

or molecule is neutral or charged. For every water molecule directly acted upon by a ray or particle of ionizing radiation one free hydrogen radical ($H^{\bullet}$) and one free hydroxyl radical ($OH^{\bullet}$) are created.

Section B of Figure 1.9 illustrates disassociation of a valence electron by ionization of a water molecule. When a valence electron in a molecule is disassociated, the chemical bonding between the elements may be altered or even lost. The alteration of the normal electron configuration of a molecule may result in modified chemical reactivity of the compound. The modified chemical reactivity may in turn cause unwanted chemical combinations not compatible with the original function of the compound. An example of the unwanted combinations of water components resulting from disassociation of electrons is the generation of free radicals and *hydrogen peroxide* (H_2O_2) shown in Section C of Figure 1.9. Hydrogen peroxide, more commonly known as just Peroxide and sometimes stereotypically associated with an individual with unnatural blonde hair, is a powerful chemical agent—bleach. Hydrogen peroxide by any name is a poison for the cell which originally required water. The production of free radicals and hydrogen peroxide from water in the human body is an example of cellular *chemical poisoning* which may be caused by exposure to ionizing nuclear radiation. The following are some details of the production of free radicals and hydrogen peroxide by irradiation of water by ionizing radiation.

An oxygen atom has 2 electrons in its inner of two shells, the K shell, and 6 in the outer shell, the L shell, for a total of 8 electrons, which is okay since oxygen has 8 protons. A hydrogen atom has only one electron shell, the K shell, holding only one electron, which is also okay since the hydrogen atom has only one proton (refer to Section A of Figure 1.9). Recall that the first shell of any atom, the K shell, can hold 2 electrons and the second shell, the L shell, can hold 8 electrons. Notice in Section B of Figure 1.9 that the oxygen atom has 2 electrons in the K shell and 8 in the L shell. That totals *10* electrons. That doesn't seem right! That is too many electrons for oxygen. There are only 8 protons in the nucleus of the oxygen atom. And with 8 protons, the oxygen atom can have only 8 electrons. Right? Not exactly. Remember, the L shell has a *capacity* of 8 electrons. Granted, with 2 electrons in the K shell of the oxygen atom, the L shell needs only 6 electrons for the oxygen atom to be electrically satisfied. However, that does not prohibit oxygen from containing more than 6 electrons in the L shell. Likewise, each of the two hydrogen atoms needs only 1 electron to be electrically satisfied but the K shell of any atom has a capacity of 2 electrons. How is it then that in Section B of Figure 1.9 there are 8 electrons in the L shell of the oxygen atom? Further,

Section B of Figure 1.9 shows actually 2 electrons in the K shell of each hydrogen atom, but the K shell of each hydrogen atom only needs one electron since there is only one proton in each hydrogen atom?

The reason for the seeming surplus of electrons in the water molecule in Section A of Figure 1.9 is that the hydrogen atoms *share* their electrons with the oxygen atom in *covalent chemical bonding*. Specifically, the hydrogen electrons become the covalent bonding electrons which hold the hydrogen atoms to the oxygen atom. The molecule of water on the right side of Section A of Figure 1.9 is electrically balanced with 10 electrons for the combined 10 protons: 8 for the oxygen atom and 1 for each of the 2 hydrogen atoms. Also, the capacity of the outermost shell of each atom is satisfied with the maximum number of possible electrons—the L shell of the oxygen atom contains 8 electrons and the K shell of each hydrogen atom contains 2 electrons.

Now, along comes alpha, beta, or gamma radiation. When either impacts with a covalent electron, the electron may be knocked off as a free electron (negatively charged ion). If a covalent electron is knocked off its parent atom, as shown in Section B of Figure 1.9, the original water molecule will have 9 electrons for the 10 protons—the water molecule has one more positive charge than negative charges—it is positively charged: $(+10) + (-9) = +1$. Equation 1-4 explains the reaction in Section B of Figure 1.9. The ionizing radiation may cause one of the valence electrons to be knocked off the water molecule, creating a positive water ion, H_2O^+, and a free electron, e^-. The positive water ion is also a charged free radical that is usually not compatible with the living chemistry of the cell which originally used the neutral water molecule. The free electron ejected from the water molecule should not have enough energy to cause ionization in another water molecule, as would beta radiation, but the free electron may be captured by another water molecule yielding a negative water ion, H_2O^- (equation 1-5). The H_2O^+ ion (free radical) from equation 1-4 may break down into a hydroxyl free radical, $OH^\bullet$, and a positive hydrogen ion, H^+ (equation 1-6). The H_2O^- ion (also a free radical) from equation 1-5 may break down into a hydrogen free radical, $H^\bullet$, and a negative hydroxyl ion, OH^- (equation 1-7). One viewpoint expresses that the change in chemical reactivity of the water due to the generation of free radicals due to ionizing radiation can create a chemically poisonous environment for the cell which originally used a complete water molecule.

Another viewpoint expresses that the electron ejected from the water molecule in equation 1-4 does not have enough energy to escape the attraction of the resulting positive charge of the parent water molecule and is therefore attracted back into the original water molecule. The original water molecule now has more energy than before the ionization event and is described as "activated", H_2O^*. The H_2O^* may then break down into a hydrogen free radical, $H^\bullet$, and into a hydroxyl radical (equation 1-8). Hydrogen free radicals from multiple events shown in equation 1-8 may combine to form free hydrogen gas, H_2 (equation 1-9). Free hydrogen in human tissues is not necessarily a harmful condition, but the next step should be harmful. Hydroxyl free radicals from multiple events shown in equation 1-8 may combine to form hydrogen peroxide, H_2O_2 (equation 1-10), which is a chemical poison for the cell which originally used the water molecule. The possible chemical reactivity changes caused by disassociation of a valence electron (ionization) may in itself cause chemical poisoning of the cell which used the previously complete water molecule, the production of hydrogen peroxide notwithstanding.

Other possible reactions of irradiated water components may cause the production of free oxygen in the human tissue which originally used a water molecule. Free oxygen can be found in many body tissues, not as a result of ionizing radiation but just as a course of life. Free oxygen in body tissues tends to increase the reactivity of water to produce hydrogen peroxide under ionizing radiation. Therefore, the free oxygen in body tissues accounts for the tendency of extra-oxygenated tissues to be extra sensitive to ionizing radiation.

Yet another viewpoint expresses that recent studies tend to indicate the primary target of radiation-induced damage at the cellular level may be in the DNA helix. Research of the effects of ionizing radiation on the DNA helix is ongoing and will not be covered in this text.

In addition, the sensitivity of tissues to radiation, *radiosensitivity*, is related to the rate of cell replication. Some cells may be damaged but not killed by ionizing radiation: damaged to the extent of reducing or stopping the ability of the cells to reproduce even though the cells continue to live. Generally speaking, the higher the rate of cell replication the higher the radiosensitivity. Radiosensitivity will be explained in more detail in Chapter 3.

In a nutshell, the modified chemical reactivity of human compounds, which may result from ionizing nuclear radiation, may result in the loss of the chemical integrity of living compounds within the cells of human tissue and the cells may:

- not be harmed
- repair the damage
- not be completely repaired and suffer dysfunction
- die

At any rate, the key event of irradiation of water in human tissues appears to be biochemical changes leading to chemical poisoning due to the creation of the highly reactive hydrogen and hydroxyl free radicals. If the chemical poisoning occurs in enough living cells, radiation injury may result. Several other possible chemical events can result from the irradiation of water by ionizing radiation. For the satisfaction of interested individuals, the book *Ionizing Radiation and Life*, 1971, Victor Arena from C. V. Mosby Company offers a straight-forward and interesting presentation of a number of possible reactions which may result from irradiation of water by ionizing nuclear radiation.

Other human compounds can also be ionized by nuclear radiation and further chemical poisoning may occur. The covalent bonding between carbon, hydrogen, and oxygen which make up the living Carbohydrates in the human body may also be ionized by nuclear radiation creating still more chemical poisoning or chemical infirmity of the molecules of living tissue.

In the Preface, I stated that radiation can destroy bacteria. Bacteria are living organisms which also depend on chemical harmony within each bacteria cell. Ionizing radiation can cause chemical poisoning in the bacteria cell the same way ionizing radiation can cause chemical poisoning in human cells.

Section 5. Relative Penetration of Nuclear Radiation

In this Section, the relative penetration of nuclear radiation into the human body will be discussed. Alpha, beta, and gamma radiations described herein each have different characteristics regarding penetration into the human tissues. However simplistic my discussion may seem to the scientist or physicist, the concepts are useful to emergency response personnel.

Radiation penetrating into the human body and its tissues must first pass through the four layers of skin tissue: an outermost layer of dead hornified skin tissue covering three layers of living skin tissue.

Imagine alpha, beta, and gamma radiations penetrating the four layers of skin tissue as the three items shown in Figure 1.10 penetrating the four staggered layers of chain-link fence fabric.

Alpha radiation is particulate radiation since it is composed of matter, namely 2 protons and 2 neutrons. Alpha radiation will travel approximately 1 to 2 inches in air. Alpha radiation trying to penetrate into the skin could be compared to trying to get a basketball through the four layers of chain-link fence fabric. The implications are that the particle itself is too large to fit between the molecules of skin tissue to allow it to pass through the skin without being stopped by giving up its energy of motion to the atoms/molecules of skin tissue.

FIGURE 1.10
Relative Radiation Penetration

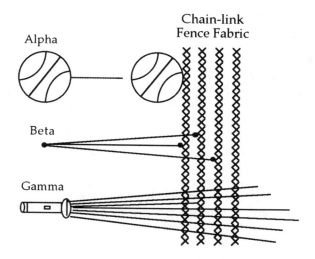

The outermost layer of hornified, dead skin cells will stop alpha radiation. Since the outermost layer of skin tissue is comprised of deal cells, as long as the alpha source remains outside the body no harm is done by the alpha radiation (no ionization of living tissue, therefore no poisoning of living chemistry). A sheet of paper, a coat of paint, even a film of water will stop alpha radiation. However, the covering of the eyeball can be damaged by alpha radiation since the covering of the eyeball is living tissue. Also, openings in the skin (exposed trauma tissue), mucous membrane, digestive linings, and pulmonary linings, i.e., any exposed living tissue, are sensitive to alpha radiation.

Beta radiation is also matter,[8] namely an electron ejected from the nucleus of a radioactive atom and as such is particulate radiation. Beta radiation can travel about 10 to 15 feet in air. Beta radiation trying to penetrate into the skin would be similar to trying to get a ping-pong ball through four staggered layers of chain-link fence

8.   For the objectives of this text, beta radiation is matter. Different experimental conditions can be established to show the beta particle as having wave (energy) properties as well as particulate (matter) properties, i.e., beta can exhibit a wave-particle duality. The wave-particle duality of beta radiation is beyond the scope of this text.

fabric. The ping-pong ball may get through the first layer and maybe even the second layer of chain-link fence fabric without being stopped. However, the chances of the ping-pong ball getting through all four staggered layers of the chain-link fence fabric without impacting a fabric wire are nonexistent. Likewise, beta radiation cannot penetrate completely through the four layers of skin tissue before it expends its energy of motion. As with alpha radiation, exposed living tissue such as eyeball tissue, mucous membranes, digestive linings, wound tissues, and pulmonary linings are sensitive to beta radiation.

Of alpha, beta, and gamma radiations, gamma is the most penetrative. Although each of these types of nuclear radiation is classed as ionizing radiation and each may be harmful to exposed living tissues, gamma radiation has the greatest range of penetration. Gamma radiation may pass well into and through living tissues. Due to the non-matter (energy) nature of gamma radiation, it may pass well into and completely through all four layers of skin tissue and well into the body as depicted by the flashlight beam in Figure 1.10 passing almost unabated through the four layers of chain-link fence fabric. In fact, gamma can pass completely through the human body.[9]

So far, alpha, beta, and gamma radiations have been presented. Another type of radiation which is not nuclear radiation may cause ionization of matter. Specifically, radiation generated from changes in the configuration of electrons...and that is the next subject.

Section 6. Radiation From Electron Shells

Recall that electrons are responsible for chemically binding elements to form compounds. Manipulation of electrons from one energy shell or level to another can also generate radiation, i.e., electromagnetic radiation. Radiation created by manipulation of electrons may be ionizing radiation, but not nuclear ionizing radiation (always remember that nuclear radiation comes from the nucleus of a radioactive atom). Light can be generated by manipulation of electrons between energy levels. Radio and Television signals are created in a similar manner. X-radiation may also be generated by manipulation of electrons.

As shown in Figure 1.4, an element of any atom has 5 possible energy shells which electrons may occupy. The total number of shells

---

9.   If a gamma ray makes it completely through the body, ionization is unlikely. Gamma does most of its damage when it is stopped. There is only one direct ionization event per gamma ray. Some energy changes may occur in the molecule/atom as gamma passes, but they are beyond the scope of this text.

occupied by electrons is determined by the number of electrons in the atom. An electron in one energy shell may be forced to jump up to the next higher energy shell, even into a previously unoccupied energy shell. Electrons being forced to jump into higher energy shells is a process called *electron excitation*. Figure 1.11 displays electron excitation using oxygen.

FIGURE 1.11
Electron Excitation

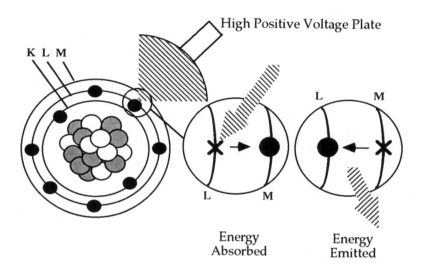

Electrons of any atom can occupy only specific energy shells or levels. Electrons *cannot* occupy space in between shells. If external energy is absorbed by one of the electrons, for example by an electron in the L shell, the electron may become excited and gain energy in excess of the range of energy allowed in the L shell. When the electron gains enough energy, the electron will instantaneously jump to the next higher energy shell, the M shell. An electron being forced out of its home energy level by absorbed energy is called *electron excitation*. The electron has a threshold before jumping to the next energy level or shell. Once the electron jumps, it jumps all the way to the next level: nowhere in between energy levels.

When the electron is knocked into the next higher energy level, an energy "vacancy" is created where the electron was originally located. The energy vacancy will seek to regain the electron it lost. The energy vacancy will draw the ousted electron back to its original energy level, i.e., the *ground level* (its home energy level).[10] When the electron falls back to the ground level , the energy the electron gained to become excited is emitted as *non-nuclear electromagnetic radiation.* The energy or strength of the radiation emitted depends on the amount of energy the electron absorbed during excitation.

A high positive voltage can be used as the external energy source needed for electron excitation and can be applied to the electrons of a particular material. The electrons, which are negatively charged, are attracted by the positive voltage due to the Coulombic law of charges which states that opposite charges attract. The electrons are "pumped" into an excited state by the energy they absorb from being attracted to the high positive voltage. Once the energy level of an electron in the L shell exceeds the range energy level permitted for occupancy in the L shell, the electron instantaneously jumps to the next higher energy shell which, in Figure 1.11, is the M shell. When the electron by nature falls back to its ground state, the energy absorbed while becoming excited is emitted as electromagnetic radiation. The emitted electromagnetic radiation can be ultraviolet light, infrared light, or ionizing radiation such as X-radiation. In Figure 1.11, oxygen is used for the sake of illustration. Other elements are actually used to generate X-radiation.

Although gamma and X-radiation are both electromagnetic radiation, gamma is different from X-radiation in that the gamma originates from the nucleus of a radioactive atom. X-radiation is generated from manipulation of electrons. Since gamma originates in the nucleus of a radioactive atom, it generally has more energy than radiation generated from electron excitation. In either case, each is electromagnetic radiation: energy with no practical mass. The lack of mass of electromagnetic radiation accounts for the ease with which gamma and X-radiation pass through matter. Recall the beam of a flashlight penetrating the chain-link fence fabric in Figure 1.10.

Section 7. When Radiation Is Stopped

In Section 5, three types of radiation penetrating into living tissue were covered, i.e., alpha, beta, and gamma. In this Section some points of interest will be presented regarding what happens when alpha, beta, and gamma radiation are stopped.

When alpha, beta, or gamma radiation bombards living tissue, ionization may occur and the damage, if any, is done. *That is all. Exposure to alpha, beta, and gamma radiation cannot make anything*

10. The *ground level* is the state of energy prior to becoming excited, regardless of the original shell or level.

radioactive nor can exposure to alpha, beta, and gamma radiations contaminate anything with the source of radiation, i.e., the radioactive material. In motion, nuclear radiation may cause harm to living tissue, but once the radiation is stopped no further irradiation from the stopped radiation can occur. Stopping nuclear radiation can be compared to firing a bullet from a pistol into a block wall. In motion, the bullet is harmful to humans. When the bullet stops, it does its damage. Once the bullet is stopped, it is no longer dangerous. The bullet cannot carry more bullets with it nor can the bullet carry the pistol with it. Neither can the ray or particle of radiation carry more radiation with it nor can the ray or particle of radiation carry any of the radiation source material with it. If the exposed material is not living tissue, no harm is done. Exposure to the levels of alpha, beta, or gamma radiation you may encounter in transportation and industrial incidents may pose a risk for living tissue but your equipment and materials are in no danger from these radiations.[11] As stated earlier, alpha, beta, and gamma radiations (as well as X-radiation) can cause ionization in electron shells. A logical question may be "What happens if the radiations collide with the nucleus?"

An alpha particle may collide with a nucleus but the force holding the nucleus together, the *near force*, is too strong to allow the alpha particle to cause other than energy changes in most nuclei. Also, repulsion between the positively charged alpha particle (2 protons, 2 neutrons) and the protons in the nucleus strongly resists permitting the alpha particle to collide with the nucleus.

A gamma ray may collide with a nucleus in the exposed material but still the intranuclear forces are too strong to allow anything but energy changes.

The beta particle, which is an electron ejected from the nucleus of a radioactive atom, has very little mass (remember $1/1845$ of a proton). Recall the examples used in Footnote 4 defining mass and you will gain perspective—a six-inch cork ball has less mass than a six-inch steel ball. The beta particle causing nuclear disruption in a physical sense can be compared to an aluminum beebee trying to break up a cluster of six-inch magnetized steel balls. If you will compare a housefly slamming at full speed into the back of Andre-The Giant, you might get the picture.

---

11. When photographic film is exposed to ionizing radiation, the film may be damaged, specifically, the radiation may cause the film to appear to have been exposed to pinpoints of light. The radiation causes a change in the chemical makeup of the film by ionization the same way light changes the chemical makeup of the film. Changes in the chemical makeup of the film is how X-radiation creates images on photographic film. The X-rays pass unabated through the light-tight jacket around the film. The different densities of objects between the source of radiation and the film, e.g., bones and tumors, cause different degrees of exposure on the film providing an image of the object.

As alpha, beta, and gamma radiations collide with or pass near the nucleus of an atom, the ray or particle may impart some of its energy into the nucleus. Energy absorbed from the radiations *does not* cause the nucleus to break apart. However, the energy absorbed by the nucleus from the impacting or passing ray or particle of radiation may excite the nucleus to a higher energy state. The higher energy state may cause secondary emission of electromagnetic radiation but the secondary radiation is not likely to be ionizing radiation.

Section 8. Neutron Radiation

So far, four types of radiation have been explained—alpha, beta, and gamma nuclear radiations, and X-radiation. Exposure to either of these radiations cannot make anything radioactive. However, one type of nuclear radiation can induce radioactivity in matter, including living tissue, specifically *neutron radiation*.

I have never heard of any transportation incident involving neutron radiation. However, some neutron generating materials are in transport today and someday an incident involving neutron radiation may occur. Also, nuclear power incidents may involve neutron exposures to utility workers who may need your services.

Neutron radiation may induce radioactivity and cause the exposed material to become radioactive. Recall the example of introducing two neutrons into a carbon-12 nucleus, causing it to become radioactive carbon-14. Neutrons *may* be absorbed by the nuclei of some human tissue elements. Should human tissue nuclei absorb neutrons, the nuclei will be changed to isotopes which *may* or *may not* be radioactive. Whether the nuclei absorb neutrons depends on the energy (speed) of the neutron radiation and on the ability of the target nucleus to absorb the neutrons.

A curious thing about neutron radiation is that the physical size the target nucleus may appear to the neutron as a different size when the neutron travels at different speeds. For example, when traveling at a sodium nucleus at one speed, the neutron may see the nucleus as a target as big as a barn. However, if the same neutron is traveling faster, it may view the sodium nucleus as big as two barns. Then again, if the same neutron is traveling even faster, the neutron may see the same sodium nucleus as less than one barn big. Traveling even faster, the same neutron may see the sodium nucleus as two barns again or even bigger. If the same neutron looks at nuclei of other elements while traveling at the same speed, the different nuclei may appear as different size targets. The nucleus of an element may even be invisible to the neutron at one speed but quite large when the neutron is traveling faster or slower. The size a nucleus appears to be to a neutron in motion is called the *neutron cross section* of the target nucleus. The cross section means the physical size the target appears to be to the neutron at a given speed. The neutron cross section of a given nucleus (target size) will change with different neutron speeds. Also, at a given neutron speed the neutron cross section of one element nucleus may be different than a nucleus of another element.

In any case, the amount of induced radioactivity, if any, due to neutron irradiation should be of lesser concern for attending personnel than the direct radiation and of even lesser concern than the medical status of the patient. While the energy of the radiation from the induced radioactivity may be as high as the more harmful radiation energies, the rate of exposure to the radiation from the induced radioactivity should be relatively low. Induced radioactivity by neutron bombardment is *not* contagious nor can any radioactivity induced by neutron capture induce more radioactivity.

A method used by specialists to determine whether the patient has been exposed to neutron radiation is to monitor any metallic objects on the patient at the time of exposure. Once it is determined that no loose radioactive contamination is present on the metal object and that there is no contamination chemically affixed to the metal object, the specialists monitor the object with special radiation detection instruments. The equipment must be super-sensitive because the radiation levels from the metallic object due to neutron-induced radioactivity might be so weak that common instruments (see Chapter 4) may not detect the radiation. Also, the equipment operator must have special training in the use and interpretation of the specialized instruments. If the instrument operator discovers radiation that is coming from the metallic objects and the radiation is not coming from radioactive contamination or chemical affixation, induced radioactivity may be suspected. Hair and nail clippings may also reveal neutron exposure but only to the specially trained expert radiological health physicist.

Section 9. "Can Radiation and Radioactivity Be Destroyed?"

"This stuff is radioactive. Let's burn it to destroy it. Alcohol kills bacteria. I'll bet it will kill this radioactive material. If not, I'll bet this Sulfuric Acid will do it. Right?"

NO

Remember, nuclear radiation comes from the nucleus of a radioactive atom. Earthly chemical and physical forces cannot touch the nucleus of an atom, therefore *nuclear radiation and radioactive materials cannot be destroyed by earthly chemical and physical means.* Fire (a chemical reaction combining oxygen with fuel) will merely change the physical form of the material. The smoke will contain the radioactive material in the form of radioactive gasses and flyash. The radioactive gasses and flyash will, of course, be diluted in the air and therefore not as concentrated as the original form of the source material, but will still be radioactive nonetheless. Acid may dissolve the material but the resultant liquid will contain radioactivity due the radioactive material becoming a chemical part of the liquid. Acid dissolving radioactive material is not induced radioactivity, it is a chemical reaction. Alcohol will not "kill" radiation or radioactive material as it will kill bacteria. Alcohol will merely transport the radioactive material in a liquid vehicle.

Regarding the statement that no earthly chemical or physical means can destroy radiation or radioactivity, if the radioactive material is subjected to the temperatures of the Sun the nucleus may become altered and the radioactive nature of the material may be altered or lost. However, solar temperatures do not exist on Earth except in thermonuclear weapons and in some ultra-special laboratory apparatus. In fact, the use of heat is how the Sun creates heat. On the Sun, nuclei are fused together by heat (nuclear fusion). Doing so in the way the Sun does it creates heat—lots of heat, and other energies too, including gamma and X-radiation.

Section 10. Natural Background Radiation

Natural background radiation is radiation bombarding all of us from everywhere all of the time; from the Earth, from outerspace, from the air, from building materials, from the food we eat. Background radiation comes from naturally occurring radioactive isotopes in everything, even our own bodies. The quantity of naturally occurring radioactive isotopes in our bodies is very small, but nonetheless, there are radioactive isotopes within us. Some of the potassium which is so vital to our living chemistry is radioactive. Some of the sodium which is also vital to our living chemistry is within us as a radioactive isotope. Even some of the carbon, the element on which life is based, that is within our bodies is radioactive. Some background radiation is likely to still be coming from nuclear weapons testing. The Chernobyl disaster has contributed to world-wide fallout as well. We have lived with background radiation since we were born. Even our fathers and mothers had radioactive materials in them and still do.

The level of natural background radiation varies widely from area to area across the world. The average background radiation in the United States is approximately 30 counts per minute on a Geiger-Mueller instrument (see Chapter 4).

Chapter 2

EXPOSURE AND CONTAMINATION

PREVIEW

Inherent with any accident involving nuclear radiation or radioactive materials, a possibility exists that incident victims have been exposed to radiation or have become externally or internally contaminated with radioactive material. In this Chapter, guidance and suggested controls regarding exposure to nuclear radiation and contamination with radioactive materials will be presented. Topics include:

- External exposure to radiation
- External contamination with radioactive materials
- Internal contamination with radioactive materials
- Contamination and exposure controls
- Personnel protective measures and decontamination techniques

It is not the intent of this Chapter to include each and every variation and detail of radiation exposure and radioactive contamination. However, the techniques described and suggested herein will provide a basis for developing your own standards of exposure and contamination controls.

In Chapter 1, alpha, beta, and gamma radiations were presented in some detail. As stated in Chapter 1, gamma radiation has the greatest penetration into living tissue and has the greatest distance of travel in air. This Chapter will be based on the properties and characteristics of gamma radiation unless otherwise indicated.

Section 1. Introduction to Exposure and Contamination

Transportation of radioactive materials on our highways occurs more often than most people realize. Radiation and radioactive materials are used more frequently than most people understand. An incident or trauma involving radiation or radioactive materials is not merely a possibility—it is a reality that may occur almost anywhere at any time. In each incident involving radiation, the victim(s) may have received external exposure to the radiation.   In each incident involving radioactive materials, the victim(s) may have become externally or internally contaminated with the radioactive materials as well as have become exposed to the radiation from them.

Radiation *exposure* is being bombarded with radiation. Radioactive *contamination* is radioactive material wherever it is not wanted. Without radiation detection equipment, it is not possible to ascertain beyond any doubt whether nuclear radiation is present.[12] Without the capability to perform specialized radiological contamination surveys with radiation detection equipment, it is not possible to ascertain beyond any doubt whether a victim has received any external or internal contamination. Eye-witness accounts and the victim himself/herself may prove helpful in obtaining incident data and information about the trauma/injury mechanisms. However, eye-witness accounts and victim statements other than "I was about 15 feet from it", "I touched it" will not likely be helpful regarding information about victim radiation exposure or contamination.

Without absolute evidence proving otherwise, you must assume the victim of a radiological incident has been:

- exposed to radiation
- externally contaminated with the radioactive materials
- internally contaminated with the radioactive materials

Section 2. Exposure and Dose

The title of this Section is not redundancy of terms. Exposure and dose are not the same. Let me explain.

A beachbody wants to get a good tan. The sun is exceptionally strong today so it should not take near as long to get a good tan as it would if the sun were not so strong. After an hour of volleyball in the sun, the beachbody has realized his goal and has a nice tan. After two hours of volleyball, the beachbody noticed his tan was even darker.

---

12. Examples of and operation of selected radiation detection equipment will be presented in Chapter 4.

In this scenario the beachbody received an exposure *to* the sun's radiation as well as a dose *of* the sun's radiation. His skin being bombarded with the sun's radiation was an *exposure*. The effect of the absorption of the sun's radiation, i.e., his tan, was a *dose*.

The magnitude or severity of the dose received from exposure to ionizing radiation depends mainly on the *type* and *energy* of radiation, the *exposure rate* of the radiation, and the *duration of the exposure*. For purposes of simplification, I will collectively describe the type, energy and exposure rate of the radiation as the strength of the radiation. The stronger the radiation and the longer the duration of exposure, the more severe the effect of the exposure, i.e, the greater the radiation dose. In the beachbody example, the stronger the sunlight and the longer the beachbody stays in the sunlight, the deeper his tan. Likewise, the stronger the ionizing radiation and the longer the individual stays in the radiation field, the more severe the effects of the exposure: the more severe the dose.

The faster the exposure is delivered the higher the exposure rate. Again using the beachbody example, the exposure rate from the noon sun is higher than the exposure rate from the early morning or late afternoon sun. The beachbody's tan will happen much sooner in the noon sun than in the early morning or late afternoon sun. The stronger the radiation, the quicker the dose (the tan) is manifest.[13]

The different *areas of the body* must also be considered when determining the absorbed dose to ionizing radiation. Also, some tissues and organs (biologic systems) of the body are less sensitive to the effects of ionizing radiation than others, i.e., different tissues and organs may have different *radiosensitivity*. Chapter 3 provides additional detail on radiosensitivity. To summarize, while the patient's *accumulated exposure* depends on the exposure rate and the duration of exposure, a patient's *accumulated dose* depends on:

- the type and energy of radiation and the exposure rate from the source material,

- the duration of the exposure (the length of time in the exposure/radiation field, once-upon-a-time the "stay-time"),

- the sensitivity of the exposed tissue to the type and energy of exposing radiation, and

- the area of the body exposed.

---

13. Although the ultraviolet light in the sun's radiation can be ionizing radiation, in this example, the sunlight is not intended to be considered ionizing radiation, just a source of radiation for purposes of illustration.

To fully explain exposure, exposure rate, dose, and dose rate, it is necessary to identify the units of radiation measurement.

- The unit for measuring *exposure* to ionizing radiation is the *Roentgen* (**R**). The Roentgen measures the total number of ion pairs produced in 1 cubic centimeter of air by gamma or X-radiation.

- The units for measuring *dose* to ionizing radiation are the *rad* (**R**adiation **A**bsorbed **D**ose) and the *rem* (Roentgen Equivalent Man). The *rad* is a unit of energy imparted to matter by ionizing radiation per unit mass of exposed material. The rad is best described as the absorbed dose of radiation. The *rem* is a special unit of dose equivalence which is numerically equal to the absorbed dose in rads multiplied by a *Quality Factor*. The Quality Factor accounts for the differences of the exposed tissue, the type of exposing radiation, and energy of the exposing radiation. The rem best relates dose to the biological effects of the dose respective of the type of radiation.

For gamma and X-radiation the Roentgen, the rad, and the rem are almost equal since the quality factor for gamma or X-radiation is approximately 1 for most tissues. For all practical purposes of emergency services, the differences between the quality factor for the different types of tissue is negligible. The units designated by the International System of Units (SI) for measuring dose to ionizing radiation are the *gray* (Gy), which is equivalent to 100 rads, and the *sievert* (Sv), which is equivalent to 100 rem. Table 2.1 summarizes the units of measuring exposure and dose to ionizing radiation.

TABLE 2.1
Radiation Exposure and Dose Units

Roentgen	Ionization in air by X- and gamma radiation
Rad	Radiation Absorbed Dose
Rem	Roentgen Equivalent Man
Gray	(Gy) 100 rad
Sievert	(Sv) 100 rem

Radiation measurement units are commonly expressed in fractions just as other units of measure are expressed in fractions, e.g., 1/16th of an inch, 1/4th of a cup, or 1/10th of a mile. The most common fractional unit of measurement is $1/1000$th. The prefix used to specify $1/1000$th is *milli*. Another fractional unit used is $1/100$th. The prefix used to specify $1/100$th is *centi*. Common units of measurement using the terms milli and centi include:

- millimeter ($1/1000$th of a meter)
- milligram ($1/1000$th of a gram)
- millivolt ($1/1000$th of a volt)
- centimeter ($1/100$th of a meter)
- centigram ($1/100$th of a gram)
- centiliter ($1/100$th of a liter)

Common fractional units to express exposure and dose measurement include *milliRoentgen, millirad, or millirem, millisievert, milligray, centisievert, and centigray*:

- milliRoentgen ($1/1000$th of a Roentgen)
- millirad ($1/1000$th of a rad)
- millirem ($1/1000$th of a rem)
- millisievert ($1/1000$th of a sievert)
- centisievert ($1/100$th of a sievert)
- milligray ($1/1000$th of a gray)
- centigray ($1/100$th of a gray)

The prefix milli is abbreviated using a lower case "m" and the prefix centi is abbreviated using a lower case "c", e.g.,

- milliRoentgen (mR)
- millirad (mrad)
- centisievert (cSv)
- centigray (cGy)
- millirem (mrem)

Units for measuring *exposure rate* and *dose rate* are expressed as *units per time*. For example:

- Roentgen per hour (R/hr)
- rad per hour (rad/hr)
- rem per hour (rem/hr)

Fractional units of exposure rate and dose rate include:

- milliRoentgen per hour (mR/hr)
- millirad per hour (mrad/hr)
- millirem per hour (mrem/hr)

Since the gray is 100 rad and the sievert is 100 rem, how many rem is a cSv? How many rad is a mGy? The answers to these questions are simple conversions of the terms as follows:

$$1 \, cSv \; = \; \frac{Sv}{100} \quad \text{and} \quad 1 \, Sv \; = \; 100 \, rem, \quad \text{therefore} \qquad (2\text{-}1)$$

$$1 \, cSv \; = \; \frac{100 \, rem}{100} \; = \; \frac{1\cancel{00} \, rem}{1\cancel{00}} \; = \; 1 \, rem$$

$$1 \, mGy \; = \; \frac{Gy}{1000} \quad \text{and} \quad 1 \, Gy \; = \; 100 \, rad, \quad \text{therefore} \qquad (2\text{-}2)$$

$$1 \, mGy \; = \; \frac{100 \, rad}{1000} \; = \; \frac{1\cancel{00} \, rad}{10\cancel{00}} = \; \frac{1}{10} \; rad$$

or 0.1 rad (100 mrad)

As stated earlier in this Section, the duration of exposure of the patient in the radiation field is as important to determining the patient's accumulated dose as the type and energy of the radiation and the exposure rate. To illustrate accumulated dose, consider the following. If the patient is in a dose rate of 100 millirem (mrem) per hour for one hour, his/her accumulated dose would be 100 mrem (100 mrem/hr x 1 hr = 100 mrem), algebraically stated,

$$\frac{100 \, mrem}{hr} \; x \; 1 \, hr \; = \; \frac{100 \, mrem}{\cancel{hr}} \; x \; 1 \, \cancel{hr} = 100 \, mrem \qquad (2\text{-}3)$$

If the patient stays in the same radiation field but for only half an hour, his/her accumulated dose would be only 50 mrem (100 mrem/hr x 0.5 hr = 50 mrem). If the patient stays in the same radiation field for only 15 minutes (quarter of an hour), his/her dose would be only 25 mrem. The following displays this information algebraically:

$$\frac{100 \, mrem}{hr} \; x \; 0.5 \, hr \; = \; \frac{100 \, mrem}{\cancel{hr}} \; x \; 0.5 \, \cancel{hr} \; = \; 50 \, mrem \qquad (2\text{-}4)$$

$$\frac{100 \, mrem}{hr} \; x \; 0.25 \, hr \; = \; \frac{100 \, mrem}{\cancel{hr}} \; x \; 0.25 \, \cancel{hr} = \; 25 \, mrem \qquad (2\text{-}5)$$

Table 2.2 provides additional examples of dose determination.

TABLE 2.2
Accumulated Dose

Dose Rate x Time = Dose

$$\frac{500 \text{ mrem}}{\text{hour}} \times 2 \text{ hours} = 1000 \text{ mrem}$$

$$\frac{200 \text{ rem}}{\text{hour}} \times 45 \text{ min} = 150 \text{ rem}$$
$$(0.75 \text{ hr})$$

$$\frac{80 \text{ mrem}}{\text{hour}} \times 6 \text{ min} = 8 \text{ mrem}$$
$$(0.1 \text{ hr})$$

Additional information for determining the patient's accumulated dose will be presented in Chapter 3.

Recall that radiation and radioactivity are not the same. As radiation is measured in units such as rem, sievert, gray, and rad, radioactivity also has a unit of measure. Radioactivity is expressed in *curies*. The curie is named after Pierre and Marie Curie for discovering polonium and radium. The curie is abbreviated as *Ci*. One curie of any radioactive material will emit 37,000,000,000 (3.7 x 10^{10}) events of radiation per second. Think of it—37 billion rays or particles of radiation per second. As radiation units may be expressed in fractional units, the curie may also be expressed in fractional units. The fractional term milli is often used with the curie. The millicurie is abbreviated mCi. Another fractional unit prefix often used with the curie is *micro*. The prefix micro (abbreviated with the Greek letter μ (Mu) means one-millionth: one microcurie (1 μCi) is $1/1,000,000$th of a curie. One μCi would emit approximately 37,000 rays or particles of radiation per second at the source.

Section 3. External Exposure and Exposure Controls:
Time, Distance, Shielding

External exposure is simply being exposed to radiation from a source outside the body. Many of us have had the opportunity to know the snuggly feeling of standing with your spouse next to a warm campfire on a cold winter night. If you have, you can understand that you cannot get too close to the fire or stand there too long else your pants may start smoking, or at least you may not be able to sit down until your pants cool off. While standing near a campfire, you are receiving an external exposure to thermal radiation.

Stand too close and your pants may start smoking. Stand too long too close to the fire and your pants may start smoking. Control of personnel and patient exposure to ionizing radiation may be achieved in much the same way of controlling the temperature of your pants while next to the campfire: minimize *time* in the area and maximize your *distance* from the source of radiation as much as practical.

Another factor of exposure control is to keep as much *shielding* (mass) between you and the source as possible. When somebody moves between you and the campfire on a cold night, you know quite soon how shielding protects you from the external exposure to the heat of the campfire. Keep in mind that implementing patient exposure control techniques before providing immediate medical service and patient stabilization may cause more harm than providing medical services and stabilization first. Table 2.3 itemizes time, distance, and shielding as features of exposure control.

TABLE 2.3
Exposure Controls

Use as much as practical:

Time	limit time in the exposure field as much as possible
Distance	stay as far away from the source as practical
Shielding	keep as much mass as practicable between the patient and the source

Exposure controls may be useful in minimizing your exposure and the exposure of the patient. If you opt to provide medical needs and patient stabilization before implementing exposure control techniques, integrate any exposure control techniques you learn herein while treating the patient. However, *the well-being of the patient should be foremost in providing medical care to the patient.* You have the luxury of controlling what is happening to you—the non-ambulatory patient does not have that luxury. The patient is depending on you.

The remainder of this Section presents each of the exposure control techniques.

Time as an Exposure Control Technique

Limitation of *time* in the exposure field is an important element of exposure control. Spend no more time than is necessary in the exposure field. Ensure that each and every movement you make is not wasted. Both you and the patient will benefit.

One example of limiting an individual's time in a radiation field is using a team approach to patient treatment and extrication. If a team approach would not jeopardize quality patient care, team 1 should provide immediate and vital life support while team 2 prepares the plan and equipment for extrication. When team 1 has stabilized the patient and readied him/her for extrication, team 2 should step in and take over. When team 2 is in place, team 1 should step out. Teamwork is easy to describe in a nice and safe textbook. But you and I both know that in a "real" incident involving the treatment of life-threatening trauma at least one medic will need to constantly apply life support while the personnel extricating the patient do their job. The ultimate point of the team approach is that if the opportunity arises in a radiation field to swap medical personnel during treatment and extrication, do so *only if it will not compromise quality care for the patient and will not cause an increase of time in the radiation field.*

Another example for limiting time in an exposure field is to step back away from the source of radiation while standing by to provide further support. Even if you step back for only a few seconds and only a few feet away, doing so will help reduce your total dose to the radiation.

Distance as an Exposure Control Technique

The previous paragraph suggested that while standing by, you should step back out of the exposure field if only a few feet away. Stepping back out of the exposure field not only reduces your time in the exposure field, it also increases your *distance* from the source of radiation. Using distance from the source as an exposure control technique is as important for medical personnel as minimizing time in an exposure field.

If you increase your distance from the source of gamma radiation, the exposure rate reaching you will decrease. Recall the beam of a flashlight. The farther away from the flashlight you stand, the less the amount of light reaching you. Try the following experiment in the dark of night. Hold a flashlight a few inches away from this book and try reading a few words. Then move the flashlight 20 feet away from the book and try to read a few other words. Reading the words is easy in the strength of the light from a flashlight held a few inches away from the book, but not so easy when the flashlight is 20 feet away. It is the same story for gamma radiation except the flashlight beam is focused where the radiation coming from a gamma source is not focused. In any case involving electromagnetic radiation, the farther you are away from the source of radiation, the less the amount of radiation reaching you. Figure 2.1 shows perspective of how the exposure rate decreases as the distance from the source increases.

A source of gamma radiation emits gamma in straight lines in all directions around the source. Envision the arrowhead lines in Figure 2.1 pointing away from the source as rays of gamma radiation being emitted from the source. Notice that bar A is intersected by 8 lines of radiation. Bar B is intersected by only 2 lines of radiation. The principle of reduced electromagnetic radiation levels at increased distances is similar, i.e., the farther you are away from the source of electromagnetic radiation, the fewer the "lines" of radiation reaching you.

FIGURE 2.1
Radiation and Distance

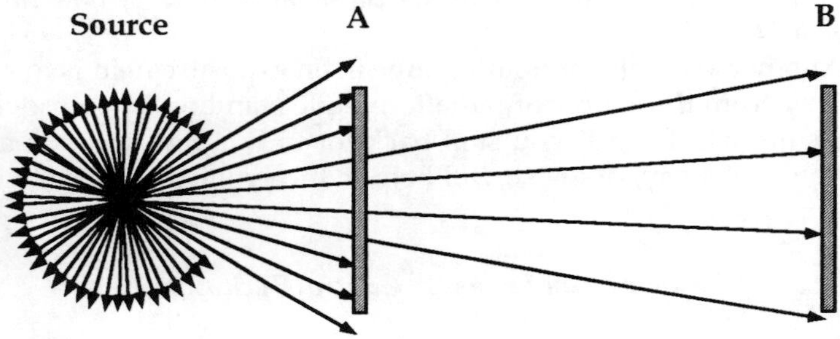

There is a specific mathematical relationship which will determine the exposure rate reaching you as you increase distance from the source. If you double the distance between the patient and the source of radiation, the exposure rate reaching the patient will reduce to a fourth of what it was at the previous location. Reduction in the exposure rate with an increase in distance is known as the *inverse square law*. For example, if the patient is located 5 feet from the source of radiation and is being exposed to 400 milliRoentgen per hour (mR/hr), moving the patient out to 10 feet (double the distance) from the source of radiation will reduce the exposure rate to 100 mR/hr (a fourth of 400 mR/hr). Doubling the distance again by moving the patient out to 20 feet from the source will again reduce the exposure rate reaching the patient by a fourth to 25 mR/hr. An exposure rate of 10,000 mR/hr (10 R/hr) at 1 foot would reduce to 2.5 mR/hr at 64 feet away. Note that the reverse applies as well. Namely, if you reduce by half the distance between the patient and the source of radiation, the exposure rate reaching the patient will quadruple. Figure 2.2 demonstrates the inverse square law.

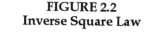

FIGURE 2.2
Inverse Square Law

The above relationships can be determined more precisely when distances cannot be so neatly segmented, i.e., 5 feet, 10 feet, and 20 feet doubling. The equation for the inverse square law can be used to determine the exposure rate at any given distance if the exposure rate at one distance is known. The exact equation for the inverse square law is:

$$\frac{(D_{Start})^2}{(D_{New})^2} = \frac{X_{New}}{X_{Start}} \qquad (2\text{-}6)$$

Where D_{Start} is the starting distance, D_{New} is the new distance away from the source of radiation, X_{Start} is the exposure rate at the starting distance, and X_{New} is the exposure rate at the new distance away from the source. Applying the inverse square law to the values in Figure 2.1:

Starting distance (D_{Start}) = 5 feet,
New distance (D_{New}) = 10 feet
Exposure rate at starting distance (X_{Start}) = 400 mR/hr
Exposure rate at new distance (X_{New}) = To be determined

$$\frac{(5\text{ feet})^2}{(10\text{ feet})^2} = \frac{X}{400\text{ mR/hr}}, \qquad \frac{25\text{ feet}}{100\text{ feet}} = \frac{X}{400\text{ mR/hr}},$$

$$\frac{1}{4} = \frac{X}{400\text{ mR/hr}}, \qquad 4X = 400\text{ mR/hr},$$

$$X = 100\text{ mR/hr}$$

Note that the inverse square law does not apply to alpha and beta radiations because they are not electromagnetic radiation. The inverse square law applies exactly to a point source of electromagnetic radiation such as gamma radiation, heat, light, and microwaves, but not to a large source of electromagnetic radiation such as gamma coming from widespread contamination. Even though the inverse square law does not apply neatly to alpha and beta radiation nor to a source of radiation coming from a large area, the farther you are away from the source or contamination, the better off the patient and you will be.

Shielding as an Exposure Control Technique

There is not much to say within the scope of this text about *shielding* as a factor of exposure control against gamma except that the more mass there is between the patient and the source of radiation, the less the amount of radiation reaching the patient. Likewise, the more mass between you and the source, the less the radiation reaching you.

Recall the definition of mass. Mass relates weight and volume. The examples used were a steel ball and a cork ball. Steel has more mass than cork because a steel ball has more weight than a ball of cork the same size (same volume). Therefore, steel will shield from radiation better than an equal volume of cork. Earth has more mass and will provide more shielding than an equal volume of air. Concrete has more mass and will provide more shielding than an equal volume of earth. Lead has more mass than steel or concrete and will provide more shielding than an equal volume of steel or concrete.

Since alpha radiation can be stopped by a sheet of paper, a coat of paint, a few inches of air, or a film of water, alpha radiation is of little concern regarding an external exposure hazard except when unprotected living tissue is involved. It is important to understand, however, that if you have instruments that detect alpha radiation and if they indicate alpha is present, there is a loss of containment of the alpha emitting material, which can be of great concern, even though alpha radiation cannot travel very far nor can it penetrate the skin.

Beta radiation can travel 4 meters (approximately 12 feet) per MeV in air and will penetrate more matter than alpha. Although beta radiation cannot penetrate completely through the skin, in strong concentrations exposure to beta radiation can cause burns to the skin which are similar to and can be treated much the same as thermal burns (heat burns). Beta can also cause epilation (loss of hair) which should eventually grow back, depending on the dose received. Just about anything metallic will shield from beta. Firefighting turnout gear will offer great protection from alpha and good protection from beta. The faceplate on firefighting headgear will stop alpha and should stop beta. A standard lab coat affords great protection from alpha and some protection from beta. While surgical gloves provide excellent protection from alpha radiation, they afford little protection from beta. The best feature of wearing surgical or other lightweight gloves is in contamination control while affording pulse palpation and tool handling. Wear as many pair of gloves as you can while still being able to palpate a patient's pulse: two or three pairs of gloves seems to be nominal.

The items mentioned above as useful for shielding against alpha and/or beta radiations are useless against gamma radiation. Almost nothing will guarantee shielding against gamma radiation. However, as a reminder, the more mass between the source of gamma radiation and the patient or attendant, the better the protection against gamma. Strategic positioning of response activities behind a concrete wall or in a convenient ditch will help shield against gamma radiation. Remember that gamma radiation travels in a straight line from the source, i.e., if you can see the source of gamma radiation, the radiation can reach you if you are within the range if its travel. Again liken the source of gamma radiation with the head of an illuminated flashlight. If you can see the head of the flashlight and are within the range of its beam—its light can reach you. However, if something is in between you and the flashlight, even if you are within its range, the beam of the flashlight cannot reach you. Remember that light and gamma radiation are examples of electromagnetic radiation and the characteristics of travel of gamma radiation and light in air are the same except that light cannot pass through solid objects while gamma radiation can. Also, light can reflect off objects while gamma radiation does not.[14]

Remember, the more dense the object the greater the mass of the object between you and the source of radiation, therefore the greater the shielding. While the best protection from gamma radiation is to get as far away from the source as practical, responding personnel must keep in mind the well-being of the patient. The chances of a transportation incident producing gamma exposure rates that even approach an acute exposure hazard level are small. Be extremely careful of risky patient movement for the sake of minimizing gamma exposure due to a suspected gamma hazard. Emergency medical support to nuclear power or other industrial facilities using radiation or radioactive materials may require a little more observance of exposure controls, but the patient's well-being should be of greater concern.

One other factor common to radioactive materials is that none of them will be radioactive forever. They will each eventually "die" and become non-radioactive due to a decay factor termed *half-life*

---

14. Gamma radiation can cause secondary electromagnetic radiation and can be likened to reflected radiation. However, the secondary radiation can be considered insignificant as an exposure hazard compared to direct (line-of-sight) exposure.

($t^{1/2}$). The half-life of a radioactive isotope is the amount of time it takes for the original quantity of the isotope to reduce to half its original strength. Figure 2.3 shows an example of half-life. If an isotope has a half-life of 10 days and on day zero the quantity of isotope emits 50 milliRoentgen per hour, 10 days later the quantity of isotope will emit only 25 milliRoentgen per hour. In 10 more days, the amount of radiation emitted will reduce to 12.5 milliRoentgen per hour, and so on until the source is no longer radioactive.

FIGURE 2.3
Radiological Half-life

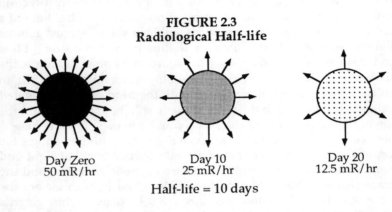

| Day Zero | Day 10 | Day 20 |
| 50 mR/hr | 25 mR/hr | 12.5 mR/hr |

Half-life = 10 days

As a bit of trivia, if the original quantity of isotope is 10 grams of radioactive cobalt-60, after the first half-life the 10 grams of cobalt-60 will decay into 5 grams of cobalt-60 and 5 grams of non-radioactive nickel. After another half-life, the 5 grams of cobalt-60 will decay to 2.5 grams of cobalt-60, leaving 7.5 grams of nickel. For your information, the half-life of cobalt-60 is 5.27 years.

There are many different radioactive isotopes. Each may have a unique half-life. The half-lives of the multitude of isotopes vary from a few fractions of a second to many years. Although any radioactive material will eventually decay to a stable (non-radioactive) state, it may take years to decay to a non-radioactive state. So, do not delay emergency medical services hoping the radioactive material will soon decay to a non-radioactive state.

Section 4. External Contamination with Radioactive Materials

Remember that exposure to alpha, beta, and gamma radiations cannot make anything radioactive whether alive or inanimate. Also remember that these radiations cannot transport the radioactive material to the exposed individual. Recall the example in Chapter 1 comparing radiation to a bullet fired from a pistol into a block wall.

In motion the bullet can be harmful, but once it is stopped, no further harm is done. The bullet cannot carry more bullets or the pistol with it nor can radiation carry any radioactive material. Therefore, *exposure to radiation cannot contaminate the exposed individual with the radioactive source material. Becoming contaminated requires physical contact with the radioactive material.*

Contamination can be caused by any mechanism which can cause the radioactive material to come in contact with an individual or equipment and tools. Such mechanisms include hands, incident debris, dust, smoke, tools, liquids, and projectiles. Few radioactive materials in transport are gaseous. Most are either solids or liquids. However, any fire involving radioactive materials must be dealt with as involving airborne radioactivity. Smoke of fire involving radioactive materials will more than likely transport radioactive flyash, dust, or minute particles of the radioactive material, diluted in the air of course, but still radioactive. Recall from Chapter 1 that fire *cannot* destroy radiation nor radioactive materials. The combustion products will be radioactive since fire is the chemical reaction of combining oxygen with the combustible material. Also recall from Chapter 1 that chemical reactions, including fire, involve only the electron shells, not the nucleus and therefore cannot alter the radioactivity in the nucleus.

A patient with external contamination by radioactive materials is a patient who has in some way received the radioactive material on the outside of his/her person, e.g., on the patient's skin, hair, or clothing. Since the patient will probably have come close enough to the source of radiation to become contaminated, the patient will probably have received an external exposure from the radioactive source as well as having become externally contaminated. There may be radiation coming from the patient but *the patient will not be radioactive—the contamination is the source of the radiation.* Partial removal of the gross, obvious contamination will help reduce the problem. Disrobing the patient is indicated in cases of external contamination—not so much as an exposure control measure but as a contamination control measure. Show all consideration practical to modesty when disrobing the patient is indicated. If you should disrobe the patient, save all items, not necessarily as a legal issue but as a contamination control measure. Place all items removed from the patient in a large plastic bag or similar waterproof container. Label the bag with, at a minimum:

- the patient's name
- the contents of the bag
- the date/time of disrobing the patient.

Chapter 7 provides greater detail into disrobing the radioactively contaminated patient.

However contaminated the patient may be, consider that disrobing the patient takes time and may cause undue manipulation of the patient's injuries. Disrobing the patient and other decontamination measures in the field may cause unnecessary delay which may cause more harm than good. It is precedence in the United States in instances of patient contamination that the level of patient contamination has been of minimal concern to attending personnel, even when the contaminated patient was generated from a nuclear power facility. An 18-year case study by Radiation Management Consultants of contaminated patients which were transported to offsite medical facilities from nuclear power facilities in the US revealed the highest dose to attending personnel from patient contamination was 14 millirem. I am not saying it is impossible to encounter a patient so contaminated with radioactive materials that he/she is an exposure danger for attending personnel, I am just saying it is unlikely.

Practical precautions should be exercised in an external contamination case to prevent the spread of the contamination. Some considerations include wrapping the patient in a sheet or blanket to help contain the contamination. It is not advisable to wrap the patient in non-porous material such as plastic. Wrapping a drill patient in non-porous plastic sheeting has been tried in a July drill and created a real patient from the drill player (hyperthermia). Contamination may be handled much the same as vermin infestation. However, remember from Chapter 1 that as most external vermin infestation can be controlled by topical antiseptics, *radiological contamination cannot be "killed" by antiseptics*. Make extra special effort to prevent the spread of the contamination to wounds or openings in the patient's body that may not yet be contaminated and to prevent further contamination of wounds or openings already contaminated.[15] Also, if wounds exist, use elastic bandages rather than tape to hold dressings in place. The use of adhesive tape is not recommended.

Although it is unlikely that anyone could receive enough contamination on his/her person to become a significant external radiation exposure risk for emergency services personnel, a contaminated patient will be a cross-contamination risk. It is likely that attending personnel will themselves become contaminated unless

---

15. Contamination can be spread very easily. In a class I attended on contamination controls, the instructors spread on handouts a harmless powder that glowed when illuminated by ultraviolet light. About 10 minutes after the start of the class, the instructors surveyed the classroom and attendees with the ultraviolet light. It was a very illuminating experience. The powder was everywhere; on noses, in hair, on faces, on lips, on clothing, on furniture, and just about everything, including me.

they each use contamination control techniques presented in Section 6 of this Chapter or similar techniques. Proper hygiene and handling techniques can limit and even prevent the spread of contamination to yourselves as well as the patient and your equipment.

Life-threatening trauma should be dealt with immediately, radiological contamination and exposure risks notwithstanding. The risk of possible self-contamination and radiation exposure should not impede vital emergency medical services. The chances of significant attendant acute radiation injury from the radiation emitted from a contaminated patient are almost nonexistent. The chances that the patient of a life-threatening injury will degrade without your help are very high. You have the opportunity to be decontaminated relatively easily, maybe with just a shower. The non-ambulatory patient does not have that opportunity.

Section 5. Internal Contamination with Radioactive Materials

A patient with internal contamination will have in some way introduced the radioactive material into his/her body, for example, through inhalation, ingestion, or entry through an opening in the body. If the patient's only contamination is internal, he/she will pose no hazard to attending personnel unless the patient has a great deal of the radioactive material inside his/her body, maybe from an explosion forcing a projectile of the radioactive material into the patient's body. If true, the patient will also have received and will be receiving exposure to the radiation from the projectile. Also, the patient will likely have received external contamination as the projectile and the fragmentation associated with an explosion peppered his/her body.

Since you will likely not have a means to identify internal contamination beyond any doubt, you should assume internal contamination is indicated in any case of contamination with radioactive materials. A sample of all body excreta should be collected and saved—*all* body excreta. The treatment of the patient of internal contamination will, to a large extent, be determined by the type of radioactive material involved. Analysis of the body excreta can reveal the type of radioactive material involved if no other means exist to make that determination.

Regarding the collection of a sample of the patient's body excreta, consider the following. In Chapter 1, you learned the properties of matter and the relationship of matter to nuclear radiation. In particular, nuclear radiation comes from the nucleus of a radioactive atom of matter and that the electrons in orbit around the nucleus and the configuration of the electrons are responsible for the chemical properties of an element. One of the chemical properties of matter is the *chemical affinity* of certain elements for particular organs or areas of the human body. Specifically, some elements when introduced into the body will tend to seek certain organs or areas of the body. For example, the element iodine when introduced inside the body will seek the thyroid. The elements calcium, strontium, and radium each having similar chemical properties tend to seek the bone tissues. Iron will seek habitation in the blood. Elements such as sodium and carbon are not so particular and may permeate the body.

Consider now if some of the above elements are in the form of radioactive isotopes. The isotope will have the same electron configuration and therefore the same chemical properties of the non-radioactive form of the element. The isotope form of the element will therefore tend to seek the organ or area for which the element has a chemical affinity. Once a radioactive isotope has found its chemical host, the isotope will concentrate in that particular organ or area. As radioactive materials concentrate in one spot, the level of radiation in that organ or area will increase, thereby causing "concentrated" effects. The chemical affinity of some radioactive isotopes for certain organs or areas of the body has been utilized in specialized controlled treatment of unwanted conditions of human tissues and organs. However, uncontrolled distribution of radioactive isotopes throughout the human body is, of course, undesirable and may cause damage to otherwise healthy tissues. The possible radiological risk involved with ingestion of radioactive isotopes is in addition to the fact that some radioactive isotopes are also chemical poisons.

If the type of radioactive isotope is known, the element will be known. If the element is known, the chemical affinity of the element for certain organs or areas of the body will be known and will alert radiological and medical personnel to which organ or area they must concentrate their attention. If you can determine the type of radioactive material involved in the incident, the attending physician in charge of patient care, in cooperation with special laboratories and consultants, may deem analysis of the body excreta unnecessary since your efforts have identified the type of radioactive material ingested by the patient. Methods of determining the type as well as the quantity of radioactive material involved in an incident will be presented in Chapter 5.

In any case, if the incident involves contamination with radioactive materials, assume the incident involves internal contamination and collect a sample of all body excreta in labeled containers. If the patient regurgitates, a sample of the vomitus should be collected and saved for isotopic analysis. Sweat wipes and other body fluid wipes should also be saved. Should dressings become blood-soaked or useless, do not discard them. They should also be saved for isotopic analysis as well as for contamination control. In cases involving extended extrication time, consider collecting samples of urine and feces should these excreta present themselves during extrication and transport.

Section 6. Personnel/Patient Protective Measures: Protective Clothing, Contamination Control, Decontamination Techniques, ALARA

Radioactive contamination is radioactive material anywhere it is not wanted, for example, on the patient, on you, on your equipment, in your ambulance, and in the hospital. Some agencies and industries specify a level of contamination before declaring the individual or object is contaminated, specifically, if there is less than a certain amount of radiation coming from the contamination, it is not to be considered contamination. In this text, the patient or object is considered contaminated if there is *any* radioactive contamination present.

In addition to time, distance, and shielding, personnel and patient protective measures include:

- protective clothing
- contamination control
- decontamination techniques

Protective Clothing (PCs)

Astronauts wear special suits to protect them from the vacuum and temperature extremes of outer space. Laboratory technicians often wear smocks to protect themselves and their clothing from caustic or acidic materials. Firefighters have developed a science of special turnout gear for maximizing personal protection from fire and heat.

Protective clothing is a set of garments which provides a measure of protection for the wearer from the environment. Sets of protective clothing are sometimes worn by emergency workers engaged in response to a radiological incident. There are variations in makeup of protective clothing (PCs) for radiation workers, but for the most part the make-up of PCs are common. Protective clothing worn by radiation workers generally consist of:

- Multiple pairs of thin rubber or plastic gloves, e.g., surgical gloves
- Fabric glove liners
- A hood over the head
- Plastic, fabric, or reinforced paper coveralls
- Rubber or plastic boot/shoe shields (covers)
- Rubber or plastic one-piece, tear-away booties
- Eye protection
- Dosimeters
- Depending on the incident atmosphere and available time, negative or positive pressure respirators, or at least a surgical mask or its equivalent

Although these PCs will not protect you from gamma or X-radiation, they will afford some protection from beta radiation and great protection from alpha radiation. The best feature of PCs is their ability to protect you from contamination and to aid in limiting the spread of contamination when used properly.

In cases where adequate time exists to don the PCs, they are useful and indicated. When PCs are indicated, they must provide the best possible seal from the outside environment. All points of mating between parts of the set of PCs should be sealed as much as possible, e.g., between the gloves and the sleeve of the coveralls to help prevent contaminants from entering your PCs. Sealing should be done using wide tape such as masking tape or duct tape. Particular care must be exercised when donning PCs to permit controlled removal of them. Controlled removal will provide for minimizing the spread of the contamination on the PCs to yourself, to the patient, your equipment, and your facility. Table 2.4 provides example techniques for donning and removing PCs.

Contamination Control

After response activities in a radiological incident are complete, treat every external surface of the protective clothing (PCs) as contaminated while removing the PCs. If you touch an external surface of contaminated PCs or equipment with clean hands or tools, your hands and tools will become contaminated. Remove the PC coveralls by rolling them down inside out and stepping out of them, leaving them inside out. Remove the booties or boot/shoe shields with a gloved hand. Remove the gloves and liners by pinching the outside of them near the wrist and peeling them off inside out, liners last of all items. Remove respirators and face masks by leaning forward and pulling down and forward with gloved hands. Be careful to not touch your face with the gloved hands when removing respiratory equipment. Let the hood fall off your head tilted back rather than pulling it over the top of your head. Place *all* removed items in containers lined with a heavy plastic bag for storage until decontaminated or disposed.

TABLE 2.4
Recommended Donning and Removal of Protective Clothing

Donning

a. Remove all outer garments except shoes.
b. Don booties.
c. Don coveralls with bootie cuffs inside the coverall leg and tape coverall chest seam closed.
d. Tape coveralls to booties.
e. Don boot or shoe shields.
f. Don eye protection.
g. Don hood, if used. If hood has chest seam, tape it closed. If a respirator is used, don it before donning the hood. As an option, tape hood face opening to the mask. If a respirator is not used, don a surgical mask.
h. Don glove liners with the cuffs inside the coveralls.
i. Don rubber gloves with the cuffs inside the coveralls. Tape the coveralls to the gloves. Don two or three more pairs of gloves untaped over the first pair.
j. Attach dosimeter to the chest of the coveralls.

Removal

a. Remove all tape.
b. Remove shoe shields.
c. Remove rubber gloves.
d. Remove hood and respirator or surgical mask.
e. Remove and read dosimetry.
f. Remove eye protection.
g. Open coveralls by inserting a finger inside the front seam and pull open. Grasp an inside surface and pull the coveralls over the shoulders and roll them down to the feet inside out. Be carefull not to touch the outside of the coveralls with the glove liners. Step out of them.
h. Remove one bootie and step on to a "clean" mat with the same foot the first bootie was removed from.
i. Remove the other bootie and step on to the "clean" mat.
j. Remove glove liners using two fingers on either hand still inside their liner to remove the opposite liner.

All material removed, except for the dosimetry, must be placed in a lined container. It is advisable to have a radiological survey of yourself performed prior to stepping off the "clean" mat.

Imagine how easily dust falls off things as they are moved and you will understand how easily radioactive contamination may fall from the PCs. Do not jerk or yank off the PCs. Carefully place removed items. Do not toss the removed items into containers as though they were a basketball because you will just scatter the contamination on the PCs and whatever contamination has collected in the containers. The next time you prepare a floured steak, toss the steak into the flour instead of carefully laying it in the flour and you will see what I mean. The tossed steak will raise a cloud of dust.

Remove the PCs in a controlled manner at the exit from the contaminated area with a clean (uncontaminated) plastic mat to step onto just outside the contaminated area. As you remove the PCs in the contaminated area, step onto the uncontaminated mat. Do not reach across clean areas with contaminated PCs just as you would not reach across a sterile field in the emergency department.

It would be difficult if not impossible in field trauma response to find the time to don all the protective gear listed in Table 2.3 let alone in the manner suggested without jeopardizing the well-being of the patient. However, there is almost always enough time for you or your partner to don at least booties, eye protection, and multiple pairs of gloves.

If you encounter a case involving radioactive materials, assume contamination is present until it is confirmed by other professionals that contamination is not present. It is unlikely a rescuer can extricate a contaminated patient without the rescuer becoming contaminated unless contamination control techniques are used.

The attending personnel must use all practical techniques to limit self-contamination and the spread of the contamination. Examples of the techniques you should use include (not necessarily in the order shown):

- Use protective clothing when indicated and when adequate time is available. Use at least booties, gloves, and eye protection when time is at a premium (as if time is never at a premium in a trauma response).

- Do not eat, drink, or use tobacco products in a contamination or radiation area, and do not handle anything unnecessarily.

- Ensure a firm control zone is established immediately to prevent entry by unauthorized personnel. Radiological health officials, law enforcement, or other personnel with the authority to deny access to the area should be charged with the responsibility for the control zone (preferably the radiological health officials).

- If self-contained breathing apparatus are used, place them in the positive pressure mode rather than demand mode in areas involving airborne radioactive materials.

- Avoid taking tools/equipment that are not absolutely necessary into the radiation/contamination area. All equipment taken into the contamination area is likely to become contaminated. Taking unnecessary equipment with you will create more clean-up headaches than are necessary. However, *if you need the piece or pieces of equipment to provide quality medical care and extrication, take it with you.* Do not be overly concerned about getting your tools/equipment contaminated—they can be cleaned or replaced.

- Communicate openly with attending radiological team personnel. Find out where hot spots may be. Find out from them where particularly contaminated areas are. However, *do not* delay vital medical care to wait for the radiological team to give you information.

- Consider radiological contamination as bacteria. Any rescue activity or action that can spread bacteria can spread radiological contamination.

- When practical, implement shielding between the patient site and the major source of radiation. Someone other than the medical personnel should place shielding. But if you can take advantage of existing items such as earthen objects or concrete embankments by moving the patient without jeopardizing his/her medical status, by all means do so.

- Limit as much as possible the time required to extricate the patient. Use deliberate actions. Make no wasted movements. Not only will the patient benefit, you will benefit as well.

- When practical, employ distance from the major source of radiation. However, keep in mind the chances of aggravating the patient's condition by moving him/her before stabilization.

- Avoid manipulating the patient's eyelids to evaluate the status of the pupils unless absolutely necessary. Your hands may be contaminated. If your hands are contaminated and you pull back the eyelids, the patient's face, mouth, nose, or eyes may become contaminated by your contaminated gloves and sleeves. For the same reason, keep your hands off your face.

- Consider any seemingly foreign material to be contamination. If a powder or liquid that just does not seem to belong there is on surfaces in the area, consider it to be contamination.

- Use a mat of plastic or similar material to provide a clean surface to lay tools on.

- Observe guidance from the radiological team personnel regarding your positioning in the radiation/contamination area as much as possible. You may need to avoid a hot spot or a particularly contaminated area. If there is a hot spot in the immediate incident area and you cannot move the patient before stabilization, try moving to the opposite side of the patient to work his/her trauma. Even the few inches farther away you would be from the source of radiation will help reduce your accumulated dose.

- Avoid allowing any part of your body to come into contact with the environment. Do not kneel beside the patient. Stoop but stay on your feet. Do not depend on the area walls or other structures to maintain balance. Do not place your hand on the floor/ground or grasp a structure when arising from a stoop. Avoid brushing against the walls or other objects/structures.

- Avoid allowing extrication equipment to come into contact with the patient's contaminated environment. For example, it has been observed in a drill that straps of a backboard were allowed to lay on the floor of a simulated contaminated area and were then allowed to lay across the patient's face. Allowing the straps to lay across the patient's face was a no-no to begin with, but if the straps were contaminated, additional patient contamination may occur.

- Drape the gurney with plastic sheeting to protect it from contamination. If a backboard is used, place plastic sheeting on the backboard before use to protect the backboard from radioactive contamination.

- All plastic sheeting must then be disposed of properly by agencies with the authority to handle contaminated waste.

Use whatever means available to provide contamination control without causing undue risk to the patient and without causing compromise in quality care. For example, if the patient has an immediately life-threatening injury or condition, taking time to don PCs may jeopardize the patient's well-being. However, if the patient's only concern is minor injuries, you might want to consider using any items of protective clothing desired.

Now you twist your face in frustration as you mutter a subtle grunt because you realize you are between a rock and a hard place. You cannot know the patient's condition without performing a patient assessment. To do that, you must get in there and do it. If you do and contamination is present, you will become contaminated and risk spread of the contamination unless you use PCs and contamination control techniques. But if you take the time to don PCs first, the patient may deteriorate while you are trying to protect yourself and prevent the spread of contamination.

A lab coat or surgical gown, surgical gloves, a surgical mask, eye protection, and booties may be all that is necessary to provide adequate protection of attending personnel from contamination and takes only seconds to don where a full set of PCs worn as suggested may take minutes to don. When time is at an absolute premium, at least booties, eye protection, and multiple pairs of gloves should be donned. If a respirator or surgical mask is indicated but do not have time to don either, inhale through your nose. The hairs in your nose can filter out some of the airborne particulates, including radioactive airborne particulates. Nasal contamination can be removed easier than lung contamination. Your partner could be donning the booties, eye protection, gloves, and a surgical mask while en route to the scene of a suspected contaminated injury. Doing so should enable at least one responder to provide immediate medical attention upon arrival at the scene.

While your partner is attending the patient's immediate medical needs, you could then don booties, eye protection, gloves, and a surgical mask before leaving the ambulance. Even if you first discover the event involves radioactive materials when you arrive at the scene by seeing a bunch of RADIOACTIVE signs and labels scattered about, it takes only seconds to don booties, eye protection, and gloves. The time it takes to don booties, eye protection, and gloves can be absorbed into the time it takes to get your jump gear readied without too much sacrifice of time. Although "adequate time" is as scarce as hen's teeth in life-threatening medical situations, you may someday be requested to provide standby medical service to a radiation incident. In such cases, adequate time should be available to don full PCs.

There are no hard-and-fast "rules" to follow regarding whether to take the time to implement contamination controls such as wearing PCs. It is a matter of judgment. However, the problem of external self-contamination can be addressed by a complete radiological survey followed by a thorough shower and washing followed by another survey and more showering if necessary. As long as you keep your hands off any of your body orfices, internal contamination is unlikely. If you absentmindedly rub your nose or eyes with contaminated hands, it may be necessary to have an analysis performed on your nasal discharge and body excreta to determine whether internal contamination is present.

In any case, major concerns of contamination controls include:

- Preventing or limiting the spread of contamination to parts of the patient's body that may not yet be contaminated.

- Preventing further contamination of areas of the patient already contaminated.

- Preventing contamination of attending personnel.

- Preventing contamination of materials, tools, equipment, and facilities so they may be maintained ready for the next patient.

- Preventing as much as possible the spread of contamination to areas beyond the confines of the immediate incident area.

Decontamination Techniques

Many variations are possible in the techniques for performing patient decontamination. Each may be as effective as the other. In most instances, field personnel will not have the opportunity to perform decontamination of the patient beyond removal of gross, obvious contamination.

Almost any method of removing foreign material from the patient which does not complicate or aggravate the patient's condition and recovery may be considered. Surgical detergents or other agents for removing foreign material from the patient should prove effective in removing gross contamination and should be satisfactory in the field. Using water freely to wash/rinse the uninjured affected area(s) should prove useful, keeping in mind the shock which may be induced or worsened by the use of fluids at temperatures less than normal body temperature. Take care in all steps of decontamination not to allow solutions or agents to flow into wounds or orifices which may not be contaminated or to further contaminate those that are contaminated. Remember that the removed contamination will contaminate everything it touches. The runoff of fluids (washwater) must also be controlled.

In Chapter 1 you saw that chemical and physical agents cannot destroy radioactive materials. In other words, they cannot be "killed." They must "die" in their own time. Radioactive materials will "die" (become non-radioactive) eventually. The amount of time it takes for a radioactive isotope to reach a non-radioactive state depends on the half-life of the isotope as discussed in Section 3 of this Chapter. Worth repeating, you must consider the radioactive material involved will remain radioactive throughout your response activities. Do not hope that the half-life of the radioactive material is short enough that the radioactive material will "die" during your activities.

Disrobing the patient may be the most effective technique of performing patient decontamination. If you should disrobe the patient, do so while wearing at least gloves, eye protection, and a surgical mask as respiratory protection. Disrobing the patient should occur in the ambulance. If disrobing the patient cannot occur in the ambulance, it will have to be done in the hospital where the contamination could spread through the hospital and to other patients as well as to other personnel and equipment. Disrobing the patient in the ambulance in the manner described in Chapter 7 keeps most of the contamination in the ambulance where the contamination on the patient's clothing may be contained and more easily controlled. When disrobing the patient, save all items in sealed containers, e.g., large plastic bags. When finished, twist the opening closed, tape it shut, fold the twist, tape it shut again, then label it as, for example, RADIOACTIVE or CONTAINS RADIOACTIVE MATERIAL. You should solicit the help of radiological team personnel, if available, to secure the contaminated clothing and personal items removed while disrobing the patient. In each case of performing decontamination, all materials and fluids used and collected must be saved in sealed containers including the drainage during washings. All personal effects of the patient must be saved for monitoring prior to release. Chapter 6 provides information on decontamination intended for emergency department procedure.

In any case of internal contamination, a consultant is indicated. The Radiation Management Consultants (RMC) of Philadelphia, Pennsylvania or the Radiation Emergency Assistance Center/Training Center (REAC/TS) in Oak Ridge, Tennessee may offer expertise in internal contamination. State radiological health departments and the US Department of Energy may also have qualified staff personnel to assist or advise. In addition to providing guidance regarding decontamination procedures, the above organizations may aid in the management of radiation accidents.

ALARA

The term ALARA stands for *As Low As Reasonably Achievable*. ALARA is a concept of employing any and all techniques available to minimize exposure to ionizing radiation. The techniques of exposure and contamination control presented in this Chapter are examples of adherence to ALARA. Any activity, non-activity, piece of equipment, or method of performing a job which would reduce the total exposure of the worker to ionizing radiation is an example of adherence to the ALARA concept.

The US Nuclear Regulatory Commission (NRC) will soon have a "big stick" to hold over the nuclear industry worker to force adherence to the ALARA concept, but the NRC cannot and will not be able to hold the big stick over private or municipal rescue and emergency department personnel while treating the radiation accident patient—you should integrate ALARA practices into medical and rescue practice voluntarily while keeping the well-being of the patient foremost. Maintain your exposure as low as *reasonably* achievable during response to an incident involving radioactive materials.

While you may be able to employ ALARA principles when providing aid to the victim of a radiation accident, the patient does not have that luxury. You must think ALARA for the patient. Anything you can do to minimize exposure of the patient to ionizing radiation will keep his/her exposures ALARA. And since you are intimately involved with the patient, you will also be reaping the benefits of ALARA when you think ALARA for the patient.

Chapter 3

RADIATION INJURIES

PREVIEW

Depending on the patient's radiation dose, it may be a long time, maybe hours to days, before radiation injuries manifest clinically in the patient. In very rare cases, the patient's radiation dose can cause clinically observable effects in less than an hour. Because of the relatively short time required to extricate the patient and to provide emergency medical care in the emergency department (usually less than an hour, the "golden hour") it is unlikely that field medical personnel will observe radiation injury symptoms. However, as you will see, knowing the time of onset of any radiation injury symptoms can be important. Some of the known and projected effects of exposure to ionizing nuclear radiation are presented in this Chapter. Topics include:

- A history of radiation injuries
- Known and projected tissue damage and effects in perspective with the radiation dose received
- Acute radiation syndromes
- 1994 changes to the methodology for making radiation dose determination
- Some late effects of radiation exposure
- Some information learned about the Chernobyl event

By now, you understand that it is redundant to use "nuclear" with the term ionizing radiation. The fact a radiation is nuclear is not the issue: that the radiation is ionizing radiation is the issue. Exposed tissues care not from where ionizing radiation comes, only that the radiation is ionizing radiation. Henceforth, I will eliminate the term "nuclear" from the term ionizing radiation unless such specification is necessary to make a point.

Section 1. Radiation Accident History

The Radiation Emergency Assistance Center/Training Site (REAC/TS) of the Oak Ridge Associated Universities in Oak Ridge, Tennessee maintains database documentation per the US Department of Energy (DOE) of reports of radiation accidents and significant exposures which occur worldwide. As part of the REAC/TS program, the data are compiled into the DOE Radiation Accident Registry (the Registry). The Registry forms a basis for assistance to survivors of radiation accidents, for development of new therapeutic protocols, and for development of training materials for health care personnel. Table 3.1 provides information complied by REAC/TS: information regarding radiation accidents worldwide from 1944 to 1991; the number of significant exposures in the accidents, the number of persons involved in the accidents, the number of accidents with fatalities, the number of fatalities, and the countries in which the accidents with fatalities occurred.

TABLE 3.1
Radiation Accident History, 1944 to 1991[a]

Number of Worldwide Accidents........ 340
Persons Involved..................... 132,928
Significant Exposures................. 3,037

Country	Accidents w/ Fatalities	Fatalities	Country	Accidents Fatalities	Fatalities
Algeria	1	2	Marshal Islands	1	1
Argentina	1	1	Mexico	1	5
Brazil	1	4	Morocco	1	8
Bulgaria	1	1	Norway	1	1
Canada	1	1	Russia	2	33
China	3	6	Spain	1	13
El Salvador	1	1	Switzerland	1	1
Germany	1	1	United Kingdom	1	2
Israel	1	1	United States	14	32
Italy	1	1	Yugoslavia	1	1
			Totals	36	116

[a] Source: DOE-REAC/TS Radiation Accident Registry

The Radiation Accident Registry revealed that between 1944 and 1991 there have been at least 340 radiation accidents throughout the world involving approximately 130,000 people: 3,000 of them receiving significant exposures ("significant" being defined by DOE and US Nuclear Regulatory Commission criteria). Thirty-six of the 340 accidents caused 116 fatalities due to the radiation exposure, the physical trauma surrounding the radiation accident, or both.

The REAC/TS uses the following criteria agreed upon by the DOE and the US Nuclear Regulatory Commission (NRC) to select significant exposures from all reports of radiation exposure:

- 250 millisieverts (mSv) to the whole-body, to active blood-forming organs, or to the gonads,

- 6000 mSv to the skin of the whole body or to the extremities,

- 750 mSv to other tissues and organs from an external source,

- an internal burden of half of the National Council on Radiation Protection (NCRP) guidelines for maximum organ burden, and

- medical misadministrations that result in a dose from a radiation source or result in a burden from a radiopharmaceutical equal to or greater than the above criteria.

A little review of Chapter 2. One sievert equals 100 rem. Therefore, 250 mSv equals 25 rem. However, much more goes into determining the magnitude of a radiation dose than simple mathematical conversion of units. For gamma and X-radiation, this estimation is fairly close, but for alpha and beta radiation, the estimation is not even close. Also, the different human tissues will exhibit different biologic response to the same numeric value of dose. Further, the same numeric value of dose to different radiations will cause different magnitudes of biologic response in the same tissue. This topic gets a little deep. Just remember that for emergency medical response activities involving doses to gamma and X-radiation, consider the rem and rad as equal.

Table 3.1 presents a summary of the information REAC/TS has complied on radiation accidents that occurred between 1944 and 1991. Data shown in Table 3.1 relate to accidents involving research and development of nuclear materials, to radioactive isotope production, industrial radiography devices, to medical uses such as X-ray and radiotherapy, and unsealed radioactive sources. None of the 32 fatalities in the US was due to radiation at commercial nuclear power plants nor was any of the fatalities in the US the result of radiation exposure received due to a transportation incident.

If you are involved in response to a radiation accident, you should provide all available data to the REAC/TS. The REAC/TS echoes me in insisting that dosimeters be worn by all personnel involved in response to a radiation accident.

Section 2. Distribution, Duration, and
Effects of Exposure to Ionizing Radiation

As explained in Chapter 1, ionizing radiation by its nature may cause damage to living tissue by causing disruption of the vital chemical harmony of the tissue cells. Specifically, biophysical changes in human cells or organs can occur due to the ionization of molecules and due to the generation of free radicals in the cells. In this Section, some information is presented on the types of injury that may be caused by tissue damage due to ionizing radiation. The scope of the information presented herein is limited to the paramedical and initial emergency department procedures.

A delay is probable from the time of exposure to ionizing radiation before the effects of the exposure appear clinically. In each case of radiation injury, a *prodromal period* will precede the manifest of the radiation injury: a period in which the effects of the radiation injury get a foothold on the biologic systems such as the blood system, the gastrointestinal system, and the cardiovascular system. The prodromal period may be from minutes for extreme doses to 48 hours for the lesser doses. The actual duration of the prodromal period depends on several factors such as the severity of the radiation dose received, the area of the body exposed, how long it took to receive the dose, the general health and fortitude of the victim, the radiosensitivity of the exposed tissue, and whether the victim receives quality medical and nutritional therapy after the exposure. The prodromal symptoms may abate or cease for a while, depending, of course, on the severity of the radiation dose. Following the cessation of prodromal symptoms, a period of lesser or no clinically observable symptoms may occur, followed by manifest of the radiation injury. The period of time between the ceasing or abating of the prodromal symptoms and the manifest of the radiation injury is called the *latent period*.

While biophysical changes in human tissues due to exposure to ionizing radiation are instantaneous, as stated above the clinically observable effects of the radiation dose a patient has received may take some time to occur except in the very rare cases of extreme radiation doses. Since extreme doses are very rare, it is unlikely field medical personnel will see prodromal radiation injury symptoms in what is usually less than one hour from the report of the exposure to the time of arrival at the hospital. However, a knowledge of the onset of the prodromal symptoms of radiation injury can be useful for prognostic purposes, especially in a multiple casualty situation where radiological triage may be necessary. Triage of radiation accident patients will be discussed in Chapter 6.

If the exposed individual eventually exhibits symptoms of radiation injury, his/her radiation injury *is not contagious*. A victim of radiation injury *cannot* transmit his/her radiation injuries to other individuals. Radiation injury, as you will soon see, may cause a reduction in the body's resistance to infection. Any infections or disease which develop due to reduced resistance may be contagious, but *the radiation radiation injury itself is not contagious*. As ionizing radiation injury is not contagious, it is also known that exposure to ionizing radiation, nuclear or otherwise, *does not introduce any new infections*. Further, *there is no convincing evidence that there exists a capability of the human species to develop adaptation to exposure to ionizing radiation*—you cannot "get used to" ionizing radiation exposure.

Some scientists have believed that injury due to ionizing radiation began at a threshold, i.e., no radiation injury occurs below a certain threshold dose. More recently, scientists believe that *any* exposure to ionizing radiation may cause some degree of radiation injury which may or may not be expressed clinically, depending on several factors. The no-threshold theory is assumed for radiation protection purposes in some organizations but there are no human data to support the no-threshold theory unequivocally. In either case, damage to living tissue can happen from ionizing radiation.

The *distribution* of radiation exposure may be as:

- *Whole-body Exposure* - means exposure to the head, lens of the eye, neck, trunk of the body, arms above the elbows, and legs above the knees. Whole-body exposure may be from destruction of a large source of radiation such as fixed radiography devices, or from nuclear power plants.

- *Extremity Exposure* - means exposure to the arms from the elbow down and legs from the knee down.

- *Localized Exposure* - means an exposure which may be received in a particular spot or area of the body, for example, from a small piece of radioactive material (a radioactive "flea"[16]), or from devices which use a beam of radiation.

Another term which has been used whether officially or unofficially is *total-body exposure* and means just what it says. The specification of *whole-body* and *extremity* will change slightly in 1994, i.e., the elbows and knees will be part of the whole-

---

16. A radioactive "flea" is a term used by the nuclear power industry to describe a small, almost invisible particle of radioactive material which is highly radioactive and has become a contaminant.

body rather than the extremities. The changes are detailed in Section 4 of this Chapter.

The *duration* of radiation exposure may be as:

- *Acute Exposure* - is that which is received in a short time, e.g., a one-time exposure. In field medical and hospital services, an acute exposure is a one-time, single event exposure.

- *Chronic (protracted) Exposure* - is that which is received over longer periods of time, e.g., months to years.

Table 3.2 itemizes the distribution (except for total-body) and duration of exposures.

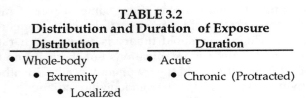

TABLE 3.2
Distribution and Duration of Exposure

Distribution	Duration
• Whole-body	• Acute
• Extremity	• Chronic (Protracted)
• Localized	

The effects of ionizing radiation on humans are grouped into three classes:

- *Somatic Effects* - are the clinical expression of radiation-induced injury in the exposed individual (vomiting, nausea, diarrhea, etc.). Somatic effects are further divided into two subclasses:

  - • *Prompt Somatic Effects* - are somatic effects observable soon after an exposure (acute somatic effects). Prompt effects are the signs and symptoms of radiation injury, the so-called deterministic effects. Their onset and severity are determined by the dose received. Prompt effects have a threshold below which they do not occur, specifically, they are *non-stochastic* effects.

  - • *Delayed Somatic Effects* - somatic effects that may be exhibited a long time after exposure (chronic or protracted somatic effects). Delayed somatic effects are expressions of gene mutations in somatic cells. The principal effect is carcinogenesis. The incidence of carcinogenesis from delayed somatic effects is related to the dose received, but no threshold is assumed and there is a probability, whether great or slight, of development of cancer in the exposed population.

- *Genetic Effects* - are radiation-induced genetic changes that may be expressed in subsequent generations

- *Teratogenic Effects* - may occur when an embryo or fetus is exposed while in utero. The effects, if severe, may not be compatible with life and may lead to prenatal or neonatal death.

Table 3.3 itemizes the effects of exposure to radiation.

TABLE 3.3
Effects of Exposure

Somatic Effects	Genetic Effects
• Prompt Somatic Effects • Delayed Somatic Effects	Teratogenic Effects

The sensitivity of cells to ionizing radiation, i.e., *radiosensitivity* is related in part to the rate of reproduction of the cells. Children are more sensitive to ionizing radiation than adults. Fetuses are more sensitive than children. Embryos are even more sensitive to ionizing radiation than fetuses. Cells showing higher sensitivity include

- Bone marrow and blood cells
- Lens of the Eyes
- Gastrointestinal tract tissues
- Gonads

and cells showing lesser sensitivity to ionizing radiation include

- Nerve Tissue
- Fatty Tissue
- Muscle Tissue
- Bone

and, except for the blood system, not necessarily in the order shown, but definitely with the blood system at the top.

Analysis of the known effects of ionizing radiation exposures and from projections reveal the somatic effects shown in Table 3.4 may occur from whole-body acute doses at the indicated levels. Table 3.4 also provides estimated ranges of dose to gamma or X-radiation which may produce the indicated results on healthy adults without receiving medical and nutritional therapy unless otherwise noted.

TABLE 3.4
Dose versus Signs and Symptoms
(Approximations)

Dose	Signs and Symptoms
0 - 50,000 mrads (0 - 50 rads)	No obvious effect, except possible minor blood changes.
80,000 - 120,000 mrads (80 - 120 rads)	Vomiting & nausea for about 1 day in 5 to 10% of exposed individuals. Fatigue but no serious disability.
130,000 - 170,000 mrads (130 - 170 rads)	Vomiting & nausea within 24 - 48 hours, followed by other symptoms of radiation sickness in about 25% of the exposed individuals. No deaths anticipated if treatment is instituted.
180,000 - 220,000 mrads (180 - 220 rads)	Vomiting & nausea within 24 hours, followed by other symptoms of radiation sickness in about 50% of the exposed individuals. Near 20% deaths if untreated.
270,000 - 325,000 mrads (270 - 325 rads)	Vomiting & nausea in nearly all of the exposed individuals on 1st day, followed by other symptoms of radiation sickness. Up to 50% deaths within 60 days if untreated. Survivors convalesce for about 6 months.
400,000 - 500,000 mrads (400 - 550 rads)	Vomiting & nausea in all of the exposed individuals on 1st day, followed by other symptoms of radiation sickness. Greater than 50% deaths among untreated patients within 2 months. Survivors convalesce for about 6 months.
550,000 - 750,000 mrads (600- 750 rads)	Vomiting & nausea in nearly all of the exposed individuals within 4 hours of exposure, followed by other symptoms of radiation sickness. About 100% deaths in the untreated population in about two weeks.
1,000,000 mrads (1000 rads)	Vomiting & nausea in all exposed individuals within 1 to 2 hours. Probably no survivors among the untreated patients.
5,000,000 mrads (5000 rads)	Incapacitation almost immediately. All exposed individuals die, mostly within 48 hours.

Quality medical and nutritional therapy can improve resilience to the non-lethal effects. The physical constitution and general health of the patient prior to exposure plays an important role in determining resilience to the effects of ionizing radiation. The patient who has a more dense body mass, i.e., more weight per unit of body volume, may exhibit greater resilience to the effects of exposure to ionizing radiation. Further, the patient's general health should also impact his/her resilience. Specifically, the better the health of the exposed individual, the better the resilience should be to the effects of exposure to ionizing radiation. Anything that is a burden to health such as stress, chronic weakness, colds, poor hygiene, poor nutritional habits, and poor general health may decrease resilience to exposure to ionizing radiation.

Note that in some instances in Table 3.4 ranges of doses and times are shown which should result in the indicated ranges of effects. For example, a range of doses from 270 to 330 rads should result in 20% to 50% deaths in the exposed population (if untreated). The range of doses relates to the range of effects. A dose of 270 rads may lead to death in 20% of the exposed population while a dose to 325 rads should lead to death in 50% of the exposed population if untreated. A term has been developed which is an abbreviation for the lethal dose. The term is LD, which stands for lethal dose. A dose of 325 rads will likely be lethal to 50% of the exposed population if the patients are not treated. Therefore, the LD term for the 325 rad dose is LD_{50}. Further, another subscript is added to the LD_{50} term to specify the time to expected death. Since the LD_{50} for the 325 rad dose is expected in 60 days, the added subscript for the 60 day period to death would change the term to $LD_{50/60}$, meaning 50% of the exposed population is expected to die within 60 days (I repeat, if untreated).

Injury caused by non-lethal dose is not wholly permanent nor additive. Specifically, the human body with its intricate healing mechanisms can repair some of the damage due to radiation, depending on the amount of dose received just as it repairs damage from traumatic injuries, depending on the degree of trauma received. The adult who is healthy before the non-lethal dose may realize approximately 90% body repair. For example, an acute whole-body dose of 25 rads should cause some damage (particularly to the blood-forming organs of the body). The body should eventually repair up to 90% (22.5 rads) of any damage. The remaining 10% of the damage (2.5 rads) may remain longer, possibly permanently as does scar tissue from traumatic injuries. The 90% figure is not constant over the range of doses shown in Table 3.4. Specifically, repair of radiation damage of smaller doses near the "No obvious effect, except minor blood changes" may be greater than 90%. However, doses near the lethal range may be less than 90%. The completeness of body repair and recovery depends in part on whether the patient receives good medical and nutritional therapy.

Section 3. Acute Radiation Syndromes

The particular vulnerability of organs and systems to ionizing radiation and the ensuing clinical effects conveniently permit grouping of the effects of radiation dose into *syndromes*. A syndrome is a set of clinical signs and symptoms characterizing a human medical condition.   I will describe the signs and symptoms characterizing the acute effects of radiation injury, i.e., the *Acute Radiation Syndromes* (ARS), adopted with permission from *The Acute Radiation Syndromes and Their Medical Management* prepared by Dr. Niel Wald published in *The Biological Basis of Radiation Protection Practice*, Mossman and Mills, by Williams and Wilkins, Baltimore, MD, 1992.

The living cell is the basic pathway for damage by ionizing radiation. Cell death and reproductive death are the main effects of exposure to ionizing radiation. Cells which have a relatively high reproduction rate are the ones most sensitive to ionizing radiation. Some blood cells have a relatively short life-span and high turnover rate in order to maintain the astronomical numbers of cells needed to maintain the level of service required of the blood. Gastrointestinal tract lining tissues also have a relatively high turnover rate and therefore a significant radiosensitivity. Although the gray matter of the brain is relatively unaffected by ionizing radiation, the vascular system within the brain is sensitive to ionizing radiation. Further, inflammation of lung tissue has apparently been caused by acute exposure to ionizing radiation. Ionizing radiation can cause damage to these crucial biologic systems causing systemic dysfunctions at the cell or organ level. Thus, the acute radiation syndrome can be conveniently subdivided into four syndromes:

- Hematologic (Bone Marrow) Syndrome
- Gastrointestinal (GI) Tract Syndrome
- Neurovascular Syndrome

Hematologic (Bone Marrow) Syndrome

The hematologic (bone marrow) syndrome is the least severe of the syndromes. The hematologic syndrome manifests at radiation doses near 300 to 400 rads dose. As provided by Dr. Shirley A. Fry, the $LD_{50/60}$ for the bone marrow is 325 rads. A dose of 200 rads to the bone marrow can lead to death in about 20% of the exposed population if untreated. A dose of about 100 rads to the bone marrow might be a threshold for declaring the patient is suffering the hematologic syndrome, but a decrease in the lymphocyte count can be observed at doses as low as 25 rads. Prodromal symptoms of the hematologic syndrome include vomiting and nausea for about 2 days. At the LD_{50}, a latent period for the bone marrow syndrome is about 14 days during which there may be no apparent clinical evidence of radiation injury. Following the latent period, further or increased evidence of blood abnormalities are likely to occur possibly leading to hemorrhage and infection. The LD_{50} to the bone marrow will deplete the blood count dramatically. A transient rise in the number of circulating granulocytes should occur within minutes to hours of the exposure, followed by a slow decrease as the cells are expended. Then, a transient attempt of the blood system to repopulate the granulocyte population should occur in the second week followed by a serious fall in the circulating granulocyte population. The serious depletion of granulocytes should be reversed abruptly as newly released mature cells enter circulation. A rapid depletion of the lymphocyte count should occur in the first 48 hours. The red blood cell count should reach a low point in about 6 weeks. A gradual fall in platelets should occur reaching a low point in about 5 weeks after exposure. After about 5 weeks, assuming the patient survives the dose, the blood system should attempt to rebuild and repopulate and the clinical evidence of radiation injury to the blood system should reduce or disappear. The LD_{50} bone marrow syndrome occurs with "surprising regularity" at the 13th day after exposure: a higher dose would likely result in the same systemic response but more condensed and more severe. A lower dose may express itself in a longer latent period with less severe results. The same response should be seen in the lymph system but faster with slower recovery.

Evidence of the hematologic syndrome includes the prodromal symptoms of nausea and vomiting for about 48 hours. The latent period of the hematologic syndrome may be followed by fever, shortness of breath, inflammation of the lungs, mucous membranes, and small intestines, and bacterial toxins in the blood. Evidence of bleeding due to the hematologic syndrome includes small, purplish red spots in the skin due to hemorrhages from the capillaries, bruising, nose bleeding, blood in the urine, feces, or vomitus, with possible bleeding in the abdomen, head, and chest. The patient of the hematologic syndrome can be very susceptible to viral, fungal, and bacterial infections and can die from the infections due to a reduction in the body's ability to fight infection due to the reduction in the granulocyte count of the blood. The underlying cause of death in the hematologic syndrome is bone marrow depression, infection, and hemorrhages. With supportive treatment while the biologic systems rebuild, the LD_{50} may be raised to approximately 450 rads.

As recovery of the blood system can be improved and expedited with proper medical and nutritional therapy, elimination of body burdens will enhance the chances and timeliness of recovery. Any body burden can tax the biological system to the extent of leaving too little strength and reserves with which to combat the effects of injury from ionizing radiation. The best possible hygiene will also improve chances for full and timely recovery. Burdens such as poor hygiene, smoking tobacco, drinking alcohol, a junk food diet, and fatigue can slow the patient's ability to rebuild the biological system after a significant dose to ionizing radiation.

Gastrointestinal (GI) Tract Syndrome

While suffering the gastrointestinal (GI) tract syndrome, the patient will exhibit the hematologic syndrome symptoms in addition to a transiently impaired or destroyed lining of the GI tract. In combination with the blood cell depletion of the hematologic syndrome, the cell depletion of the intestinal tract may lead to irreversible effects, including death. The GI tract syndrome is manifest around 1000 rads while patients with 500 rads or greater dose have exhibited symptoms of GI tract dysfunction. In addition to the effects of the hematologic syndrome, the GI syndrome may be evidenced by lesions in the lining of the GI tract. The latent period of the GI tract syndrome may be from 4 to 9 days and includes the symptoms of the hematologic syndrome plus diarrhea. The GI tract syndrome may manifest with signs of malnutrition, infection, fever, electrolyte imbalances, and inflammation of the small and large intestines. Circulatory collapse may occur in the GI tract syndrome. Denudation and ulceration of the GI tract is likely in the more severe cases of the GI tract syndrome.

Neurovascular Syndrome

The neurovascular syndrome (previously thought of as the central nervous system (CNS) syndrome) is the most dramatic form of acute radiation syndrome. Fatal manifestation (LD_{100}) of the neurovascular syndrome occurs at or near 2000 rads dose and above. Within minutes to hours of the 2000 rad dose, the patient may exhibit altered states of consciousness from apathy to lethargy. The patient will likely have difficulty sleeping and may be hyperexcitable. The cardiovascular system becomes increasingly incapable of maintaining vital functions thereby leading to dysfunction. Although fatality occurs only at very high doses, a transient response of the nervous system may be caused at much lower doses, for example, beginning at

100 rads and affecting almost all patients at 300 rads, resulting in loss of appetite, nausea, and vomiting occurring within a few hours and lasting for about 48 hours. At the 2000 rad level, tremors and convulsions as well as gait disturbances may appear. The cardiovascular system is likely impacted as a part of the neurovascular syndrome and is relatively unresponsive to even vigorous therapy. Death may result within hours to a couple days. Dysfunctions of the central nervous and cardiovascular system due to doses causing the neurovascular syndrome are likely to be irreversible. Normal regulatory control systems are interrupted and damage to the blood vessels in the brain is expressed as convulsions and coma. While the brain gray matter is affected very little, evidence of cerebral edema may be found due to the damaged blood vessels.

Other Syndromes and Tissue Damage

Although not included in the above discussions of acute radiation syndromes, radiation burns to the skin associated with exposure to ionizing radiation are similar to and can be treated much the same as thermal burns. Ionizing radiation burns may develop from a high level dose of gamma, beta, or X-radiation but principally from beta by comparison. There is no biological warning of radiation burns: ionizing radiation burns are not as painful as thermal radiation burns. Although radiation burns may resemble thermal burns, burns due to ionizing radiation are generally much deeper than thermal burns, affecting the skin's supporting tissues and resulting in poor healing. The endothelial cells lining the small arterioles may over compensate for cell death due to the ionizing radiation and may "clog" the arterioles. Symptoms of severe radiation burns from extreme doses *may* appear as tingling and itching at the time of exposure. Of the more severe cases of radiation skin burns, prodromal symptoms of reddening (erythema) and possibly blistering may appear lasting 2 to 3 days followed by no symptoms at all for 3 to 5 days during the latent period. Then the reddening may renew followed soon by blistering. The blistering may dry and peel after about 3 weeks. Then dark red wart-like spots may appear. A high protein diet, multiple vitamins, and antibiotics may promote recovery. Dr. Wald pointed out that the skin as an organ with its appendages and sweat glands may suffer erythema in about 50% of the population exposed to 600 rads with erythema appearing at lesser dose as well. Blistering may occur at about 2000 rads and dermal necrosis may occur at doses over 3000 rads.

Doctor Wald also pointed out that another form of the acute radiation syndromes was the pulmonary syndrome. The pulmonary

syndrome has been observed in some therapeutically irradiated
patients 1 to 3 months after a dose of 800 to 900 rads to the chest. The
pulmonary syndrome was diagnosed in Chernobyl victims who
suffered interstitial edema and respiratory failure within three days.

Specification that a syndrome at Chernobyl was due to a certain
level of radiation dose is difficult since the Chernobyl victims also
suffered physical trauma from fighting the fire and from other
emergency response efforts. Vigorous therapy also confused the
determination that a medical condition was due to a radiation dose:
not to physical trauma and the ensuing therapy.

TABLE 3.5
Acute Radiation Syndromes
(Approximations)

Hematologic Syndrome	
Chief Determining Organ	Bone Marrow
Syndrome Threshold	150 rads
Latent Period	14 days at the LD_{50}
$LD_{50/60}$	325 rads (w/o treatment)
Characteristic Signs and Symptoms	Malaise (discomfort), fever, dyspnea (shortness of breath), fatigue, leukopenia (reduction in white blood cells), thrombopenia (decrease in platelets), with a decrease in lymphocytes at near 25 rad
Gastrointestinal (GI) Tract Syndrome	
Chief Determining Organ	Small intestine
Syndrome Threshold	500 to 700 rads
Latent Period	4 to 9 days
$LD_{100/14}$	1000 rads
Characteristic Signs and Symptoms	In addition to hematologic symptoms, , diarrhea, GI malfunction, fever, electrolyte loss, , platelet dereangement, GI denudation and ulceration.
Neurovascular System Syndrome	
Chief Determining Organ	Central nervous and cariovascular systems
Syndrome Threshold	1700 rads(LD_{50})
Latent Period	15 minutes to 3 hours
$LD_{95/48 hours}$	5000 rads
Characteristic Signs and Symptoms	Apathy, mental drowsiness, tremors, convulsions, failure of muscular coordination, hyperexcitability.

The hematologic, the gastrointestinal, and the neurovascular acute radiation syndromes described are tabulated in Table 3.5, which is modified from a format prepared by Dr. Z. L. Olkowski as Associate Professor of Radiation Oncology of the Emory University School of Medicine from a paper he prepared for training. Input for the modifications were provided by Doctors R. C. Ricks, S. A. Fry, and N. Wald. The somatic effects shown in Table 3.5 are determined from or are projected to result from acute exposures. In Table 3.5, the *Chief Determining Organ* is the main organ in which the radiation syndrome would manifest itself. The *Syndrome Symptoms* suggests a dose at which the syndrome should appear in most individuals. The *Characteristic Signs and Symptoms* are those most likely to be exhibited in the exposed individuals. The *Latent Period* and the *LD* factors have already been explained.

In preparing material for the US Nuclear Regulatory Commission's Reactor Safety Study of 1975, Dr. Wald and his associate, Dr. J.A. Watson, determined an estimate of the effect of LD_{50} dose from radiation accident and medical therapy data available at the time. Doctors Wald and Watson believed that the $LD_{50/60}$ was approximately 340 rads for a patient with no treatment or with minimal treatment. However, patient support treatment was believed to raise the $LD_{50/60}$ to near 510 rads, with bone marrow transplantation raising the estimated $LD_{50/60}$ even higher than 510 rads to some unknown level. In a 1989 update of the model used in the 1975 report, reanalysis the relevant data revealed the human $LD_{50/60}$ may be about 450 rads *with* supportive treatment. Within Dr. Wald's *The Acute Radiation Syndromes and Their Medical Management*, he revealed that Dr. T.M. Fliedner and his associates suggested the human $LD_{50/60}$ may be raised by a factor of 1.5 to 2.0 with supportive therapy, and with bone marrow transplantation the human $LD_{50/60}$ could be raised to 1350 to 1800 rads. For the Chernobyl victims, the average LD_{50} was around 520 rads but thermal burns and other physical trauma complicated their medical condition such that confidence was low that their radiation dose was the main contributor to their medical condition.

The information in Table 3.5 may impart a feeling of dire anticipation, but understand that available material indicates that serious radiation doses are rare in the United States. Individuals who wish to investigate radiation sickness syndromes further the should read *Clinical Radiation Pathology* by Phillip Rubin and George Casarett, published by W. B. Saunders Company, 1968, pages 850 to 865, or any of the publications listed in the References and Suggested Reading section of this book.

Section 4. 1994 Changes to the Methodology
of Dose Determination

Radiological health physicists and governmental radiological health professionals perform determination of the dose of ionizing radiation a patient has received using the terms and methods described in Chapter 2 and this Chapter. However, by January 1, 1994, all personnel responsible for making human dose determinations must use a new methodology required by the US Nuclear Regulatory Commission (NRC). The new methodology is detailed in Title 10 of the Code of Federal Regulations, Part 20, *Standards for Protection Against Radiation* (10CFR20). The new methodology is borne of information gathered over 30 years regarding the effects of exposure to ionizing radiation and is endorsed by the International Commission on Radiation Protection (ICRP). Adherence to the new methodology is required of occupational radiation workers (explained later) but is not required of emergency medical services (EMS) personnel since we are not the ones responsible for making patient dose determination. However, I provide to you the basics of the new methodology and terms to help ensure a common language between EMS and health physics personnel so we may all speak in familiar terms.

So far I have explained that radiation dose determination is performed using, for example, acute exposure, whole-body exposure, extremity exposure, and localized exposure in terms of somatic effects (prompt and delayed). Inherent with the new methodology of dose determination will appear a new language for quantifying and declaring patient radiation dose. This Section presents a summary of the pending changes to patient dose determination so that you will not feel totally intimidated and confused when radiological health professionals mingle about mumbling "TODE", "TEDE", "DDE" and so on.

The new methodology, henceforth the new regulation since adherence to the new methodology is a Federal requirement (for those who perform patient dose determination), specifies two categories of health effects: *non-stochastic* and *stochastic*.

Non-stochastic effects are the known effects experienced by the exposed patient when he/she receives a specific amount of radiation dose at or above a given threshold level, the higher the dose is over the threshold level, the more severe the effects become. The radiation effects shown in Tables 3.4 and 3.5 are non-stochastic effects. Another example of non-stochastic effects includes a sunburn. Using the non-stochastic effect of a sunburn as an example, the beachbody who stays too long in the sun may get a sunburn after the pre-burn tolerance threshold of his/her skin is exceeded. The sunburn is the non-stochastic effect of exposure to the sun.

Stochastic effects are those which have no specific threshold. Radiation leukemogenesis is an example of a stochastic effect. The specific dose at which radiation leukemogenesis is likely to occur is not known, nor is the specific length of time it takes for radiation leukemogenesis to manifest itself. Stochastic effects exist with any level of radiation dose: the lower the dose the lesser the risk of stochastic effects. Again using exposure to the sun as an example, short-term (acute) exposure to the sun's radiation can increase the risk of skin cancer to the exposed individual. However, long-term exposure to the sun's rays can dramatically increase the risk of cancer.

Since ionizing radiation can cause cancer and inasmuch must be classified as a carcinogen, the radiation dose concerns in the new regulation are centered around minimizing the risk of cancer due to exposure to ionizing radiation. All personnel who, by occupation, work with radiation and radioactive materials which require a license to use or possess, i.e., all radiation workers, are currently subject to a guidance of the NRC to maintain their exposures to ionizing radiation As Low As Reasonably Achievable (ALARA) as discussed in Chapter 2 to minimize the risk of cancer. Adherence to ALARA, albeit currently a guidance and not a requirement for the radiation worker, encourages the radiation worker to implement any and all reasonable practices to minimize his/her radiation exposure (recall Time, Distance, and Shielding from Chapter 2). However, beginning January 1, 1994 all radiation workers will be *required* to adhere to ALARA principles. Deviation from ALARA principles after January 1, 1994 may result in enforcement action. Although adherence to ALARA is not and will not be enforced of private and municipal primary patient care personnel such as EMTs, medics, police, fire, first aid, rescue, and emergency department staff members, adherence to ALARA is most assuredly recommended.

The new regulation still uses the rem and rad as terms of measurement of radiation dose. However, the nomenclature for the different types of doses and how they are determined will change.

Recall the term whole-body exposure which means exposure to the trunk of the body, the head, the lens of the eye, the arms above the elbows, and the legs above the knees. Also recall that extremity exposure means exposure to the arms at the elbow and below and to the legs at the knee and below. The new regulation redefines the whole-body and extremity to include the elbow and knee as part of the whole-body. So, if you hear that a patient from a nuclear plant (after January 1, 1994) has received a whole-body exposure you will know what parts are included in the whole-body. You will also know that if you are told the patient has an extremity exposure to the leg, he/she has received the exposure below the knee. The new regulation relates whole-body exposure to determining external exposure to gamma radiation with *Deep Dose Equivalent* (DDE) as measured by dosimeters.

A term is used to describe the dose to the skin of the patient, i.e., the *skin dose*. In the new regulation, the term skin dose will be replaced with *Shallow Dose Equivalent* (SDE) and will involve the skin of the entire body. As the skin dose will have its own measurement, the eyes will also have their own measurement, specifically, the *Eye Dose Equivalent* (EDE), which will be the actual dose the eye receives taking into account any eye protection used by the exposed personnel.

The new regulation will require determination of the specific internal radiation doses received by individual organs from breathing or ingestion of radioactive material. The dose to the individual organ will be the *Committed Dose Equivalent* (CDE) for the subject organ. The CDE will be converted to an equivalent internal whole-body dose called the *Committed Effective Dose Equivalent* (CEDE) by assigning a *weighting factor* (W_f) to each organ. The weighting factors for the individual organs are presented in Table 3.6.

TABLE 3.6
Organ Weighting Factors, W_f

Organ	Weighting Factor
Gonads	0.25
Breast	0.15
Red Marrow	0.12
Lungs	0.12
Thyroid	0.03
Bone Surface	0.03
Remainder of Organs	0.3

Example: The patient has inhaled sufficient cobalt-60 to receive a Committed Dose Equivalent (CDE) of 100 millirem to his/her lungs. To determine the whole-body overall effect of the lung dose, i.e., the Committed Effective Dose Equivalent or CEDE, multiply the 100 millirem CDE times the weighting factor of 0.12 for the lungs to reveal an overall whole-body effect of 12 millirem. This means that the 100 millirem lung dose has the same overall internal dose effect on the whole-body as 12 millirem, expressed algebraically,

$$\text{CEDE} = (W_f)(\text{CDE}) \tag{3-1}$$
$$\text{CEDE} = (0.12)(100 \text{ millirem}) = 12 \text{ millirem}$$

It is important to note that whenever you hear the term *effective* when used with dose values, for example, Committed Effective Dose Equivalent, remember that it relates the dose to an equivalent uniform whole-body dose.

Another term you may hear after January 1, 1994 is *Total Organ Dose Equivalent* (TODE) which I pronounce "toad-ee." The TODE is the sum of the Deep Dose Equivalent (DDE) plus the Committed Dose Equivalent (CDE). Algebraically stated:

$$TODE = DDE + CDE. \tag{3-2}$$

One of the most effective tools of the new regulation in determining total dose is the summing of internal and external doses, i.e., the sum of the DDE and the CEDE for each organ exposed. The sum of the DDE and the CEDE yields a new term called the *Total Effective Dose Equivalent* (TEDE), affectionately pronounced "ted-ee" as in teddy bear. The TEDE is calculated as follows:

$$TEDE = DDE + \sum[(W_f)(CDE)_{for\ each\ organ}] \tag{3-3}$$

or, substituting $(W_f)(CDE)$ with CEDE (see equation 3-1)

$$TEDE = DDE + \sum CEDE_{for\ each\ organ}$$

Table 3.7 summarizes the new terms.

TABLE 3.7
Terms of Dose Determination

DDE	Deep Dose Equivalent - external whole-body exposure as measured by dosimetry
SDE	Shallow Dose Equivalent - external exposure to the skin
EDE	Eye Dose Equivalent - external exposure to the lens of the eye
CDE	Committed Dose Equivalent - the dose of an organ due to the uptake or radioactive material
CEDE	Committed Effective Dose Equivalent - the equivalent amount of whole-body dose due to individual organ uptakes (CDE)
TODE	Total Organ Dose Equivalent - the sum of the DDE and the CDE
TEDE	Total Effective Dose Equivalent - the sum of the DDE and the CEDE (for each organ)

There are other terms you may hear as the new regulation is implemented, but the other changes are primarily for the onsite radiation workers at nuclear power or utilization facilities and are not presented herein.

The bulk of the information provided in this Section is intended to expand the knowledge of emergency medical personnel. As stated before, it is unlikely that field medical personnel will see any radiation injury manifest itself clinically in the patient: this is why I have covered radiation injuries only briefly. Even if the field personnel observe the onset of prodromal symptoms, there is little they can do to treat radiation injury other than providing symptomatic treatment including emergency life support if needed and trying to reduce emotional stress which is likely when the victim knows he/she has been exposed to ionizing radiation or radioactive contamination. Relieving emotional stress as well as physical burdens should enhance the patient's recovery.

Section 5. Late Effects of Radiation Exposure

Ionizing radiation can cause cancer. Inasmuch, it must be classed as a carcinogen. With chronic exposure to ionizing radiation (it is not know what level of dose), a consistently low count of white and red cells may develop. The book, *Ionizing Radiation and Life* by Dr. Victor Arena,[17] provides a great deal of information regarding the effects of ionizing radiation on living tissues.

Leukemia

One of the possible late effects on blood that may be realized from ionizing radiation is radiation leukemogenesis (radiation-induced leukemia). Leukemia is characterized by an abnormally high distribution of white blood cells in the blood. The leukemogenic properties of ionizing radiation have been demonstrated in laboratory animals.

Life-span Shortening

The effects of ionizing radiation on the human life span is controversial. It is expected that smoking tobacco does more damage than ionizing radiation, but nonetheless ionizing radiation may

---

17. Dr. Arena's material and review-for-comment of this Chapter 3 manuscript by Dr. Olkowski were the source of much of the information regarding the late effects of ionizing radiation on living tissues.

shorten one's life. In some animal experiments, rodents lost as much as 5% life-span per 100 rads dose. Experiments on beagles have revealed a shortening of life-span as much as 20% for 300 rads. In other experiments, ionizing radiation has had no effect on the life span of the subject. It is, however, generally agreed that life shortening due to ionizing radiation exposure can be almost totally accounted for by the increases in deaths due to radiogenic malignancies.

Sterility

A dose of 600 rads to the testes of the male is suspected of inducing permanent sterility. A dose of 12 rads has been observed to cause a temporary reduction in the sperm count in males. The following report is quoted from Dr. Arena's *Ionizing Radiation and Life*, page 482:

> "The victim, a 34-year old man, had been exposed to an estimated dose of 416 R; he suffered acute radiation sickness from which he recovered. Seven months after the accident, his semen was aspermic. After 10 months, biopsy showed normal sertoli cells, but no spermatogenesis. Signs of recovery appeared later; the sperm count began increasing and reached almost normal values 58 months after the accident, when this man fathered a child."

It is suspected that doses between 320 and 625 R may induce permanent sterility in females. In a group of 72 women, a single dose of 635 rads was suspect for causing permanent sterility. As opposed to the male testes which can produce sperm "as needed", the female is born with a given number of eggs which are not replaced. Once the eggs are gone, there will be no more.

Cataracts

A disorder of the lens of the eye which manifests itself as increased opacity is known as cataracts. It has been observed that ionizing radiation can cause cataracts, which are clinically and pathologically different from the cataracts which develop spontaneously, i.e., due to old age. Doses as low as 15 rads can cause cataracts in mice, but it is suspected that a direct dose of 200 rads to the lens of the eye is the threshold for cataract development in man. Cataracts are one of the delayed effects of ionizing radiation since cataracts due to ionizing radiation may take as long as 3 to 4 years to develop in man. Studies of the Japanese victims of the World War II detonations of the atomic bombs in Nagasaki and Hiroshima revealed that children of the victims while in utero have been victimized by impaired visual acuity. Studies of the Nagasaki and Hiroshima children provided evidence of the greater radiosensitivity of fetal tissues than the tissues of older humans.

Section 6. Chernobyl

"THE NUCLEAR ACCIDENT AT CHERNOBYL WAS THE WORST IN THE HISTORY OF NUCLEAR POWER. IT TESTED THE ORGANIZED MEDICAL RESPONSE TO MASS RADIATION CASUALTIES... THE UNITED STATES WOULD BE WELL ADVISED TO ORGANIZE ITS RESOURCES DEFINITIVELY TO COPE WITH FUTURE NON- MILITARY ACCIDENTS."

The above is quoted from an article which appeared in the Journal of the American Medical Association (JAMA), August 7, 1987. Volume 258. The article was prepared by Dr. Roger E. Linnemann of Radiation Management Consultants, Inc., Philadelphia, Pennsylvania.

Although the design of United States commercial nuclear reactors does not provide the same physical geometry and conditions that led to the Chernobyl accident, improved organization of mass-casualty medical response resources may be prudent. I do not intend to influence anyone's evaluation of commercial nuclear power in the United States—it takes much more information than can be provided in a single text to formulate an educated evaluation. However, no matter how slight the risk of wide-spread high-level contamination, the risk exists.

Much of this Section contains material taken from the JAMA article, a copy of which was provided to me by Dr. Linnemann, in an attempt to increase awareness of the lessons learned to as many professionals as possible. Following is a summary of Dr. Linnemann's experience from participation in the Chernobyl post-accident review meeting and by interviews with personnel involved in the event.

The Soviet medical plan involved three stages of care; rescue and first aid at the plant, emergency treatment at regional hospitals, and definitive care at specialized centers. There were 135,000 people evacuated as a result of the Chernobyl event. Three-hundred and fifty people were evaluated for acute radiation syndrome. The most serious and immediate problems involved thermal burns of plant personnel. One of the plant personnel died in a little more than five hours. Another individual was presumed killed by the explosion and buried by falling debris. Two-hundred and three individuals were hospitalized. Of the 203 hospitalized personnel, 29 died from a combination of thermal burns and ionizing radiation injuries. Thus, the total number of personnel who were killed as a result of the Chernobyl event is 31.

Blood counts were obtained every few hours on the individuals hospitalized. A rapid drop in cell counts indicated acute doses in the lethal range. Erythema (reddening of the skin) was another indication of acute dose. Radiation erythema tends to peak within hours then abate over the few days after exposure. Early radiation erythema can be distinguished from erythema of thermal burns since thermal burns are painful. Erythema due to ionizing radiation is not as painful as erythema due to thermal burns. Erythema due to exposure to ionizing radiation that appears within 24 hours or less may be due to lethal or near-lethal doses to gamma radiation.

Doctor Linnemann was able to determine four groupings of exposure of the hospitalized patients and the relation of deaths to the groupings. Table 3.8 provides the groupings of the deaths of the personnel who were hospitalized and excludes the two plant personnel who were killed almost immediately.

TABLE 3.8
Exposure Groupings

Group	Deaths[a]	Range (rad)
1	0	100 - 200
2	1	200 - 400
3	7	400 - 600
4	21	600 - 1600

[a] Severe skin damage was a significant factor of the deaths.

Some attendants received doses due to handling contaminated persons. Attendant doses should be expected from handling so many contaminated persons in terms of hours. Doctor Linnemann imparted in his article that attendant doses were believed to range from 4 to 5 rads whole-body and 35 to 40 rads to their hands. As implied by Tables 3.4 and 3.5 and by Dr. Linnemann's findings, the 4 to 5 rad whole-body doses and the 35 to 40 rad extremity doses are of minor concern regarding ill acute effects.

It is unproven that US commercial reactors could produce contamination levels as severe as the Chernobyl event: Three-mile Island did not. The inventory of nuclear material in US reactors may be as great as the Chernobyl reactor but the design of US reactors will not permit them to react as did Chernobyl. Also, US reactors have far more sophisticated safety features than did the Chernobyl reactor. Furthermore, the Chernobyl design did not provide for a sealed reactor containment building as do all commercial US reactors.

The level of dose by the Soviet emergency workers are in excess of the doses allowed for US radiation workers. The US Nuclear Regulatory Commission (NRC) has established laws and regulations regarding radiation worker doses. The dose limits in the US are typically 3 rem for whole-body dose in any calendar quarter (no more than 5 rem per calendar year) and 18.75 rem to the hands per calendar quarter. These dose limits are due to change on January 1, 1994 but will be more conservative. Note that the dose allowances for radiation workers is not to be construed as allowable doses for radiation accident patients. There is no defined allowable dose for radiation accident patients. Nor are you as medical and paramedical personnel to construe the allowable doses for nuclear industry workers as allowable doses for yourselves. *Keep all exposures As Low As Reasonably Achievable* (ALARA).

As the engineering and technological aspects of the Chernobyl disaster are now understood, it will take quite some time, maybe decades, to obtain all possible sociological and medical data and to compile and analyze the data into a scientifically complete database. Interested individuals should consider monitoring the development of the information as it becomes available and as it matures. Doing so should provide for integration of the lessons learned into training and into practice in as timely a manner as possible. Emergency medical service providers are encouraged to solicit developments as they become available from State radiological health departments or other credible sources.

There are a great many publications prepared explaining a number of aspects of the Chernobyl event. There are so many that I felt it counterproductive to list each of them in the References and Suggested Reading section of this book. Most of the articles and publications I reviewed provided a scientific or engineering perspective of the explosion and the events leading to the explosion. Many provided an in-depth discussion of the impact of the radiological releases to the populace near Chernobyl. One article echoed my estimation of years to compile the sociological and medical data into a scientifically complete database. Few articles and publications I reviewed captured my interest from a paramedical response perspective. Of all the articles on Chernobyl I've reviewed, in my opinion Dr. Linnemann's article came closest to providing information which I felt was most useful to the paramedical community. You should, however, not rely on one individual's opinion to satisfy your curiosity about the single most disastrous incident in the history of commercial nuclear power. I recommend you evaluate for yourself whether the various articles and publications on the Chernobyl event can contribute to your medical and paramedical service needs. If you have been apprehensive about getting more than superficially involved with the Chernobyl event due to unfamiliarity with the "language" used, the background provided by this book should help you to draw more information from the articles and publications.

The International Atomic Energy Agency (IAEA) published in 1992 a broadsheet summary of some of the Chernobyl findings in a pamphlet titled *The International Chernobyl Project*. The project was directed by an International Advisory Committee comprised of scientists from 10 countries and 7 international organizations and involved around 200 experts of 25 countries and 7 international organizations: experts including medical doctors and physical and social scientists from outside the nuclear industry. The project involved investigation of 825,000 people from 3 republics. The assessment of the radiological impact to the people of the Chernobyl area was centered around the protection of the people still living in the area and excluded people who had been evacuated to uncontaminated areas and excluded the decontamination workers. Some of the information provided by the IAEA in the broadsheet summary is provided below as general information.

Regarding environmental contamination, project teams found that their findings correlated well with official maps of contamination distribution. By measuring water in lakes and rivers, in food, and in drinking water, the teams found that the levels of cesium and plutonium in soil samples confirmed the official findings, but the levels of strontium found by the teams were lower than the official levels. Drinking water and food contamination was found to be generally below international guidelines with water often being below detection limits.

Radiation doses were calculated for seven contaminated settlements using specialized dosimetry devices. Doses of 8000 residents were assessed by film badges and 9000 residents were provided with a whole-body monitoring. External exposure was the major contributor to the radiation doses received by the residents, but evaluation of the 8000 film badges revealed 90% of the results were below the limit of detection of 0.2 millisievert (0.2 millisieverts = 200 millirem). For 9000 residents in 9 settlements, theoretical models for estimating the amounts of cesium in the bodies of residents by environmental transfer, metabolism, and dietary intake generated results which were greater than the result revealed by whole-body monitoring. Official values of radiation doses were higher than the estimates determined by project teams. The teams could find no health effects directly attributable to the radiation doses. However, the report indicated that "it is possible that increases in thyroid cancer may be detected in the future", that " increases in other cancers would be difficult to detect" and that "The accident had substantial psychological consequences in terms of anxiety and continuing uncertainty."

The project team found that where the actions of the authorities could be evaluated, the action of the authorities seemed to be "reasonable and consistent with internationally established standards." The team did recommend, however, that better public information is needed.

Much more information is available in *The International Chernobyl Project - an Overview*, and *The International Chernobyl Project - Technical Report*, both available through the International Atomic Energy Agency.

Chapter 4

RADIATION DETECTION

PREVIEW

In this Chapter, the basics of radiation detection will be presented. After studying this material the student will have the background to undertake operation of radiation detection equipment with only supplemental classroom instruction and study of the manuals specific to your instruments. Topics include:

- Principles of radiation detection
- Examples of instrumentation
- Radiation energies applicable to radiation detection

Section 1. Principles of Radiation Detection

Recall from Chapter 1 the topic of ionization. Ionizing radiation causes the loss of an electron from its parent atom or molecule, thereby creating an ion pair. In the example of lithium used in Figure 1.5, the parent lithium atom minus one of its electrons is the positive ion of the ion pair and the electron knocked out of its orbit is the negative ion. Figure 4.1 illustrates ion pair production in the path of radiation. In Figure 4.1, the +'s and -'s indicate the positive and negative ions created in the path of the ionizing radiation.

FIGURE 4.1
Ion Pair Production

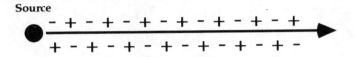

Radiation detection depends of the occurrence of ionization. As a ray or particle of radiation proceeds through matter, ion pairs are created in its path. Radiation detection equipment detects the ion pairs created. In fact, radiation detection equipment "counts" the ion pairs created. Radiations of different type (alpha, beta, and gamma) and of different energy will create different numbers of ion pairs per path of radiation. In air, gamma radiation may create only one ion pair per ray path. Beta radiation may create as many as 10 ion pairs per particle path in air. Alpha may create as many as 20 ion pairs per particle path in air. The reason for the greater number of ion pairs per path of alpha and beta radiation is due to the particulate nature of alpha and beta. Alpha and beta radiation possess more energy of motion (kinetic energy) than gamma since they are matter. Gamma is energy only (electromagnetic radiation). Generally speaking, particulate radiation will impart more force on the target than electromagnetic radiation, thereby creating more ion pairs in its path.

In addition to the type and energy of the radiation, the type of material exposed to the radiation will play a part in how many ion pairs are created per path. In addition to the type and energy of the radiation, the density of the exposed material will determine the number of ion pairs per path and the path length (depth of penetration). The more dense the exposed material, the more the interaction of the radiation with matter, therefore the shorter the distance of travel (less penetration). Different electromagnetic radiations have different energies. Radiation of different energies will create different numbers of ion pairs per path in a given material, therefore different distances of travel in the material (penetration).

Radio and television signals each carry a multitude of channels because radio and television signals each have a multitude of frequencies. Light comes in different colors because light comes in different frequencies. Radio and television signals and light are examples of electromagnetic radiation. Hidden in the first two sentences of this paragraph is that electromagnetic radiation follows a spectrum of frequencies. To explain frequency, the concept of waves needs to be explained.

Electromagnetic energy is a wave motion entity. Waves are expressed in terms of cycles, meaning they repeat themselves in subsequent units of time. The concept of electromagnetic wave motion, or propagation, can be likened to tossing a pebble into water as illustrated in Figure 4.2.

FIGURE 4.2
Wave Motion/Propagation

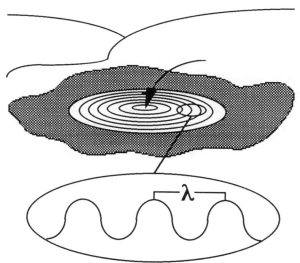

Side View, as if looking at the waves through a
vertical piece of glass at water level

$\lambda =$ Wavetop to wavetop, one cycle, one wavelength

The effect of tossing the pebble in the water propagates as waves from the point of impact on the surface of the water. A wave is the point-to-point distance from wavetop one wavetop to the next.

The point-to-point distance between wavetops is also called the *wavelength*. A point-to-point distance, or one wavelength, is one *cycle*. Wavelength is expressed in terms of meters or fractions of a meter. The *frequency* of the waves is the number of point-to-point distances (cycles) that pass a fixed point per unit of time, e.g. seconds. Waves are therefore expressed in terms of *cycles per second* (cps). Note that another term more often used than cycles per second is the *hertz (Hz)*—one cycle per second equals one hertz. As the number of cycles in each unit of time (cycles per second or hertz) increases, the frequency increases. When the frequency of waves increases, so does the energy of the waves. When the number of cycle events in one unit of time increases (when the frequency increases), the energy must increase to cause the events to occur at the increased rate. Therefore, as the frequency of electromagnetic radiation increases, the energy of the radiation increases.

To help explain the concept of wave propagation further, consider sound. Sound is defined as that which is perceived by the human ear. Sound propagates from the source as waves of high and low pressure. A speaker cone makes sound by the cone starting at its rest position then moving forward to the maximum distance of forward cone travel, then reversing motion back through its rest position to the maximum distance of cone travel backward, then back to its rest position. One journey of the speaker cone out from its starting position then in then back to its starting position is one cycle of the speaker cone. Repetition of this cycle makes sound. As the cone moves out from the rest position, a high pressure wave is created in the air. The high pressure wave moves away from the speaker just as the wavetops in the water move away from the point of impact of the pebble in the water. As the cone moves back in and beyond the rest position, a low pressure wave is created in the air. The low pressure wave also moves away from the speaker just as the wave troughs in the water move away from the point of impact of the pebble with the water. The ear perceives the pressure waves created by the cone movement as audio. The rate of the cone movement is in direct proportion to the source of audio, e.g., a voice in the microphone, the guitar string, or the drum head. The faster the cone moves the higher the pitch. The higher the pitch, the higher the frequency. High pitch sounds require more energy than the low pitch sounds—another example of how the frequency of the waves determines the energy of the waves.

Electromagnetic radiation energy follows a spectrum of frequency and energy as shown in Figure 4.3. Section A of Figure 4.3 identifies the spectrum of light as it falls within the spectrum of electromagnetic radiation shown in Section B. Recall the examples used earlier of electromagnetic radiation, i.e., heat, light, radio/television signals, microwave, and nuclear (ionizing radiation—each falls within the electromagnetic spectrum in Section B of Figure 4.3 Heat falls within the Infrared light band. Nuclear radiation falls within the range labeled Gamma (gamma only since Figure 4.3 is a spectrum of electromagnetic energy: Alpha and beta are particulate radiations).

Proceeding from left to right in the spectrum, the energy of the radiations increase. The increase in radiation energy is due to an increase in the frequency of the radiation due to the shortening of the wavelengths. The shorter the wavelength (the higher the frequency) of the radiation, the higher the energy of the radiation. The spectrum in Section B of Figure 4.3 illustrates the wavelength of the radiations.

FIGURE 4.3
Electromagnetic Radiation Spectrum

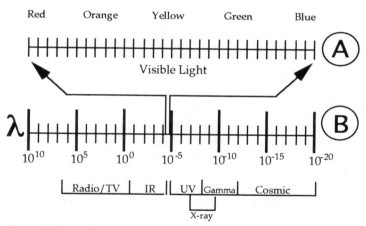

From left to right, wavelength in centimeters shortens, therefore, frequency and energy increase

Radio/TV - Communications signals. IR - Infrared light.
UV - Ultraviolet light. Cosmic - from outer space.
λ - Wavelength (wavetop to wavetop) in centimeters

For example, gamma radiation has a band of wavelengths centered around 10^{-10} centimeter: each gamma wave is 0.0000000001 centimeter long. A wavelength of 10^{-10} centimeter equates to a frequency of 3×10^{20} hertz which is 30,000,000,000,000,000,000 hertz—and that is just the center of the band. Audio has a maximum audible frequency of 20,000 hertz. Maybe the frequency of gamma helps explain why gamma has so much energy? On the left end of the light spectrum in Section A of Figure 4.3, in the red light band, is the lower end of light frequency/energy. Proceeding to the right of the light spectrum through yellow and blue light, the frequency and energy increase.

Alpha and beta radiations are particulate matter and are not expressed in terms of frequency. The matter nature of alpha and beta radiations accounts for their capability to produce more ion pairs in their path than gamma radiation. Their energies are determined by their velocity and their physical and electrical parameters. For those of you who have taken college physics, I cannot include within the scope of this text the wave/particle duality of matter in motion mentioned in footnote 8.

The energies of electromagnetic radiations are measured in terms of electron-volts (eV). The energies of electromagnetic radiation can be as low as a few thousand (kilo) electron-volts (KeV) and can reach as high as a few million electron-volts (MeV). The energy of one eV is quite small. The energy of one electron-volt can be likened to the amount of energy expended by a flea doing a push-up in the weightlessness of outer space. However, millions of eV per particle or ray of radiation combined with millions and millions of rays or particles of radiation can have a serious effect on human tissues. The average electromagnetic radiation energy of one million electron-volts (1 MeV) will be the basis for statements of radiation detection within this text unless otherwise specified.

Remember that electromagnetic radiation such as gamma radiation has many possible energies. One energy of electromagnetic radiation may cause a different response in radiation detection instruments than another energy. For example, an instrument that is calibrated to measure gamma radiation at 1 MeV will not measure 500 keV gamma—the instrument will *detect* the 500 keV gamma and will certainly indicate radiation is present but the instrument will not *measure* it. Specifically, if an instrument calibrated to 1 MeV gamma reads 1000 mR/hr, it will not read 500 mR/hr for gamma half as strong (500 keV). Only specialists can accurately interpolate the indication of the instrument from an energy different from that which the instrument is calibrated to read. Imagine a radio receiver than is tuned to 94.1 megahertz. The radio's antenna and circuitry will receive many frequencies but the radio will produce program audio only at the frequency the radio is tuned ("calibrated") to receive. Similarly, a radiation detection instrument will detect several energies of radiation passing through its detector and will show response on the instrument but will measure only the energy it is calibrated to measure.

Section 2. Survey Rate Meter Radiation Detection Principles

As discussed in Section 1, radiation detection equipment use the production of ion pairs to detect radiation. Figure 4.4 shows the Geiger-Mueller rate meter or survey meter (GM Counter or Geiger Counter) principle of detecting the *rate of exposure* to radiation.

In a GM type survey meter, a constant high DC voltage is applied across a volume of gas. The enclosed gas volume is contained in a metal Geiger-Mueller tube (GM tube). The GM tube has a wire passing from top to bottom through the center of the tube. The center wire (the anode in Figure 4.4) is charged with a high positive DC voltage. The outside of the tube is charged with a high negative DC voltage.

The high positive DC voltage pulls on the outer electrons of the gas atoms. The pull on the outer electrons is just weak enough not to cause the electrons to leave orbit. The pull by attraction of opposite charges is constant as long as the instrument is turned on. Many of the GM type instruments use 900 volts DC. Although not an electrocution problem, the 900 volts DC is most certainly an attention-getter. I speak with the voice of experience.

FIGURE 4.4
Geiger-Mueller Radiation Detection

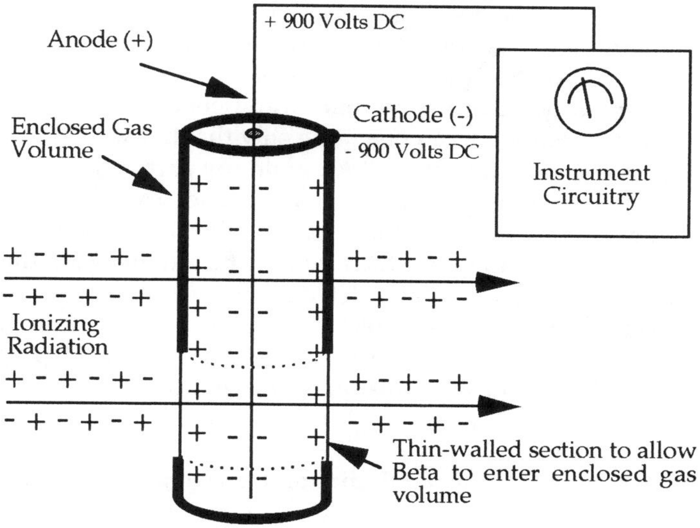

As radiation passes through the enclosed volume of gas, ionization of the atoms occurs. When one of the electrons is knocked out of its orbit (when it is *ionized*) by the ray or particle of radiation, the ionized electron then collides with a second atom which is ready to lose an electron due to the pull of the high positive voltage. The energy of the ionized electron is enough to cause the second atom to give up one of its electrons. While on its way to the positive voltage, the freed electron from the second atom will collide with another atom under the same conditions. The atom the second electron collides with also gives up an electron which will collide with another atom which will give up one of its electrons, and so on. The collisions are repeated in a surge throughout the atoms in the enclosed volume of gas and creates what is called an *avalanche* of electrons.[18] The positive terminal (anode, + terminal) attracts the electrons. The deluge of negative electric charges caused by an avalanche of electrons is conducted by the anode and constitutes a pulse of electric current. The pulse of electric current is amplified by the electronics of the instrument and sent to the meter. Thus the ray or particle of radiation is counted. The avalanche occurs in a tiny fraction of a second. The short duration of each avalanche event allows the atoms of the enclosed gas to claim replacement electrons to be ready for another ray or particle of radiation to cause another avalanche of electrons. The more the rays or particles of radiation, the greater the number of avalanche events and the greater the number of counts. Although the avalanche duration is very short, it is possible for the instrument to be in a radiation field with a high enough rate of exposure that the enclosed gas volume will saturate and become useless until the instrument is turned off and taken out of the exposure field. Once removed and turned off, the instrument should regain operability. Gamma radiation can penetrate any area of the GM tube. Beta radiation can penetrate only the thin-walled section of the tube. Alpha radiation cannot penetrate any part of the GM tube.

There is another type of radiation detection called the *ionization chamber* or *ion chamber*. The ionization chamber instrument also uses ion pair production to detect the rate of exposure in much the same way the GM survey rate meter detects ion pair production but at a lower voltage and with a different enclosed gas. The ionization chamber type instrument is typically used to detect much higher rates of exposure than the Geiger-Mueller instrument.

Section 3. Dosimeter Radiation Detection Principles

As the Geiger-Mueller and ion chamber survey rate meters are used to detect the rate of exposure to radiation by detecting the rate of

---

18.   The avalanche effect is *not* a nuclear chain reaction.

ion pair production, another type of instrument is used to detect *accumulated exposure* to radiation. The instrument used to detect accumulated exposure is called the *dosimeter*. The dosimeter operates by accumulating the effect of ion pair production on an electrical charge. You may assume that if the dosimeter receives a certain amount of radiation, the individual wearing the dosimeter has received the same amount, at least at the location on the body the dosimeter was worn.

There are basically three types of dosimeters the *self-reading dosimeter (SRD)*, the *film badge*, and the *thermoluminescent dosimeter (TLD)*. The operating characteristics of the self-reading dosimeter will be presented herein. A brief discussion of the film badge and the thermoluminescent dosimeter are also presented.

The *self-reading dosimeter (SRD)* is the first to be presented. The operation of the SRD is based on what is called the *electroscope effect* displayed in Figure 4.5.

FIGURE 4.5
Electroscope Radiation Detection

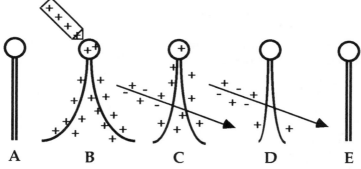

The electroscope in Figure 4.5 is two flexible metal strips electrically connected to a metal ball. The metal strips will hang down parallel to each other when there is no electrical charge on them, i.e., when neutral.

If a glass rod is rubbed with a silk cloth or a fur, a static (electrical) charge will build up on the rod. For the sake of illustration, let's say the static charge is positive. If the charged rod is touched to the metal ball of the electroscope, the static charge will transfer to the metal ball, sometimes as a spark. The positive electrical charge would then be conducted equally to each of the metal strips. When the flexible metal strips both possess an electrical charge of the same polarity, they will push away from each other and flare out from straight down. They do so in accordance with the law of charges which requires that opposite charges attract and like charges repel. In Figure 4.5, each metal strip has a positive charge (two objects with like charges) and will push away from each other.

Step A of Figure 4.5 shows the electroscope in the uncharged position. In step B where the charged glass rod touches the metal ball, the positive charge is conducted to the metal strips which then push away from each other. The distance the metal strips reach away from each other depends of the amount of charge on each strip. The stronger the charge, the stronger the repulsion and the farther away from each other the strips will move. If ionizing radiation passes through the area of the metal strips, the negative charges created by the ionizing radiation will neutralize the positive charges on the metal strips. The greater the number of negative ions, the greater the neutralization of positive charges. The stronger the radiation field or the longer the duration of exposure, the greater the number of ion pairs produced in the vicinity of the electroscope. Steps C and D portray additional ionizing radiation passing through the area creating additional negative ions which neutralize more positive charges.   After enough ionizing radiation has passed by the electroscope, all positive charges will eventually be neutralized as shown in Step E of Figure 4.5.

The information to remember from the electroscope is that a physical change in the position of the metal strips can be caused by:

• the effect of like electrical charges, and
• neutralization of the charges by ionizing radiation.

The principle of operation of the self-reading dosimeter (SRD) uses the electroscope principle of operation. Both the SRD and the electroscope use the ion pair production to detect radiation and both use a change in physical position due to neutralization caused by ion pair production. Referencing the cross-section of a self-reading dosimeter in Figure 4.6, a SRD consists of an ionization chamber (an enclosed gas volume), a flexible horseshoe-shaped quartz fiber attached parallel to a fixed metal horseshoe-shaped electrode, a microscope of about 125X magnification, and a metal bellows-type switch.

The horseshoe electrode and its quartz fiber operate in the same way as the two metal strips of the electroscope: one strip as the horseshoe electrode and the other strip as the quartz fiber. The horseshoe portion of the electrode and the quartz fiber are in effect an electroscope and are sealed in the ionization chamber (an enclosed gas volume). The SRD is readied by charging with a DC voltage between 50 to 250 volts from a dosimeter charger which will be presented later in this Chapter. The voltage is applied across the horseshoe electrode and the metal case of the dosimeter. Positive voltage is applied to the horseshoe electrode and negative voltage is applied to the metal case of the dosimeter. As the positive voltage is applied to the horseshoe electrode, the positive voltage is identically applied to the quartz fiber. Recall from the electroscope in Figure 4.5 how the electrical charge is applied equally to both metal strips of the electroscope due to the configuration of the metal strips. In accordance with the law of charges which states that like charges repel, the positive voltage on the horseshoe electrode and the positive voltage on the quartz fiber will repel each other. The repulsion between the electrode and quartz fiber causes the flexible fiber to move away from the fixed horseshoe electrode in direct proportion to the amount of positive charge applied.

FIGURE 4.6
Self-reading Dosimeter

Side View

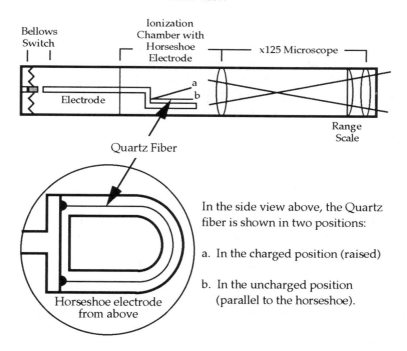

In the side view above, the Quartz fiber is shown in two positions:

a. In the charged position (raised)

b. In the uncharged position (parallel to the horseshoe).

The quartz fiber is viewed through the 125 power microscope which magnifies the fiber to a visible size. A graduated range scale is superimposed over the image of the fiber in the viewfield of the microscope (the scale will be covered later in this Chapter). Different voltages provided by a dosimeter charger will position the quartz fiber away from the horseshoe electrode in proportion to the amount of voltage on the electrode and fiber. The change in position will be apparent against the viewfield scale, i.e., the fiber will move across the scale in the viewfield as the voltage on the fiber and horseshoe electrode varies. The voltage on the electrode and fiber changes as the voltage adjustment knob of the dosimeter charger is rotated. Setting the fiber on the zero of the scale with the dosimeter charger is called *zeroing* the dosimeter. A zero setting represents a full charge on the dosimeter.

As radiation passes through the enclosed gas volume (ion chamber), ion pairs are created in the path of the radiation within the enclosed gas volume. The positive voltage on the electrode and quartz fiber attract the negative charges created by the ionizing radiation in the same way the positively charged metal strips of the electroscope attracted negative charges created by ionizing radiation. As more and more negative charges are collected by the positively charged electrode and fiber, the amount of positive charge on the electrode and fiber is reduced. As the amount of positive charge is reduced, the amount of repulsion between the electrode and fiber is reduced. As the amount of repulsion is reduced, the position of the fiber will move toward its uncharged position which is parallel to the electrode. When parallel to the electrode, the fiber will appear at the high end of the scale or will disappear off-scale at the high end. The fiber will not move from the position set by the dosimeter charger or from an after-exposure position until the dosimeter is recharged or is further exposed to ionizing radiation or unless the dosimeter leaks the charge. The electroscope design feature of the self-reading dosimeter is what permits it to detect the *accumulation* of radiation rather than the rate of radiation exposure.

Most self-reading dosimeters will drift (leak their charge) without exposure to ionizing radiation. It is recommended that if any SRD you have leaks more than 5% of full scale in 4 days or less, the dosimeter should be replaced.

Although the dosimeter is designed to detect accumulated exposure of the wearer, it may also be used as an exposure rate device. Place a SRD in an unknown exposure rate field for a given period of time. It may be assumed that the reading of the dosimeter represents the exposure in the location of the dosimeter for the time it was there. For example, place a SRD in the exposure field for one hour. If the SRD reads 100 millirem, it may be assumed the exposure rate in the location the dosimeter was placed averaged 100 millirem per hour. If the dosimeter was worn by someone, it may also be assumed that the wearer received the same dosage the dosimeter received, definitely at the location the dosimeter was worn on the body and likely over the entire body of the wearer.

The *film badge* operates by ionizing radiation causing exposure of photographic film while encased in a light-tight jacket. Gamma, beta, and X-radiations will cause ionization in the chemistry of the film causing the film to be exposed in the same way light causes the film to be exposed. By placing squares of material of different opacity to X- and gamma radiations in the badge housing in front of the film, the degree of exposure under the squares will reveal the amount of X- and gamma radiation received by the badge (and presumably by the wearer). By providing a window in the badge housing which allows beta radiation to penetrate the light-tight jacket, the degree of exposure to beta radiation can be measured. Alpha radiation cannot penetrate the light-tight jacket of the film badge.

The *thermoluminescent dosimeter (TLD)* operates on a different principle. In a strip of special chemicals, ionizing radiation will cause a change in the chemical make-up of the material by exciting the chemical molecules (recall electron excitation in Chapter 1). As ionizing radiation passes through the chemicals, ionization occurs and creates a condition where, when heated, the excited molecules of the chemicals will emit minute pulses of light. A special device for heating the chemical strip also detects the minute pulses of light. Thus, the amount of exposure received by the TLD can be determined by the amount of light emitted from the chemical strip. The TLD is so accurate that its reading may be used as a legal record of the exposure received by the wearer.

Film badges and TLDs may not be practical for emergency field personnel since each requires special processing on a periodic basis by specially equipped laboratories. Recurring costs are involved as well.

Now you may understand the importance of ionization due to radiation. Not only may ionization cause injury to living tissues, ionization provides a means of detecting and measuring ionizing radiation.

Section 4. Instrument Examples

Examples of radiation detection instruments which will be presented are *survey rate meters* and *self-reading dosimeters*. The types of survey rater meters presented are:

- CDV-700, 0 to 50 milliRoentgen per hour rate meter
- CDV-715, 0 to 500 Roentgen per hour rate meter

The types of dosimeters presented are:

- CDV-138, 0 to 200 milliRoentgen dosimeter
- CDV-742, 0 to 200 Roentgen dosimeter

Survey Rate Meters (Survey Meters)

Survey rate meters are used to detect the rate of exposure to radiation in the area where the instrument is positioned. Survey rate meters are provided with an indicating meter on the face of the instrument which provides a visual indication of the radiation field in the area. Some are provided with a headphone or speaker to provide an audible indication of the radiation field. Portable survey meters provide a convenient means of radiation detection since they are powered by batteries. Each model has different scales which provide different ranges of radiation detection.

Many different vendors of survey rate meters are available; some are expensive, some are not so expensive. Some have price ranges that may be prohibitive, e.g., several hundreds of dollars each. However, your State and/or local Civil Defense or Emergency Preparedness Agency may have survey rate meters which may be made available to State, county, and municipal emergency medical service providers. Although the Civil Defense or Emergency Preparedness survey rate meters may not necessarily be dependable as accurate *measuring* devices, each of them is excellent for *detecting* radiation. The instruments may not tell you exactly how much radiation is there, but they will certainly tell you there is radiation present, which is extremely valuable since none of the five human senses can detect ionizing radiation—*radiation cannot be seen, felt, heard, tasted, nor smelled.* As presented in Chapter 3 there may be some evidence that extremely high rates of exposure to ionizing radiation may be sensed as tingling and itching. However, you should *never* trust this speculation for an indication of the presence of ionizing radiation. There are too many things that can cause tingling and itching—depend only on instruments.

CDV-700 Survey Rate Meter

The CDV-700 survey rate meter will detect gamma and/or beta radiation. The CDV-700 will not detect alpha radiation unless it is equipped with a special detector. Stock instruments are provided with a Geiger-Mueller tube (GM tube) as the detector. CDV-700 instruments will operate as designed in exposure rates between 0 and 50 milliRoentgen per hour. In addition, the CDV-700 is so sensitive that it will detect background radiation coming from naturally occurring radioactive isotopes and outer space.[19] Exposure rates between 50 milliRoentgen per hour to near 1 Roentgen per hour will cause the CDV-700 to read off-scale high end. If the radiation field the detector is in exceeds approximately 1 Roentgen per hour, the Geiger-Mueller tube will saturate, read zero, and become useless until turned off and removed from the radiation field (recall the discussion of the avalanche of electrons in Section 2). Figures 4.7 and 4.8 display the physical features of the CDV-700.

The GM tube inside the probe of the CDV-700 is connected to the electronics of the instrument via a cable. The probe nests in a cradle which also serves as the instrument handle. The top half of the probe is a rotating sleeve called the *beta shield*. Cut into the beta shield are openings called *beta windows*. When the beta shield is rotated so the beta windows are open, exposing the GM tube inside to the environment, both beta and gamma may enter into the GM tube. When the beta shield is rotated to close the beta windows, the beta shield prevents beta from entering into the GM tube. Therefore the beta shield provides a means to determine if beta or gamma or both beta and gamma are present. If there is a difference between a reading taken with the beta shield closed and a reading with the shield open, both beta and gamma are present. If there is no difference, only gamma is present. No indication with the beta shield closed and an indication with it open indicates beta only.

Beta Shield Open	Beta Shield Closed	Radiation(s) Indicated
40 mR/hr	25 mR/hr	Both beta and gamma
40 mR/hr	40 mR/hr	Gamma only
40 mR/hr	≈ 0 mR/hr	Beta only

When responding to a radiation incident, the beta shield should be kept open and the probe held perpendicular to the direction of radiation with the beta windows facing the source. *Do not* point the probe at the source. Only if you need to determine whether beta or gamma or both gamma and beta radiation is present would you need to close the beta shield. It would be best, anyway, to let the radiological health physics personnel determine what type or types of

---

19. Background radiation is radiation coming from radioactive isotopes naturally present in our food, in the air, in the ground, in building material, and in ourselves. Some evidence exists that supports nuclear weapons testing provides minor contribution to the background radiation. Background radiation. is discussed further later in this Section

radiation is involved. Your main need-to-know is whether radiation is present and from where it is coming, not the type of radiation, particularly, if the radiation is coming from radiological contamination on the patient, or if the radiation is coming from a radiological source near the patient (and you).

FIGURE 4.7
CDV-700 Survey Meter

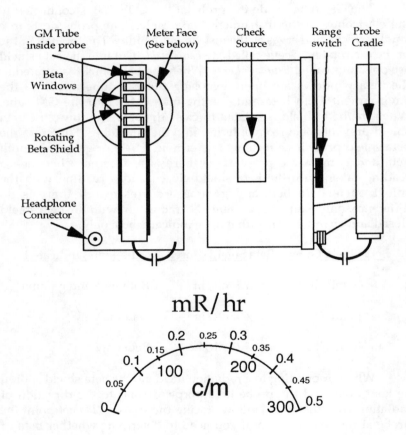

An indicating meter with two scales is located on the face of the CDV-700. The needle on the meter moves upscale as the radiation field increases. In order to provide a stable and non-frantic meter response to radiation, bouncing with every count[20], the meter

---

20. Due to physical constraints, many Geiger-Mueller instruments will count only 1 in 10 rays of gamma radiation. The ratio for beta is better than 1:10 but still not 1:1.

integrates and averages the rate of counts detected. Integrating and averaging the counts electronically may require a few seconds. Therefore, it may be a few seconds before the meter needle stabilizes and properly indicates the level of radiation being detected. However, as you will see later in this Section, the CDV-700 and similar instruments are provided with a headphone which provides an instantaneous audible indication of radiation. The scale on the top of the meter face reads in milliRoentgens per hour (mR/hr). The scale on the bottom reads in counts per minute (c/m or cpm). The cpm scale is used for calibrating the instrument. The 0.05, 0.15, 0.25, 0.35, and 0.45, labels corresponding to the minor scale divisions on the meter face in Figure 4.7 are not shown on the actual meter face of the CDV-700, but are shown to improve comprehension of the meter scale.

The range switch under the probe cradle provides three operating ranges, specifically, X100 (times 100), X10 (times 10), and X1 (times 1). The X100, X10, and X1 mean whatever the meter needle is pointing to times the range multiplier of 100, 10, or 1. The operating ranges of the CDV-700 are:

- 0 to 50 mR/hr in the X100 range
- 0 to 5 mR/hr in the X10 range
- 0 to 0.5 mR/hr in the X1 range

Below are a few examples of interpretations of the meter indications of the CDV-700:

Needle Position	Range Multiplier	Approximate Indication
0.05	X10	0.5 mR/hr
0.35	X100	35 mR/hr
0.5	X100	50 mR/hr
0.05	X100	5 mR/hr
0.25	X10	2.5 mR/hr

In the lower left corner of the top of the instrument is a connector for a headphone. The headphone provides an audible click as ray or particle of radiation is counted. As the radiation field changes, the number of audible clicks change (the frequency of clicks changes). The audible clicks are an instantaneous indication of radiation. While the meter needle may take a few seconds to stabilize, the headphone provides an immediate indication that radiation is present and whether the radiation field is increasing or decreasing by a change in the frequency of clicks. Another positive feature of the headphone is that listening to the headphone to detect changes in the rate of audio clicks allows the user to keep his/her eyes on what he/she is doing rather than on the meter face. The audio from the headphone is not affected by the range selector switch.

If a responder must know what the meter face indicates, he/she should enter the radiation field with the Geiger-Mueller instrument switched to the highest range. As the radiation field is encountered, as indicated by the audio response, the responder should step the range switch down through the ranges to one that provides on on-scale meter indication.

It is always advisable to perform an *operational check* of the CDV-700, as well as all other instruments, prior to each use and once per calendar quarter during storage. The CDV-700 is provided with its own check source on the side of the instrument. To perform an operational check on the CDV-700, hold the probe with the beta shield open and flush against the check source with the middle beta window directly over the check source. With the range switch set to the X10 scale, the check source should provide a reading of between 1.5 to 2.5 milliRoentgen per hour, depending on the age of the check source isotope.[21] Refer to Figure 4.8 while reading the following instructions for performing an operational check on the CDV-700. Most Geiger-Mueller instruments may be checked in the same manner.

1. Connect the headphone if not already connected.

2. Set the selector switch to the X10 position

3. Lift the probe from its cradle and rotate the beta shield open.

4. Place the probe flush against the operational check source on the side of the CDV-700 with the middle beta window fully open and directly over the check source.

5. Note the meter reading. The meter should indicate somewhere from 1.5 mR/hr to 2.5 mR/hr, maybe less, maybe more, depending on the age of the check source and whether the instrument has been calibrated.

6. The audio should sound like popping corn.

7. Move the probe away from the check source and back again a few times to note the change in the frequency of audio clicks as the probe is moved relative to the source.

21.   Recall the discussion on half-life in Chapter 2.

FIGURE 4.8
CDV-700 Operational Check

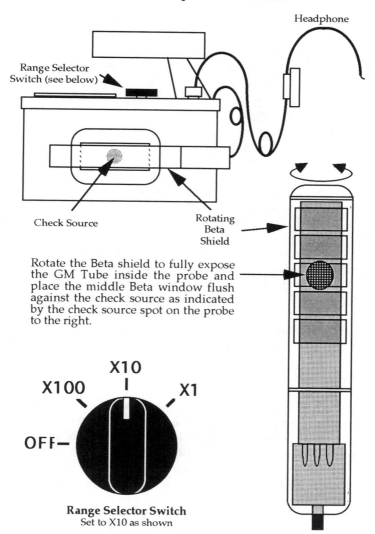

Headphone

Range Selector
Switch (see below)

Check Source

Rotating
Beta
Shield

Rotate the Beta shield to fully expose
the GM Tube inside the probe and
place the middle Beta window flush
against the check source as indicated
by the check source spot on the probe
to the right.

X10

X100   **X1**

OFF—

Range Selector Switch
Set to X10 as shown

8. When finished with steps 1 through 7, rotate the beta shield
to fully close the windows and return the probe to its cradle,
turn the selector switch to OFF, and disconnect the
headphone. Snap the probe into the cradle with the cable
end of the probe over the meter face. Doing so should help
prevent damage to the cable at the cable end of the probe.

Once these steps have been performed with satisfactorily results, you have determined that your CDV-700 is operational. The operational check only takes about one minute to complete. If the meter does not seem to operate correctly but the headphone works well, you can still use the instrument in a pinch to determine if radiation is present—just depend on the headphone.

One malfunction of the CDV-700 simulates high radiation. Specifically, if the Geiger-Mueller tube or the high voltage transformer starts arcing due to age or damage, the meter will peg offscale and give the operator the impression of high radiation. The headphone will probably sound off with a very high-pitched squeal when arcing occurs, also giving the operator an impression of high radiation. If arcing occurs, do not try to use the instrument. Turn it off and take it out of service for repair.

Geiger-Mueller radiation detection instruments such as the CDV-700 are so sensitive that they will respond to natural background radiation. With the Geiger-Mueller instrument turned on, with the probe in its cradle, with the beta shield open or closed (open or closed makes no difference since background radiation is electromagnetic radiation), and with the headphone connected, you will hear clicks in the headphone with no radioactive material near the probe. Each click represents a detected count of radiation. The clicks are due to natural background radiation. Natural background radiation in the United States averages about 30 counts per minute. Thirty counts per minute equates to approximately 100 millirem per year. The biological effect of a whole-body dose of 100 millirem spread over a year is not detectable, let alone an acute exposure hazard.

The audio clicks due to natural background radiation will not be evenly spaced and regular like a timepiece, but will be completely sporadic and random. You may hear one click, followed by a moment of silence, then one or two more clicks close together, followed by a few moments of silence, then three or four clicks close together. You may hear several clicks, some close together, some not close together, then a few moments of silence followed by another random sequence of clicking. You may even hear seemingly regular clicks for a moment or two, then several sequences of random clicks or individual clicks. The sequencing of clicks due to background radiation cannot be predicted accurately.

With the discovery of radon gas (a naturally occurring radioactive gas) in some building materials, radiological health personnel have reevaluated the 100 millirem exposure due to background radiation. Radiological health personnel now believe the annual estimate of exposure due to background radiation to be near

300 millirem. Although a 300 millirem dose spread over a year exposure is not an acute exposure hazard, as you learned in Chapter 3 ionizing radiation is a carcinogen. Therefore, naturally occurring radon gas may be contributing to the incidence of cancer. Unfortunately, the average Geiger-Mueller instrument such as the CDV-700 is not the proper instrument for detecting the presence of radon gas.

CDV-715 Survey Rate Meter

The CDV-715 shown in Figure 4.9 is a high range ion chamber gamma detection instrument.

FIGURE 4.9
CDV-715 Survey Meter

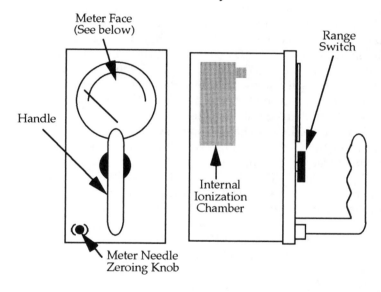

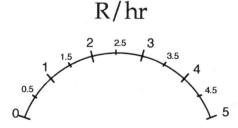

The CDV-715 indicates radiation levels by detecting the rate of ion pair production much like the Geiger-Mueller instruments, but at a much lower voltage and with a different enclosed gas. The paint on the outside of the instrument will stop alpha radiation from reaching the internal ionization chamber. The metal case of the instrument will stop beta.

The CDV-715 will *measure* 1 MeV gamma up to 500 Roentgen per hour (R/hr) if it has been calibrated. If it has not been calibrated, it is a great detector of high levels of gamma radiation up to the 500 R/hr level. The CDV-715 is not provided with a probe. The detector of the CDV-715 is an internal ionization chamber. Whereas the CDV-700 will saturate and become temporarily inoperable at exposure rates near or above 1 R/hr, the CDV-715 will typically peg off-scale high in exposure rates above of 500 R/hr and stay there and will not read zero until removed from the radiation and turned off.

The CDV-715 is not provided with a headphone since the rate of audio clicks due to ion pair production in the ranges of the CDV-715 would be above the range of human hearing (20 to 20,000 hertz). The meter face of the CDV-715 shown in Figure 4.9 is similar to the meter face of the CDV-700 except the CDV-715 meter shows only one scale. The 0.5,1.5, 2.5, 3.5, and 4.5, labels corresponding to the minor scale divisions on the meter face in Figure 4.9 are not shown on the actual meter face of the CDV-715, but are shown to improve comprehension of the meter scale.

The CDV-715 also has a range switch under the instrument handle, but the CDV-715 range switch provides four ranges rather than the three ranges of the CDV-700. The four ranges of the CDV-715 are X100, X10, X1, and X0.1. As with the CDV-700, the ranges mean whatever the meter needle is pointing to times the range multiplier. The operating ranges of the CDV-715 are:

- 0 to 500 R/hr in the X100 range
- 0 to 50 R/hr in the X10 range
- 0 to 5 R/hr in the X1 range
- 0 to 0.5 R/hr in the X0.1 range

Below are a few examples of interpretations of the meter indications of the CDV-715:

Needle Position	Range Multiplier	Approx. Reading	Needle Position	Range Multiplier	Approx Reading
1.5	X0.1	0.15 R/hr	4.0	X10	40 R.hr
4.5	X0.1	0.45 R/hr	2.5	X0.1	0.25 R/hr
3.5	X100	350 R/hr	5.0	X100	500 R/hr

Since the CDV-715 is calibrated by the State Radiological Maintenance and Calibration shops, the CDV-715 can be used to measure gamma radiation but only if the energy of the radiation the instrument is responding to is 1 MeV. Even if the radiation the instrument is responding to is 1 MeV gamma, readings should not be taken with the CDV-715 when the meter needle is in the lower 10% of the scale set by the range switch. Specifically, not in the area of the meter face corresponding to less than the first minor scale division (between the zero and the 0.5 mark). The CDV-715 is less accurate in the lower 10% than in the upper 90% of the same scale. If the CDV-715 meter needle is falling within the lower 10% of the scale the instrument is switched to, switch the scale to the next lower scale.

A meter indication at the first minor division of the CDV-715, the 0.5 R/hr mark, in the X0.1 scale equals 50 mR/hr (0.5 R/hr x 0.1 = 0.05 R/hr = 50 mR/hr), which happens to be the upper limit of the CDV-700. So, if your CDV-715 is reading below the 0.5 mark in the X0.1 range (in the lower 10% of the X0.1 scale), use the CDV-700. A combo of a CDV-700 and a CDV-715 will provide the capability to detect gamma radiation from approximately zero mR/hr to 500 R/hr (500,000 mR/hr). Since the CDV-700 will saturate and become inoperable in exposure rates at or near 1 R/hr, a CDV-715 would be valuable for alerting you to exposure rates above 1 R/hr. Although it is unlikely that the exposure rate at a trauma incident could even approach hazardous levels, I would prefer to have *both* a CDV-700 and a CDV-715 turned on, both in the highest range, when entering a radiation field of unknown exposure rate, just in case...

The CDV-715 operational check is merely turning the instrument on to any range, letting it warm up for a minute, and setting the meter needle on zero with the needle zeroing adjustment knob in the lower left corner of the face of the CDV-715. Setting the meter needle on zero after instrument warm-up should be done prior to each use. Doing so provides a bias for instrument readings. Setting the bias point for instrument readings means setting a starting point or threshold from which the electronics begins measuring radiation. If this is not done, the indication of the meter may be off as much as the zero setting is off.

Self-Reading Dosimeters (SRDs)

As discussed earlier, self-reading dosimeters (SRDs) are devices that provide an immediate visual indication of the accumulated exposure received by the instrument which is likely to be the accumulated exposure of the wearer. Dosimeter costs can be prohibitive but dosimeters may be available through your State/local

Civil Defense or Emergency Preparedness Agency. A multitude of vendors are available for SRDs as well as for survey rate meters. The following are the operating characteristics of two SRDs: the CDV-138 and the CDV-742.

The operating characteristics of the CDV-138 and the CDV-742 are the same except the range of the CDV-138 is zero to 200 mR and the range of the CDV-742 is zero to 200 R. Recall the construction of the SRD in Figure 4.6. Except for the difference in range scales, the two dosimeters are constructed the same. The scales of the CDV-138 and the CDV-742 look the same except the CDV-138 scale label reads milliRoentgens and the CDV-742 scale label reads Roentgens. Figure 4.10 shows the *viewfield* of the CDV-138 and the CDV-742.

FIGURE 4.10
Dosimeter Viewfield

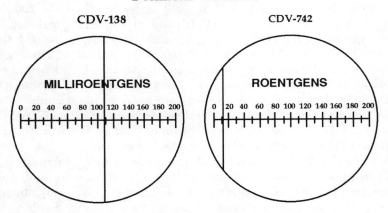

The vertical line (hairline) spanning the viewfield is the quartz fiber.

Self-reading dosimeters are read by pointing the charging end of the dosimeter toward a light. A translucent substance suspending the electrode permits light to pass into the dosimeter and illuminate the field of vision inside the SRD. The light reveals the position of the quartz fiber through the microscope. The fiber appears as a vertical line (hairline) passing through the horizontal scale. The scale indicates the amount of exposure accumulated by the SRD. The CDV-138 fiber in Figure 4.10 is indicating approximately 108 milliRoentgens and the CDV-742 fiber is indicating approximately 12 Roentgens.

Of alpha, beta, and gamma radiations, each SRD is capable of measuring approximately 1 MeV gamma radiation only. The SRD may respond to gamma radiation of weaker or stronger energy and the SRD may respond to strong X-rays, but it will not measure electromagnetic radiation energies above or below approximately 1 MeV. The metal case of each SRD will prevent beta radiation from entering the ionization chamber. The paint on the outside of each SRD will stop alpha from entering the ionization chamber.

The SRD is provided with a charge using a dosimeter charger. An example dosimeter charger is shown in Figure 4.11. The SRD is charged by pressing the charging end of the SRD down on the charging pedestal of the dosimeter charger. Pressing the SRD down against the charging pedestal will:

1) light an internal lamp illuminate the field of vision, and

2) energize the charging circuitry inside the charger.

FIGURE 4.11
Dosimeter Charger

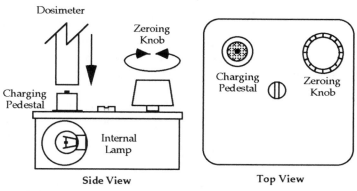

Side View   Top View

Lightly pressing down on the SRD will turn on the internal lamp and will energize the charging circuitry but will not close the metal bellows switch inside the SRD. Therefore, pressing the SRD down lightly on the charging pedestal will not provide electrical continuity between the fixed electrode, the quartz fiber, and the charging circuitry, but will illuminate the internal lamp to provide light to read the SRD if no outside light is available. To provide electrical continuity with the charging circuitry, you must press down firmly on the SRD. Pressing firmly on the charging pedestal will close the metal bellows switch inside the SRD and will provide an electrical path for the charge from the dosimeter charger to get to the horseshoe electrode and the quartz fiber inside the SRD.

Once continuity is established between the horseshoe electrode and the quartz fiber and the charger, rotate the zeroing knob of the dosimeter charger to set the SRD fiber. Rotating the zeroing knob varies the voltage of the charging circuitry. As the charging voltage varies, the charge on the horseshoe electrode and the quartz fiber varies. As the voltage on the electrode and fiber changes, the position of the quartz fiber will change. By careful adjustment of the charging voltage, the fiber can be set on zero. Once zeroed, the SRD is ready for use. Although starting a mission with the SRD set on zero is preferable, it is not essential. If the quartz fiber is set on a readable value, record the value at the start of the mission and subtract the starting value from the reading of the SRD at the end of the mission. The difference between the mission start reading and the mission end reading will be the mission exposure.

Whereas you may use the internal lamp to read the SRD, trying to use the internal lamp may destroy any reading of the SRD. The amount of pressure needed to turn on the internal lamp and charging circuitry of the charger may be so near the amount of pressure needed to close the metal bellows switch inside the SRD that the bellows switch may close at the same time or before the internal lamp and charging circuitry energize. If the charging circuitry energizes while trying to read your exposure, the reading of the SRD will be altered, possibly off scale before you could read the SRD, then you would not know what your mission exposure was. Use the lamp inside the charger only to zero the SRD, do not use the internal lamp to read your SRD unless no other light source is available. An outside light source is almost always available. For example, use the light from your headlights, a flashlight, flood lamps, or your visibar beams. Red light is a little weak to read the SRD but blue light is great. Amber light is also great. White is best. Please do not use the light from a match or cigarette lighter—they are not bright enough. Again I speak with the voice of experience. Besides, the flame does nasty things to the translucent material suspending the electrode inside the SRD.

A factor common to all SRDs is that they are *geotropic*. Geotropism is a property which will cause the fiber to change positions due to gravity when the SRD is rotated while held horizontal. The geotropic effect may be observed when the SRD is pointing to the horizon with the viewfield scale horizontal, and then rotating the SRD until the viewfield scale is vertical. When rotating the SRD, the fiber appears to "fall" up. Actually, the fiber falls down because of gravity but due to the focal inversion of the microscope, the fiber appears to fall up. The geotropic shift due to gravity may be as much as 10% of full scale. It is important to read the SRD using ambient light with the dosimeter and its viewfield scale horizontal.

Another common factor of the SRD is that when the SRD is removed from the charging pedestal of the dosimeter charger, the fiber may shift to the right of the attempted setting as much as 10% of full scale. The shift in the fiber position may be caused by:

1) the voltage between the SRD and the charging pedestal not remaining constant as the dosimeter is removed from the charging pedestal, and

2) a resistance of the SRD to accepting a quick charge.

The factors which cause fiber shift may be due to a layer of dust and/or corrosion on the outside of the charging pedestal and the inside of the SRD, and due to charger component corrosion or failure. Also, months to years may have passed since the last charging. Actions that may correct the shift to the right of the attempted setting are:

1) While pressing the SRD firmly down against the charging pedestal, rotate the SRD several times.

2) At the same time you are rotating the SRD, rotate the zeroing knob from fully clockwise to fully counterclockwise a few times.

The above techniques will probably break through any dust and corrosion and will allow a little more time for the dosimeter to accept a good charge. The above techniques will also exercise the charge storage component in the dosimeter. If the dosimeter you use still shifts to the right after you have tried the above restoration techniques, try setting the fiber left of the desired setting (ostensibly on zero) an amount equivalent to the amount of shift. Some dosimeter manufacturers anticipated the SRD fiber shift problem and have provided a small division to the left of the zero division as a mark for setting the fiber to compensate for the shift of the fiber when removing the SRD from the charging pedestal.

Read your SRD as often as you can throughout your mission. If the mission exposure rate is high enough, the SRD may peg off-scale before you finish your mission, and you would have no idea what your mission exposure was. For example, if you start your mission with your 0-200 mR SRD set on 100 mR and the exposure rate at the site of the patient is 200 mR/hr, the SRD would peg off-scale in 30 minutes. I do not know of any transportation incident which produced exposure rates of 200 mR/hr at the patient site, but there are locations within nuclear power plants with 200 mR/hr and greater—and personnel work in these areas, therefore an injury can occur.

Realize that if your approach to the patient took 3 minutes and you received 5 mR exposure during your ingress, your egress will likely take as long or longer with the inherent additional exposure. Specifically, if it takes as long to get to the patient as it takes you get him/her out of the exposure field, you would receive as much exposure coming out of the radiation field as you received going into the radiation field. Incorporate ingress and egress times into your plan for extricating the patient from a radiation field.

For those who are extra curious or for the electronics types, a capacitor inside the SRD is used to maintain the charge. Unless the capacitor is fully charged, it will act as a drain of the charge. The capacitor is the component which provides for different ranges of the SRD: different capacitor values for different ranges.

Section 5. Instrument Training

Most radiation detection survey meters and dosimeters operate in the same manner as the Civil Defense instruments. Review of the vendor manuals specific to the instruments you may acquire coupled with Sections 1 through 4 of this Chapter should be adequate to provide a solid foundation for working with the instruments. However, a working knowledge gained by reading texts is inadequate to fully prepare the user for actual use of the instruments. Initial and periodic classroom training is necessary to maximize immediate recall of the knowledge gained. Periodic exercises using the instruments obtained are also necessary to develop short- and long-term memory and to maintain proficiency in the use and operation of the instruments. Your State/local Civil Defense or Emergency Preparedness Agency should be prepared to provide or assist with training in the use and operation of Civil Defense instruments. They should also be prepared to conduct or advise on training in an actual radiation field to minimize simulation. Vendor representatives may be capable of providing training on the use of the instruments they supply.

I strongly recommended, whether you use Civil Defense instruments or others, that you obtain hands-on training for the instruments you select for use in your service. The hands-on use of radiation detection instruments in an actual radiation field provides an experience and observation not possible any other way. You can read all the books there are about driving an earth-mover, but you will not be able to drive it well until you get on it and do it. Likewise, you cannot be expected to be proficient in the operation of radiation detection instruments until you actually use them in a radiation field, first in a training exercise, then in "real life" when need be.

Having conducted many classes in radiation detection instrumentation in an actual radiation field, I can testify that I have received no observable ill effects by the levels of radiation exposure received in the classes (neither has with my super-smart, very healthy young-un born after the exposures). The radioactive material used as the training radiation source set the State/local Civil Defense or Emergency Preparedness Agencies use will probably be a sealed source set of cobalt-60 or cesium-137. Both are of sufficient quantity to provide a readable level of radiation using Geiger-Mueller instruments but are small enough to present no significant hazard when used under the control of a qualified instructor. There are many ways to conduct instrument operation training in an actual radiation field: a few of the training techniques are discussed in the remainder of this Section.

Prior to the training using one of the cobalt-60 or cesium-137 source sets, your instructor should provide dosimetry for monitoring exposures received, if any, by the class attendees. Forms should also be provided by your instructor to record any readable exposure you receive during the training. The reason I say "readable" is that in all of my classes, the largest credible exposure received by any of the attendees was no more than 3 milliRoentgen, which is approximately a fiber width on the CDV-138. Most student exposures were unreadable on the CDV-138. Their SRDs read zero before and after the training exercises

Figure 4.12 shows one technique for conducting instrument operation training in an actual radiation field provided by the cobalt-60 training source set. Figure 4.12 suggests a matrix of numbered paper cups on a grid pattern, a few of which each hide one of six sealed capsules of the cobalt-60 source set. The matrix exercise is intended to prompt the attendees to identify which of the cups hide a capsule. In a classroom setting, the matrix should be on a 6 foot by 6 foot grid. Smaller grid patterns are just as efficient provided the cups which hide capsules of radioactive material are not so close that the students cannot differentiate locations of the cups hiding the radioactive material. If a smaller grid is required, use fewer capsules under fewer cups. Use an even number of capsules if the two-member team approach to this exercise is used so each member of the team has an opportunity to find an equal number of capsules. There is no need to use all six capsules of radioactive materials. Using fewer capsules is just as efficient. Figure 4.12 uses only 4 capsules as indicated by the shaded cups which, of course, in an exercise should not stand out from the rest of the cups which do not hide radioactive capsules. Two capsules would even be enough…maybe even one capsule as long as each team member has an opportunity to participle in the exercise. Just do not tell the attendees which or how many cups hide capsules.

FIGURE 4.12
Matix Survey Exercise

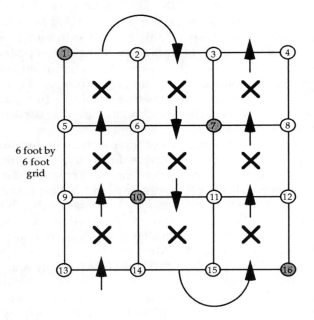

Prior to the exercise, the instructor should place one capsule under each of six cups. While away from the matrix of cups hiding the cobalt-60 capsules, the students should form teams with two members in each team. *Boldly* instruct, for fear of expulsion from the exercise and training, that the attendees *do not* pick up any cup to find out if their suspicion that the cup is one that hides a capsule is correct—as the instructor you are the only individual authorized to handle the capsules, who must do so with long tongs.

Team member one would walk through the grid formed by the pattern of cups with a Geiger-Mueller instrument such as the CDV-700. Team member one should pause at each "X" long enough to get a feeling of the rate of audio clicks from the Geiger-Mueller instrument, three or four seconds should be long enough. While team member two is standing away from the matrix, team member one should announce his/her findings at each "X" to team member two. Team member two should record the findings on a chart of the matrix. If team member two takes notes well, team member one might not have to stop at each "X": team member one may be able to slowly walk the grid pattern. Since the purpose of radiation detection instrumentation for field medical personnel is just to find out whether radiation is present and where the radiation is coming from, not to find out how much radiation is there, it is not necessary to try to take a reading from the meter of the instrument.

When team member one finishes half of the grid, team two member should trade places with team member one so team member two would have an opportunity to use the instruments in an actual radiation field. The technique of trading places would also minimize the student exposures in the exercise. A team approach to the matrix exercise would mimic team activities in an actual radiation emergency.

When located at an "X", the students should sweep the area around him/herself about 3 feet off the ground with the probe of the radiation detection instrument and note where the probe is located when the instrument provides the highest frequency of audio clicks. It is not necessary to observe the meter indication in a survey to simply discover if radiation is present and from where it is coming, the headphone indication is adequate. Observing the meter indication takes more time than just listening to the headphone since the headphone sounding is instantaneous while the meter indication may take a few seconds to stabilize. If the students take time to observe the meter indication, they are spending more time in the radiation field than is necessary. As the students determine which cups they feel hide a capsule, they should then record their findings on a chart of the grid. As teams finish the exercise, they should wait in an area away from the exercise area while other teams complete the exercise.

After each student has completed the exercise, the instructor should collect the capsules, return them to the master container, then evaluate the matrix charts completed by the students. Once the matrix charts have been evaluated, the instructor should conduct a critique of the training session with the students. The critique should solicit feedback from the students regarding the efficiency of the training and the instructor, and should solicit student opinions for improvements. The critique statements must be individually evaluated by the instructor and reviewed by the organization sponsoring the training. Results of the critique evaluations should be shared with the students. Without feedback from the students, training programs cannot mature and can fail quickly.

The matrix type of exercise may involve establishing a matrix grid in an outdoor field and placing the capsules at landmarks such as under a bush or in the fork of a tree limb. When set in an outdoor field, more attention to detail is necessary to estimate where the cobalt-60 capsules are hid since the greater distances between the capsules will yield lesser exposure rates and lesser frequency of clicks. The outdoor matrix survey exercise would well simulate a transportation incident involving the spread of radioactive cargo. It is not often that packages of radioactive materials are so destroyed that the contents of the packages are spilled or released to the environment. However, as you will discover in Chapter 5, each package containing radioactive material will emit some radiation, and these packages must be found and secured after a transportation incident. The amount of radiation allowed to escape the packaging may be quite small and almost undetectable. Thus is revealed the utility of an outdoor matrix exercise: that attention to detail to the lower rate of clicks due to greater distances involved in the scattering of radioactive cargo is important to locate the scattered packages. As emergency medical and rescue personnel are not normally involved in such a search-and-find effort, they may be requested to assist or support such an activity, especially when you now have some expertise in the subject.

Another style of instrument training utilizes hiding the capsules of cobalt-60 in or behind familiar office or household objects. The "hidden source" training exercise would simulate contamination due to an explosion or other dispersing force in a laboratory or storage facility.

A third style of instrument training may include a mock-up of a transportation accident. Placement of the cobalt-60 capsules in various locations on the transport vehicle would simulate vehicular contamination or scattering of radioactive cargo. If live personnel are employed as simulated patients to exercise emergency medical services, it is not advisable to place the cobalt-60 capsules on or near the simulated patient(s): doing so would not be in accordance with Federal guidance which insists on maintaining personnel exposures *As Low As Reasonably Achievable (ALARA)*. Also, if live personnel are employed as simulated patients, stage the live personnel after placement of the radioactive training capsules. Do not place the capsules in the same vehicle compartment as the patient. Put the capsules in boxes in the transport compartment of the vehicle or scatter the boxes around the rear end of the vehicle. If simulated contamination of patients is desired, use Coleman® lantern mantles placed on the simulated patients. Coleman lantern mantles provide a strong enough beta radiation to provide a readable indication on the

CDV-700 or similar instrument with the beta shield open, even while the mantle is inside the plastic envelope it comes in. The beta from the Coleman lantern mantles is strong enough to penetrate clothing and are excellent for simulating patient contamination. Although the beta from Coleman lantern mantles is strong enough to penetrate clothing, it is not dependable that the beta will penetrate boots, car seats, any glass, plexiglass, or other material of similar mass. Neither can beta radiation penetrate metallic materials such as the car or truck body.

The techniques for instrument training described so far will not provide meter deflection on a CDV-715 high range survey meter or equivalent. One way to observe the response of a CDV-715 survey meter or equivalent would be for the qualified instructor to place all sealed capsules in the small container provided with the source set (the source set comes with a smaller container which fits inside the large container). All six capsules placed together *inside the smaller container* will provide a radiation field strong enough to provide a reading on the CDV-715. The source sets I used provided approximately 1 Roentgen per hour when the bottom of the CDV-715 was placed flush against the opening of the smaller container so that the radiation beam from the capsules would pass through the ion chamber directly beneath the meter. Figure 4.13 shows how to configure the capsules, the instrument, and the student.

If the technique shown in Figure 4.13 is used, the students must *not* be allowed to place their heads or hands directly above the CDV-715 while reading the meter. The students must move their head back away from above the container to a location outside of the cone-shaped range above the capsules as shown in Figure 4.13. The students should place their dosimetry at the neck level or above if the instrument training technique shown in Figure 4.13 is used. Providing headgear to personnel for mounting their dosimetry on should ensure maximum efficiency of monitoring student exposures. Students should spend no more time in this exercise than is necessary to measure the radiation level from the cobalt-60 capsules: five to ten seconds should be adequate. The position of the small cobalt-60 container with the six capsules should be as far away from the gathering of personnel as practical. For example, conduct this exercise in the parking lot while the students wait in the classroom for their turn. Students should have a CDV-715 readied in the X1.0 range and should handle the instrument with one hand at an arm's length using two or three fingers to hold the CDV-715 by the vertical portion of the handle. Once a student is finished, he/she should return to the classroom.

FIGURE 4.13
CDV-715 Survey Meter Exercise

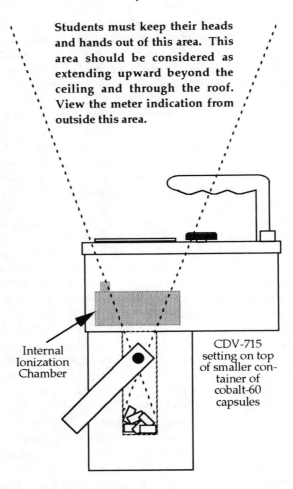

Students must keep their heads and hands out of this area. This area should be considered as extending upward beyond the ceiling and through the roof. View the meter indication from outside this area.

Internal
Ionization
Chamber

CDV-715
setting on top
of smaller con-
tainer of
cobalt-60
capsules

An alternate to using an actual source of radiation to provide hands-on training in the use of radiation detection instruments is available. A special detector actuated by a radio signal is installed into various radiation detection instruments. The transmitter is operated manually by the instructor. This system requires constant operation by an instructor who must increase and decrease the signal strength as the student approaches and moves away from the intended (simulated) source of radiation. While this system is not as good as using an actual source of radiation, it does not involve any radiation, hence, no exposures to ionizing radiation will occur.

However you obtain training in the use and operation of radiation detection instruments, it is questionable to rely entirely on book-learning. It is almost imperative that your training include the use of actual instrument response of some sort. A sense of instrument response is provided best using actual radiation: a sense that cannot be gained any other way. Using only Coleman lantern mantles as a radiation source is better than no radiation source at all. Use of the radio actuated instruments is better than no instrument response at all.

Chapter 5

RECOGNITION OF
RADIOACTIVE MATERIALS

PREVIEW

Ionizing radiation cannot be smelled, heard, tasted, seen, nor felt. Instrumentation is necessary to ascertain beyond any doubt that radiation is or is not present. However, package labeling, vehicle placarding, and room/area signs can alert emergency response personnel to the presence of radioactive materials or sources of radiation. Unless excepted, each package containing radioactive materials is required to be so labeled and each room or area housing a radiation source or radioactive materials must be posted with a sign so stating.

This Chapter is devoted to the media which provide notice of radiation and radioactive materials to anyone in the proximity of the possible hazards. Topics herein include:

- Packaging and package labeling
- Transport of radioactive materials and vehicle placarding
- Room and area posting signs

Section 1. Package Labels

For transportation purposes, radioactive material is defined as any material having a specific radioactivity of greater that 0.002 mCi per gram of material.[22] Unless excepted, Federal regulation requires that any package that contains radioactive material must be labeled stating the package contents.

All packages containing radioactive materials will in fact emit radiation. How much radiation emitted varies with the contents of the package and the package itself. Radiation emitted from the packages is permissible in the transport of radioactive materials but only to a certain level, depending on the contents and the package.

Package labels are coded in accordance with the exposure rate at any external surface of the package and at one meter from the package. This Section presents the required labels and the limits of radiation coming from the packages. Figure 5.1 illustrates the package labels.

FIGURE 5.1
Radioactive Materials Package Labels

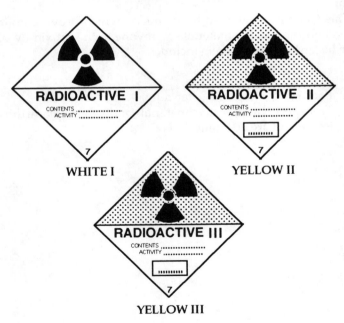

22.   Recall the definition a curie (Ci) in Chapter 2, Section 2

The label names are:

- Radioactive White I (White One)
- Radioactive Yellow II (Yellow II)
- Radioactive Yellow III (Yellow III)

The color included in the term for a label (*White* I, *Yellow* II, *Yellow* III) refers to the background color in the upper half of the label. Specifically, the White I label has a white background in the upper half of the label. The Yellow II and Yellow III each have a yellow background in the upper half of the label. The trefoil, or three-bladed cross, is the international symbol for radiation/radioactive and is black on package labels. The numerals I, II, and III next to the word RADIOACTIVE in the lower half of the label are red. The lower half of each label has a white background. The Figures 5.2, 5.3, and 5.4 explain the labels.

FIGURE 5.2
Radioactive White I Label

Radiation from packages with this label must be less than 0.5 milliRoentgen per hour at any accessible point on an outside surface of the package.

FIGURE 5.3
Radioactive Yellow II Label

Radiation from packages with this label must be less than 50 milliRoentgen per hour at any accessible point on the outside surface of the package and less than 1 milliRoentgen per hour at one meter from the package.

The Yellow III label shown in Figure 5.4 has special applications regarding whether the carrier transporting the radioactive material is hauling the radioactive material as non-exclusive use or exclusive use. A non-exclusive use shipment means the transport vehicle is hauling things other than and in addition to radioactive materials. An exclusive use shipment means the transport vehicle is hauling *only* radioactive materials for a single consignor and for which all initial, intermediate, and final loading and unloading are carried out in accordance with the direction of the consignor or consignee. In addition, exclusive use vehicles must be loaded or unloaded by personnel who have radiological training and appropriate resources for safe handling of the radioactive materials.

FIGURE 5.4
Radioactive Yellow III Label

Non-exclusive Use
If the carrier is hauling a non-exclusive use load, radiation from any package bearing this label must be less than 200 milliRoentgen per hour at any accessible point on the outside surface of the package and less than 10 milliRoentgen per hour at one meter from any accessible surface of the outside of the package.

Exclusive Use
If the carrier is hauling only radioactive material, radiation from any package with this label must be less than 1000 milliRoentgen per hour at any accessible point on the outside surface of the package. Further, radiation from an exclusive use shipment vehicle must be less than 200 milliRoentgen per hour on any external surface of the transport vehicle, e.g., the trailer of a tractor-trailer rig. Also, radiation levels less than 2 milliRoentgen per hour are permitted in any compartment occupied by personnel.

If you have radiation detection instrumentation when responding to an incident involving the transport of radioactive materials, it is not advisable to rely on the readings of the instruments as accurate. As stated in Chapter 4, radiation detection instruments must be calibrated to the energy of radiation being detected to be reliable as *measuring* instruments. Radioactive materials in transport are widely varied. It would be chance if the radiation coming from the radioactive material involved in an incident was the same energy your instruments were calibrated to measure. The purpose of specifying herein the exposure rates permitted for each label is merely to alert response personnel to the relative amounts of radiation that is allowed to escape the packaging.

Although probably not accurate, if the Geiger-Mueller instruments you have indicate radiation is present in response to a trauma case, move out to an area where the instruments indicate the exposure rate is less than 2 milliRoentgen per hour, assuming of course that such movement will not jeopardize the patient's well-being. An area of less than 2 mR/hr can be used as a radiologically "safe" area as long as contamination is not present. Although it is chance that your Geiger-Mueller instruments are calibrated to the energy of the radiation coming from the radioactive material in a transportation incident, if the instruments have passed an operational check with the check source supplied with the instruments, they should be relatively close when they indicate as low as 2 milliRoentgen of gamma radiation.

In responding to a transportation incident involving the shipment of a uranium fuel rod assembly for a nuclear submarine, I was certainly glad to have instruments available. Even though the instruments were not calibrated to uranium radiation energies, the instruments revealed by contamination survey that there was no breech in the fuel assembly containment. While evaluating the results of a structure fire involving a cobalt-60 source set, the instruments I used revealed by contamination survey that no cobalt-60 had escaped containment. The instruments I used in the structure fire survey were calibrated to the cobalt-60 gamma energy but the greatest value of the instruments was in determining by contamination survey that cobalt-60 had not escaped containment. It is some comfort to at least know that your equipment is useful while standing under a creaking, burned out floor with 12-inch charred and sagging timbers groaning at you. I then became keenly aware of a small taste of what firefighters must face. Hats off to them. The two scenarios above provide excellent examples of the best use of radiation detection instruments in emergency medical and fire situations—to *detect* radiation, not to measure radiation.

Section 2. Vehicle Placarding, Room/Area Signs, Transport Packaging

As a requirement of the US Department of Transportation, each vehicle transporting any package of radioactive materials which requires a Radioactive Yellow III label must be placarded with the RADIOACTIVE vehicle placard. The vehicle placard is shown in Figure 5.5.

FIGURE 5.5
Vehicle Placard

FIGURE 5.6
Room or Area Sign

The vehicle placard has a yellow background in the upper half of the placard and a white background in the lower half. The trefoil is black. When placarding of the transport vehicle is required, a placard must be placed on each of the four sides of the transport vehicle. If the vehicle is a tractor-trailer rig, the placard must be placed on each of the four sides of the trailer rig. If two trailers are being towed in tandem, each side of each trailer bearing radioactive cargo must be placarded. Further, if a shipment involving radioactive materials is an exclusive use shipment regardless of which package labels are used, the vehicle must have the RADIOACTIVE placard on all four sides of the transport vehicle(s). Railway cars must also be placarded with the RADIOACTIVE placard if the car is hauling a Yellow III labeling package or is an exclusive use car. Aircraft are not required to display the RADIOACTIVE vehicle placard.

The sign in Figure 5.6 is an example of a posting sign for an area in which radioactive materials is stored or is in use. Other examples of postings include signs which state:

- CAUTION - RADIATION AREA
- DANGER - HIGH RADIATION
- RADIATION IN USE
- X-RAY IN USE
- LOCKED HIGH RADIATION AREA
- GRAVE DANGER - VERY HIGH RADIATION AREA
- AIRBORNE RADIOACTIVITY AREA

The posting signs should have a yellow background with a black or magenta trefoil. These signs are to alert personnel in the immediate area that a hazard may exist in the room or area and that they should stay clear and avoid unauthorized entry.

Should you encounter a radiological incident at a facility which displays a danger sign, for example, a metal-working factory which uses a radiography device or a source of radiation to detect flaws in the metal, an individual usually called the Radiation Safety Officer should be available to provide important data regarding the radiological hazard. Any facility or business which possesses a licensed radiation source must have knowledgeable individuals to supervise and control use of the materials.

Three types of packaging are specifically designed to transport radioactive materials:

- Strong, tight container (STC) for smaller quantities
- Type A
- Type B

Approximately 95% of all shipments are low level waste, and are shipped using strong, tight containers (STC) or Type A packages. If all the radioactive materials contained in a STC or Type A package were released from containment, there would be no significant exposure hazard or environmental impact. When liquid radioactive materials are shipped in STCs or Type A packages, there must be enough absorbent material in the container to absorb twice the volume of liquid contained. Examples of STCs and Type A packages include cardboard boxes and wooden crates.

Approximately 5% of radiological shipments involve high radioactivity, possibly of high level radiation and are for the most part shipped in Type B packages. The Type B package must provide sufficient shielding and containment to lower the external exposure rates to allowable limits. Type B packages must withstand several performance-oriented tests without loss of containment integrity. For example, a shipment of spent fuel rods from a nuclear reactor may contain extremely radioactive material. The actual radioactive material in the shipment may weigh only 25 to 50 pounds. However, the cask used as the container weighs approximately 22,500 pounds and is just as massive as the weight implies. The cask must withstand a drop test onto a 6-inch steel pin from 40 inches without losing containment integrity. The cask must also be dropped from 30 feet onto an infinitely rigid surface without losing containment integrity. Further, the casks must withstand submersion in at least 3 feet of water for at least 8 hours without leaking and must also be subjected to fire of temperatures as high or higher than may be expected in a transportation incident without losing containment integrity. A prototype of the cask must undergo the tests before the design may be approved for use in shipping. It is evident the containers do not rely on an accident not happening, the containers appear to rely on their ability to survive accidents.

Section 3. "What Is This Stuff? How Much Is There?"

'The signs indicate it's radioactive, but what is it? How much of 'it' is there? The captain will want to know."

• *A reasonable question* •

Not only the captain, chief, boss, or the like will want to know, *radiological response team personnel will need to know.* They will need to know exactly what 'it' is so they can determine special response measures, if any. Special response measures might include which type of instruments to bring. For example, if the radiological response team can be told that the material involved is cobalt-60, they will know that they need to use instruments capable of responding to gamma and beta. For incidents involving cobalt-60, alpha detecting instruments would not be necessary. If they are informed of the type of radioactive material involved and if they can be told the amount involved, they can estimate the radiation exposure rates generated by the radioactive materials. You can help them find out precisely which radioactive materials and how much are involved. Refer to Figure 5.7.

FIGURE 5.7
Package Contents and Activity

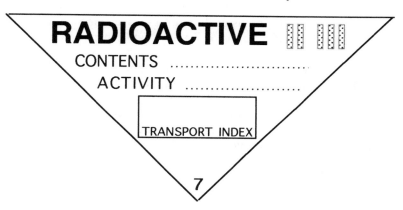

Information regarding the type of radioactive material and how much is contained in a package is required to be placed on the package label itself. In the lower half of each package label, there are blanks for entering the type of radioactive material, the *contents*, and the amount of radioactive material, the *activity*.

The Contents are entered by the name of the isotope shown with the atmoic mass of the element, for example, cobalt-60, strontium-90, and sodium-24. The name of the isotope may not be spelled out, the element symbol may be used, e.g., Co-60 or ^{60}Co for cobalt-60, Sr-90 or ^{90}Sr for strontium-90, and Na-24 or ^{24}Na for sodium-24. Whether you understand the symbolization is not important: that you report the Contents exactly as shown to the radiological response team is important.

Under the blank for Contents is a blank titled Activity for the number of curies contained in the package. As with the Contents information, the Activity information may be abbreviated. For example, 0.030 Ci or 30 mCi means 30 millicuries, 1.9 mCi means 1.9 microcuries. As with the Contents information, it is not important whether you understand the abbreviations. Merely report the information exactly as shown.

Running around checking each label of a bunch of boxes or crates scattered about to determine the type(s) and quantity(ies) of radioactive material(s) involved may not be acceptable. If the shipping papers are accessible, they will indicate the type(s) and quantity(ies) of radioactive materials involved in the shipment. Shipping papers are usually found in the tractor of a tractor-trailer rig or in the cab of other vehicles.

The block at the bottom of the Yellow II and Yellow III labels in Figure 5.7 is for entering the *transport index*. The Transport Index is determined by the total of exposure rates at one meter from each package in the shipment. The transport index cannot exceed 50 per shipment. For example, envision 10 packages in a shipment and each package has an exposure rate of 3 milliRoentgen per hour at one meter from the package. By adding the exposure rates at one meter of all packages, the total is 30 (not 30 milliRoentgen per hour, just 30). If each package had an exposure rate at one meter of 5 milliRoentgen per hour, the shipment would have the maximum allowable Transport Index of 50. Special authorization is required for transport of radioactive materials above a Transport Index of 50. The shaded II and III to the right of the word RADIOACTIVE in Figure 5.7 merely indicate the applicability of the Contents and Activity to the Yellow II and Yellow III. The Transport Index is not used on White I labels (remember the White I labels may emit only 0.5 milliRoentgen per hour at the surface of the package). The White I label has one red I to the right of the word RADIOACTIVE on the label.

At the time of printing, the information in this Chapter was in accordance with Federal regulation and guidance. Federal regulation and guidance can change at any time. Regardless of the current regulations and guidance, radiation is likely to be encountered in a radioactive materials transport incident. Use your instruments to find out whether radiation is present and from where it is coming, not how much radiation is present.

Chapter 6

EXTRICATION AND TREATMENT

PREVIEW

In this Chapter, various aspects of prehospital and emergency department services in view of possible radiological risks will be presented. The emergency department procedures herein for handling and treatment of radiation accident patients have been adopted and modified from guidance developed by numerous professional radiological and medical personnel and are offered for consideration. The only aspects of emergency department patient treatment which will be covered are those which may require special consideration due to the radiological conditions. I do not wish to contradict medical procedures which depend on the judgment and expertise of a physician. The physician-in-charge has final authority on how medical procedures are performed and which medications are administered. Topics herein include:

- Field extrication of radiation accident patients
- Basic treatment of multiple radiation accident patients
- Emergency department handling and treatment of radiation accident cases
- Response to incidents at nuclear power facilities

Section 1. Field Extrication of Radiation Accident Patients

Consideration for the patient beyond basic life support or advanced life support regarding radiological incidents is actually application of common sense and good house-keeping. Special consideration, if any, beyond life support may be required to minimize personnel/patient radiation exposure and radiological contamination.   Special equipment is essential to maximize on-the-scene radiological controls and to provide on-the-spot alerting of response personnel to radiological risks.

Some basic preparation for responding to radiological incidents is necessary to maximize protection of personnel and patients. Preparation includes procuring equipment, developing response plans and procedures, providing training, and drills. Frequent drilling is necessary to maximize radiological response expertise and to maximize immediate and long-term recall of skills and knowledge learned.   As rescue providers respond to incidents involving non-radiological medical emergencies 20 to 30 times a month, response to radiological incidents will be much less frequent. Repetition from drills is the best method of maximizing retention of knowledge and skills so infrequently used.

Equipment

Following is a suggested "shopping list" of equipment for preparing for radiological prehospital response activities:[23]

- Radiation detection instruments, minimum one Geiger-Mueller type and one ionization chamber type survey meter, e.g., a CDV-700 and a CDV-715. In addition, one low range and one high range dosimeter. The CDV-138 and the CDV-742 dosimeters or equivalent should be adequate.

- Protective clothing (PCs) referenced in Chapter 2. The minimum recommended are:

    •• Multiple surgical gloves
    •• Booties/waterproof shoe covers
    •• Eye protection
    •• A surgical mask

- Vehicle floor and seat protective covering

---

23.   The "shopping list" excludes medical support equipment

Procedures

Following are suggested procedures and guidelines for prehospital radiological incident response (not necessarily in the order shown).

- All equipment procured for responding to a radiological emergency must be stored in an area easily and quickly accessible. All personnel must maintain memory of the operation of the equipment and where the equipment is located. Of course, it is best to keep the equipment on the response vehicle, but usually the more often needed inventory takes all the available space in the vehicle. At any rate, the equipment for radiological response must be kept readily available.

- All attendants should don PCs before leaving. If it is not practical for all attendants to don a full set of PCs before leaving, at least one attendant should don at least booties, multiple gloves, eye protection, a surgical mask, and dosimeters en route to the incident.

- Place protective covering on the floor of the ambulance and on the seats prior to leaving the garage to help protect the ambulance from contamination.

- Turn on radiation detection equipment and perform operational checks on the instruments en route to the incident.

- Upon approach to the incident site, avoid wet spots and liquid trails, and accumulations of dust or granular materials. Anything that seems foreign may be radiological contamination. Also, avoid approaching the incident site into the wind. Upon arrival at the incident site, take the instruments with you as you leave the response vehicle.[24] As you approach the patient site, observe the instrument

---

24. Some radiological incident control measures have been published which include the establishment of a control zone around the incident prior to performing emergency services. Establishment of a control zone is not your job if patients are involved. You cannot determine the patient's condition until you perform patient assessment. You cannot assess the patient in a timely manner if you are running around barking directions to support personnel—let the radiological health, law enforcement, or firefighters do that. Your duties are to the patient.

indications.[25] This action is only to alert response personnel to any radiation in the area. Indication of radiation should not cause the responding personnel to hesitate or delay emergency services. I cannot justify that a radiation area can be equated to an immediately life-threatening environment such as a working fire or other similar immediately life-threatening risk unless it has been determined by radiological professionals that the radiation field is strong enough to cause ill acute effects in what is usually minutes the responding personnel will be in the incident area.

- Once it has been determined that radiation and/or radioactive materials are involved, request that the radiological health agency in your state be notified. If at all possible, determine the type and quantity of the material(s) involved (reference: Chapter 5) and relay the information to the agency.

- Upon arrival at the patient site, perform patient assessment and treat injuries as indicated in accordance with your medical training. Incorporate into your medical and extrication activities any special considerations appropriate to the radiological conditions. Record the distance the patient is from the source.

- Once the patient is stabilized, or if movement of the patient will *not* jeopardize his/her condition or chances of complete recovery, remove the patient from the radiation area to continue life support activities or to transport the patient to medical facilities. Document the amount of time the patient was in the radiation area, if known, and when he/she was removed. Handling the patient with tools or materials which have come in contact with the immediate environment is not advisable since the tools or materials will likely become contaminated from the contaminated environment. Using waterproof (plastic) sheets to drape the gurney or other patient transport device prior to placing the patient and backboard on the gurney will help control the spread of contamination. Also, removing an outer pair of gloves as they become contaminated will help control the spread of contamination. Further contamination controls should include placing a plastic sheet on the ground or floor

---

25. Remember to rely more on the audio response of the CDV-700 or equivalent than on the meter face.

of the contaminated area to place your jump kit or other jump gear on to prevent them from becoming contaminated. Realize that whenever a tool such as scissors is used in response activities in a contaminated environment, they will likely become contaminated. Common sense and good house-keeping will maximize contamination control.

- Request the radiological health, law enforcement, or firefighting personnel to obtain names and addresses of bystanders and support personnel involved in the incident.

- Remind the radiological health officials to establish and maintain a control zone and ensure that nothing is handled by unauthorized personnel and that nothing is removed (except the patient, of course) until the radiological health officials have monitored the material for contamination. The radiological health officials should be allowed the authority to retain the vehicle which was transporting the radioactive materials until they can determine it may safely be released. No matter how slight the incident, the radiological health officials should monitor the vehicle prior to its release. The radiological health officials should also be allowed the authority to control access to any structure involved in a radiological incident.

- Request radiological health officials to report to the medical facility to assist with radiological controls and decontamination activities at the facility. The radiological health officials should coordinate decontamination of the hospital and patient transport equipment with a hospital official. The hospital official who should coordinate with the radiological health officials should be titled the Radiation Safety Officer. The duties of the Radiation Safety Officer are presented in Section 3.

- Once prepared to transport the patient, place him/her in the transport vehicle in accordance with your medical training. Keep in mind that if you are contaminated, whatever you touch should be considered contaminated unless determined otherwise. Placing disposable plastic sheets such as Herculite® on the floor of the transport vehicle prior to placing the patient in the vehicle will also aid in contamination control since it may be assumed the wheels of the gurney as well as your booties are contaminated after leaving the contaminated area. If time and the patient's condition permit, replace your booties with a clean pair before stepping into the ambulance. Even when dry, three sheets of plastic (2 booties and the floor covering) can be slippery, therefore it is not recommended to don two pair of booties when donning PCs. Remember to remove an outer pair of gloves or don clean gloves after you remove contaminated booties.

- Notify the hospital in advance of arrival with an estimated time of arrival and whether the patient is contaminated.

Classroom Training

After coordinating draft procedures and techniques with agencies and personnel impacted by the procedures, and after the procedures have been finalized and approved, training must be provided to all personnel involved, including outside support personnel and organizations. Training must include classroom and testing (cognitive) on every possible element of radiological medical response in the field and in the hospital. Unless all personnel involved have been trained on how things are to be done, coordination efforts might fail.

Drills

Drills are supervised periods of instruction with observations by a qualified instructor who stands ready to provide on-the-spot correction of erroneous or questionable performance: who stands ready to stop the drill and have the participant repeat performance until satisfactory performance is demonstrated. The drill instructor must also be capable for demonstrating the desired performance. Objectives of the drills are must be performance-based. Without drills, the level of skills/knowledge possessed by personnel cannot be adequately measured. Once procedures have been approved and once training has been completed, drilling is without a doubt the most important management and proficiency maintenance measure of response activities. Drills should be conducted in both a classroom refresher environment and in the field minimizing simulations as much as possible. The drill instructor should observe performance of personnel and equipment thoroughly. Feedback from the students must be solicited. Student feedback must be evaluated with a professional attitude, not allowing personal tastes or feelings to interfere with credible and rational reports.

Students should be requested to offer recommendations for change or improvement in equipment and procedures, and offer comments on the performance of the instructor and the training program. Students should be advised to avoid useless comments such as "It ain't good enough" or "This stinks" or "I don't wanna be here." Rather, the students should provide proposed solutions to the problems the students identify.

Drills should be conducted frequently enough to maintain a level of proficiency which maximizes immediate and long-term recall as much as possible. Semiannually is not frequent enough since the expertise provided by this training activity will probably be used infrequently. A partial drill and refresher training should be conducted at least once per calendar year. In addition to the partial drill and refresher training, a full-scale exercise should be conducted each year with participation by each agency and individual having any responsibilities to the effort.

Section 2. Treatment Basics

This Section presents the basics for evaluating, for establishing triage, and treatment of radiation accident patients. This Section is a distillation of material prepared by Dr. Niel Wald in *The Acute Radiation Syndromes and Their Medical Management*, published in *The Biological Basis of Radiation Protection Practice*, Williams and Wilkins, 1992, and of material in *Ionizing Radiation and Life*, 1971, by Dr. Victor Arena. Although the efficacy of treatment of radiation accident syndromes is not well defined, knowing the time of the onset of radiation injury symptoms can enable the physician to determine which clinical course the radiation injury should take and the appropriate patient support needed.

Table 6.1 is a scheme for anticipating a course of the radiation injury based on the time of the onset of the symptoms—ask the ambulance personnel if they observed any symptoms of radiation injury, explaining to them what you need to know, and what time the symptom occurred. Daily blood counts are also necessary to support the evaluation process. Table 6.2 provides an estimated minimum dose required to cause the indicated pretreatment finding based on the patient history and the time of onset of the symptom(s).

The Gastrointestinal (GI) system post-exposure is a good indicator of the dose an individual has received. Lesser levels of dose may cause anorexia and nausea. Vomiting, if any, may be delayed for more than 5 hours. Should any vomiting begin between 1 to 5 hours after exposure, it is likely the patient received a significant dose and a serious course should be anticipated—medical and nutritional therapy would be indicated. Should vomiting begin within an hour or so, it is likely the patient has received a near-lethal dose. If vomiting occurs within minutes and is not due to other stimuli or conditions, the patient has more than likely received a lethal dose.

TABLE 6.1
Evaluation Procedures[a]

Findings	Potential Outcome
Nausea, vomiting, diarrhea within <u>minutes</u>. Faliure of muscular coordination, disorientation, shock, coma in <u>minutes to hours</u>	Neurovascular Syndrome
Nausea and/or vomiting and some blood count derangement in <u>2 days</u>	Minor Hematologic Syndrome
Marked leukocyte and lymphocyte count derangement in <u>3 days</u>	Major Hematologic Syndrome
Diarrhea within <u>4 days</u> and marked platelet derangement within <u>6 to 9 days</u>	Gastrointestinal Syndrome

[a] Reproduced with permission from *The Acute Radiation Syndromes and Their Medical Management* in *The Biological Basis of Radiation Protection Practice*, Williams and Wilkins, 1992

TABLE 6.2
Radiation Injury Evaluation Procedures and Their Results in Relation to Time and Magnitude of Radiation Exposure[a]

Procedure	Finding	Time of Onset	Approx. Min. Dose Required
History	Nausea, vomiting	Within 48 hours	150 rad
Physical exam	Erythema	Within hours-days	300 rad
	Epilation	Within 2-3 weeks	300 rad
Blood count and differential	Lymphocytes <1000/mm^3	Withing 24-48 hours	100 rad

[a] Reproduced with permission from *The Acute Radiation Syndromes and Their Medical Management* in *The Biological Basis of Radiation Protection Practice*, Williams and Wilkins, 1992

As provided in Table 6.2, another indicator of the dose received by the patient is his/her lymphocyte count after exposure. The lymphocyte count change is a more sensitive indicator of the dose received than the GI system's response to exposure. Differential counts in the lymphocytes, if any, should present themselves within 24 hours. Table 6.3 "fine-tunes" some of Dr. Wald's material in Table 6.2. Doctor Victor Arena indicated in *Ionizing Radiation and Life*, that apparently only clinical observation of patients is indicated if the lymphocyte count remains above 1200 per cubic millimeter in the first 24 to 48 hours. Should the count fall to near 500 within 24 hours, a significant dose is likely and a serious course requiring medical and nutritional therapy should be expected. If the lymphocyte count is not measurable 6 hours after the exposure, the patient has almost certainly received a lethal dose. Table 6.3 provides these human dose indicators in tabular format. Table 6.3 is not to indicate that medical and nutritional therapy is not warranted in the cases of questionable or unlikely recovery. Medical and nutritional therapy may be indicated in all situations of radiation exposure, depending on the judgment of a physician.

TABLE 6.3
Human Dose Indicators[a]

Gastrointestinal System		Blood System	
Vomiting	Recovery[b]	Lymphocyte Count	Recovery[b]
> 5 hours	Likely	≥ 24 hours, >1200/mm^3	Likely
1 to 5 hours	Medical and Nutritional aid	<24 hours, ≤500/mm^3	Medical and Nutritional aid
≈ 1 hour	Questionable		
In minutes	Unlikely	In 6 hours, not measurable	Unlikely

[a] Reproduced with permission from Ionizing Radiation and Life, Dr. Victor Arena.
[b] Following appropriate treatment

The basics of treatment of a radiation accident patient with a likely serious clinical course consists mainly of

- maintaining a clean environment for the patient
- antibiotic therapy
- blood support
- vigorous infection fighting

The clean environment for the patient may include internal cleanliness as well as external cleanliness. Air filtration should be considered if the patient must be placed in a bacteria-free environment. Filtration should be capable of removing E. coli bacteria. The suggested activities of the hospital engineer in Section 3 provides for filtration of the return air from the room occupied by the radiation accident patient, specifically the Decontamination/ Treatment Room, to remove airborne radiological contaminants from the air returned to the hospital's forced-air system. If the physician-in-charge determines a bacteria-free environment must be maintained for the patient, it should also be the responsibility of the hospital engineer to install proper filtration, preferably establishing a positive air pressure environment for the patient. A positive air pressure environment for the patient should better ensure outside microbiological organisms are kept out of the patient's environment. If necessary, the patient can be placed in a "life island" with air flow from his/her head to toes.

Internal cleanliness may be as important to the patient's recovery as external cleanliness. Vigorous antibacterial, antifungal, and antiviral therapy should improve the patient's chances of full recovery, or at least support the patient's life while his biological system rebuilds itself. The patient's food and water must also be biologically "clean." Use canned or packaged foods and prepare the foods in the patient's room. To further ensure internal cleanliness and freedom from new infections, skin perforations should be kept at a minimum with extra care to maintain a sterile field when skin perforations must be made.

The patient with a depressed hematopoietic system will likely need blood component support since his/her blood counts will likely be reduced due to exposure to ionizing radiation as discussed in Chapter 3. Intravenous nutrients and blood fractions including red cells, platelets, and possibly white cells must be made available to support the patient's hematopoietic system while awaiting spontaneous regeneration of blood components.

Bone marrow transplantations have been tried with, as Dr. Wald described, "not impressive" results. However, some success has been realized illuminating the need for consideration of bone marrow transplantation for a patient with life-threatening doses on a benefit versus attendant risk evaluation by a skilled physician.

Hematopoietic growth factors have been used in seriously exposed patients, but use of the growth factors is still in relative infancy.

Once the physician-in-charge is satisfied that decontamination can begin, either concurrently with emergency treatment or after treatment is complete, the RSO and the Decon Room staff should begin decontamination of the patient as suggested in Section 3. After each attempt to decontaminate the patient, the RSO should monitor the cleaned area for persistent contamination. Initially, the level of decontamination will likely decrease rapidly with each decontamination event. As decontamination attempts continue, the yield of decontamination efforts will decrease, eventually to almost no yield or no yield at all. Therefore, the rate of audio clicks of a

Geiger-Mueller instrument due to the radiation coming from the contaminated area will initially decrease rapidly, with the decrease in clicks slowing as decontamination continues. *Any activity that can transport bacterial, viral, or fungal contamination can transport radiological contamination.*

Section 3. Emergency Department Handling of Radiation Accident Patients

The Joint Commission on Accreditation of Healthcare Organizations (JCAHO) has mandated that emergency departments of hospitals have procedures in place to handle radiation accident patients. The following provides suggested guidelines consistent with the standards of JCAHO[26] for hospital administrators and emergency department personnel for meeting the needs of a radiological trauma incident. The suggested guidelines have been adopted from procedures developed by recognized professionals in the field of radiological emergency medical response and from personal observation and experience. The recognized experts in the field from which I have adopted the following guidelines include Doctors Ralph B. Leonard, Robert C. Ricks, Niel Wald, and Roger E. Linnemann. Each has established himself as a valued mentor of radiological emergency medical response and has developed an expertise of providing guidance in the field.

Although every hospital emergency department may one day be required to handle a contaminated injured trauma patient, few emergency departments have had first-hand experience. Each emergency department should obtain professional assistance in adapting these guidelines to a system specific to their facility. Such a system would require several key elements and personnel. Examples of the key elements and personnel are presented herein.

Radiation Safety Officer (RSO)

An individual established as the Radiation Safety Officer (RSO) supported by a small staff should be designated to supervise and control non-medical activities in response to a radiological trauma incident. The RSO should have the authority and expertise to execute the responsibilities of conducting and/or coordinating radiological monitoring and decontamination of the patient, the ambulance and its equipment, the hospital and its equipment, support personnel, and any other response personnel or equipment which may become

---

26.   Emergency Services Standard ER.5.1.2.20, Accreditation Manual for Hospitals.

intimately involved in response to the radiological incident. The RSO should also be the medical facility point-of-contact for outside professional support services and should have the authority to coordinate hospital resources and activities with outside support services. The RSO should be further responsible for collection, containment, and disposition of radiologically contaminated wastes, samples, and articles of value, e.g., patient personal effects. The RSO must have the expertise and authority to provide such support. The RSO should also have the responsibility for issuing or directing issuance of dosimeters to staff and support personnel.

The RSO would coordinate with the ambulance personnel, the physician in charge, the hospital administrator, other hospital support personnel, and radiological emergency response team personnel from outside sources such as the State's radiological health agency. The RSO should be responsible for developing and maintaining a functional area for admitting patients who may be contaminated, specifically, the *Radiation Emergency Area* (REA). The RSO should also be responsible for coordinating the development of the REA operations plan and procedures, and for coordinating radiation accident patient drills and exercises involving the hospital/REA. An example layout of a Radiation Emergency Area is provided in Figure 6.1 at the end of this Section. Figure 6.1 should be referenced as you read the remainder of this Section.

Decontamination Team

A Decontamination Team (Decon Team) must be designated to perform patient decontamination support during medical treatment of the patient. The individual in charge of the Decon Team is the physician in charge of the patient services. The RSO would monitor patients as they are admitted and would direct that the contaminated patient be taken to a Decontamination and Treatment Room (Decon Room) where medical and decontamination services are provided for the contaminated patient.

In addition to the RSO and the physician in charge, members of the Decon Team should include two nurses. One assisting nurse should be dedicated to collecting specimens and samples which may be contaminated and assisting the physician with medical treatment of the patient. The assisting nurse should stay in the Decon Room with the physician-in-charge until patient decontamination activities are complete and until monitored for contamination and decontaminated as necessary.

A second nurse should be designated as the circulating nurse and should handle materials to be transferred into and coming out of the Decon Room. The circulating nurse will not enter the actual Decon Room and will stay in an area designated as the Buffer Zone. She/he will also be responsible for assisting with labeling samples and specimens. The circulating nurse (Buffer Zone nurse) should also be valuable for recording information learned by the RSO, the physician-in-charge, and the assisting nurse.

Decontamination/Treatment Room

A Decontamination/Treatment Room (Decon Room) should be established within the REA to treat patients who may be radiologically contaminated. The Decon Room is an area that is prepared for the ingress of contaminated patients. At least, the Decon Room should be a room that has materials nearby to rapidly prepare the area for the ingress of contaminated patients. A single room should be used for both emergency treatment and decontamination. Once the patient's medical needs are met and once patient decontamination is complete, the patient may be discharged from the Decon Room and admitted to the medical facility for definitive care, observation, and further radiological evaluation such as collection of urine and fecal samples for radiological analysis.

The Decon Room should be isolated from the emergency department or at least isolated from ingress and egress of non-contaminated patients. If a room that can be isolated is not available, the Decon Room should be one with immediate or near-immediate access to the outside of the hospital. In this way, the contaminated patient may be transported to the Decon Room without contaminating passageways that non-contaminated patients would use. The pathway from the ambulance to the Decon Room must be covered with waterproof sheeting and then roped off and policed to deny access by unauthorized individuals. Once the Decon Room is isolated and the pathway covered with protective sheeting, an emergency department/REA gurney should be draped with waterproof protective covering to accept the patient for transport from the ambulance bay to the Decon Room. If the patient's condition permitted the ambulance personnel to disrobe the patient,[27] his/her contaminated clothing will remain in the ambulance, keeping most of the contamination in the ambulance. However, some contamination may remain on the patient's body after disrobing the patient, and the ambulance gurney will likely be contaminated. When transporting the patient from the ambulance to the Decon Room, use a second gurney rather than the ambulance gurney. Using the emergency department/REA gurney will prevent contamination on the

27. Details for disrobing a contaminated patient are described in Chapter 7.

ambulance gurney from entering the hospital. However, if the ambulance personnel were able to only partially disrobe the contaminated patient in accordance with Chapter 7 (the ambulance personnel could not roll the patient to his/her side or the patient was on a backboard), there will likely be pieces of the patient's contaminated clothing under the patient.

Materials that should be prepared for the Decon Room include:

- Precut plastic floor coverings. The floor coverings should be adequate to cover any area traversed by any personnel and mobile equipment involved in the handling and treatment of the radiologically contaminated patient. Yellow floor covering is recommended since yellow is the nuclear industry standard to indicate contaminated. When treatment and decontamination activities are complete, a radiologically "clean" floor covering of a different color should be laid over the yellow floor covering in the path of egress of the patient from the decon/treatment table to the Buffer Zone—white is recommended. The white floor covering should not be laid until after the patient has been treated, decontaminated, and is ready to leave the Decon Room. All personnel involved in treatment and decontamination activities must not walk on the white egress path floor covering.

  The Buffer Zone area floor should be covered with a different color to provide easy identification of the demarcation between the possibly contaminated yellow decon/treatment area and the Buffer Zone clean area. Green has been used by the nuclear industry for radiologically clean areas.

- Yellow and magenta spiraled into a rope or yellow ribbon ("rad rope") with a magenta longitudinal stripe in the middle of the ribbon (visible from both sides) to provide elevated lines of demarcation between contaminated or possibly contaminated areas and radiologically clean areas. The rope or ribbon should be supported by stanchions, not taped to walls or tied to door knobs. Yellow and magenta spiraled into a rope or yellow ribbon with a magenta longitudinal median stripe is the nuclear industry colors for radiological warning barricades.

- RADIATION/RADIOACTIVE signs to hang on the rope or ribbon and to attach to the door(s) in the REA and ambulance bay. Although not essential, if a doorway provides access to the Buffer Zone, an over-and-under door (Dutch door) would aid in control of unauthorized traffic into the Buffer Zone

- Wide tape for securing the floor coverings. The tape should be wide enough to permit secure anchoring of the floor covering to the floor. Two-inch duct tape is adequate. Paper tape tears too easily and is not as waterproof as duct tape.

- A patient decontamination tray or makeshift mechanism to direct decon washwater to special containers. The tray should be supported by a treatment table. An adjustable gurney with locking wheels is adequate for the treatment table. Together, the decontamination tray and table are the decon/treatment table. The height of the decon/treatment table assembly should be adjustable to compensate for different heights of decon/treatment personnel.

- Several sealable waterproof jugs or barrels to receive drainage from the decon/treatment table. The drainage should be directed to the waterproof barrels with a waterproof drainage tube, not just allowed to drip from the drain hole. When finished with decontamination activities, the drainage tube should be fully inserted into the last barrel used. Use yellow plastic barrels and drain tubes.

- Heavy sealable plastic bags of assorted sizes to collect contaminated articles such as specimens, swabs, gauze, dressings, clothing, patient personal effects, and PCs. Yellow bags are commonly used for this purpose.

- Large waterproof refuse barrels to fit the collection bags.

- Sealable glass or plastic tubes of assorted sizes to receive and contain samples, specimens, and swabs.

- Cotton swabs and gauze.

- Lead storage containers to hold contaminated sample/specimen tubes.

- Anatomical outline charts to record patient contamination areas and the levels of contamination.

- Decontamination agents, e.g., Lava soap®, a mixture of 50% Tide® and 50% cornmeal (kept refrigerated and sealed), 3% hydrogen peroxide (H_2O_2), 1% citric acid solution, and Clorox®. Betadine surgical scrub kits may be used.

- Soft scrub brushes and scrub suits for the decon team. The suits must be large enough to fit over street clothes and should be lightweight and waterproof.

- Waterproof surgical gowns or aprons.

- Surgical hoods, masks, and gloves of assorted sizes.

- Eye protection.

- Sterile saline for wound irrigation.

- A water supply hose from a sink faucet with warm water and with an aerated nozzle to supply decontamination washwater. A garden hose and nozzle have been used due to their compatibility with most sink faucets, but overpressure discharge is easy when using a garden hose nozzle unless special adaptation is used to prevent overpressure discharge .

- Waterproof booties/shoe covers.

- Dosimeters, both film badges and self-reading dosimeters. TLDs should be considered.

- Radiation detection instruments with extra batteries. At least two Geiger-Mueller instruments and one high range ion chamber instrument should be provided. An alpha detection instrument should be considered.

- RADIATION/RADIOACTIVE adhesive labels for labeling contaminated samples, specimens, and swabs. *Do not* use labels that must be wetted to adhere. Someone may lick the labels as a habit. If the labels or the user's hands are contaminated, the user may receive internal contamination.

- Assorted sizes of placards and tags with the trefoil "radiation" symbol (three-bladed cross) for labeling rooms, bags, and barrels of contaminated materials.

The above materials should be maintained in a lockable storage cart, cabinet, or storage room and should be inventoried and operationally checked frequently to ensure the availability and operability of the materials and equipment. If a mobile storage cart is used, it should be maintained within seconds of the Decon Room. The RSO should be responsible for periodic inventories and operational checks of the Decon Room materials and equipment.

After Receiving Notification

"Emergency department. This is unit 2. I am en route to your facility with a male patient approximately 42 years of age with multiple trauma about the chest, upper arms, head, and neck resulting from a MVA. Patient was the driver without restraint and has a Glasgow coma score of 13. Vital signs are BP 165 over 90, respirations 24 per minute, pulse 120 and regular. Pupils equal and reactive to light. Patient complains of a headache. *Patient is possibly contaminated with radioactive materials*."

Outside of notification of a school bus accident, this may be the most alarming incoming message an emergency department may ever hear. The hospital may not be equipped to handle and treat a radioactively contaminated patient, but this may be a scenario from a transportation accident on just about any highway in the country. This may also be a scenario from a nuclear laboratory or nuclear power facility. In effect, a radiologically contaminated patient may be a reality almost anywhere in the country. This Section provides guidance on preparing for, receiving, handling, treating, and decontaminating a radioactively contaminated patient, and for discharging the patient from the decontamination/treatment area of the Radiation Emergency Area.

Once the call has been received that a patient with confirmed or suspected radiological contamination is en route to the emergency department, a shift in posture is necessary. Several preparatory actions must be taken. To prepare for admitting the patient, the following actions are suggested (not necessarily in the order shown).

Before Patient Arrival

- The individual who receives notice of the event should notify the Radiation Safety Officer (RSO). The RSO should:

• • notify or direct notification of the emergency department staff, the hospital security supervisor, the hospital engineer, the hospital administrator/emergency department supervisor, and the State/local radiological health agency or other preestablished radiological support service that a patient with suspected or confirmed radiological contamination will be arriving at approximately _____.
                                                              (TIME/DATE)

• • direct the hospital engineer to configure the ventilation system to isolate the Decon Room from the rest of the hospital. At a minimum, a filter should be affixed over the return air duct in the Decon Room to minimize introduction of possible airborne radiative materials into the hospital's forced air system. If filtration of the breathable air for the patient is needed, install supply air filtration capable of removing E. coli bacteria. Also direct hospital engineering, maintenance, or custodial personnel to lay the protective floor covering in the Decon Room and in the path of the patient from the ambulance. After the protective floor covering is placed, attach the decon water hose to the sink and adjust the water to near body temperature.

• • direct the hospital security supervisor to implement access control throughout the REA.

• • ensure the demarcation rope/ribbon ("rad rope") is stretched to isolate the areas the possibly contaminated patient may traverse and to separate the Decon Room from the Buffer Zone. Rad rope should also be placed to isolate the ambulance arrival area from unwary personnel. Enough rad rope should be provided to enclose the ambulance and the pathway from the ambulance to the Decon Room.

• • ensure RADIATION/RADIOACTIVE signs are hung at the REA and Decon Room entrance(s), and on the rad rope.

• • place the REA supplies cart near the Decon Room, preferably in the Buffer Zone.

• • ensure the patient decon tray or make-shift device is placed on a table in the Decon Room, preferably on an adjustable gurney with the locking wheels locked.

•• place protective covering such as tape over permanent equipment, e.g., light switches and door knobs, where hands will touch them.

•• place a radioactive refuse barrel in the immediate area where decontamination services will be provided to the patient. Be careful when removing the lid to the refuse barrel when it contains contaminated items. Removing the lid hastily can cause turbulence inside the barrel, thereby scattering loose contamination.

• If the configuration of your REA provides patient services on a routine basis, the emergency department supervisor should coordinate the movement of the emergency department patients to other areas of the hospital. All female patients of child-bearing age should be evacuated from the REA due to the ultra-sensitivity of fetal tissues to ionizing radiation. The emergency department supervisor should coordinate with the security supervisor to ensure that the areas between the ambulance and the Decon Room are evacuated of non-essential and unauthorized personnel. All jewelry should be removed from attending personnel as well as from the patient.

• The decontamination team should suit up as soon as possible with PCs and dosimeters while preparing to receive the patient. Dosimeters should be worn on the upper chest with the film badge (if available) inside the PCs and the self-reading dosimeter on the outside of the PCs. Finger ring film badges are available which provide measurement of extremity exposures.

Upon Patient Arrival

• After donning PCs, the physician in charge and the RSO should meet the ambulance in the bay. The physician in charge should examine the patient while in the ambulance to determine if the injuries are critical. The RSO should begin monitoring the patient immediately if doing so does not delay vital medical services. If the patient is contaminated, if the patient's injuries are not critical, and if his/her clothes have not yet been removed, they should be removed in the

ambulance.[28] Once the patient with non-critical injuries is
disrobed, he/she should be taken to the Decon Room. If the
patient is contaminated and his/her injuries are critical, the
patient should be immediately taken to the Decon Room for
treatment. If the patient is not contaminated, implement
standard services for the patient. The medical condition of
the patient should be the only driving force whether to
disrobe the patient in the ambulance.

- The RSO should observe transfer of the patient to the
  REA/Decon Room to ensure the ambulance crew follows the
  correct path to the Decon Room. If, for whatever reason, the
  crew strays from the marked path, the RSO must note the
  spot and prevent anyone from touching it until monitored
  for contamination.

- Once the patient is under the care of the physician-in-charge,
  the ambulance personnel should stay in the ambulance or in
  the area set up for receiving the ambulance. Contaminated
  ambulance personnel occupying space in the Decon Room
  may add to the contamination that may be brought in by the
  patient, the backboard, and the gurney. The ambulance
  personnel and the ambulance itself must be taken
  out-of-service until monitored for radioactive contamination
  and decontaminated as necessary. Once the RSO or
  radiological health officials have determined the ambulance
  and ambulance personnel are no longer contaminated, the
  personnel and the ambulance may be returned to service.
  Returning the ambulance and its crew to service before
  monitoring for contamination would not be wise.

- The RSO should perform a detailed monitoring of the patient
  (see Chapter 7). A Heparinized 10cc or similar vacutainer of
  the patients's blood should be taken for isotopic analysis and
  dose determination by chromosome aberration analysis by
  special laboratories. This should be done prior to the
  inducement of any medications or other intravenous
  solutions: such substances may reduce the accuracy of the
  chromosome aberration process. The sample should be kept
  cool at all times but not frozen.

---

28. Chapter 7 provides more detail on disrobing the contaminated patient.

Patient Decontamination

- *After first attending to the patient's serious or life-threatening injuries,* swab samples of the patient's ears, mouth, and nostrils should be obtained. The samples should then be placed in sealed glass or plastic tubes. Handling of the glass or plastic tubes and their stoppers (as well as any other sample container) should be done with clean (uncontaminated) gloves to prevent contaminating the containers. Before passing contained samples and swabs to the Buffer Zone nurse, the RSO should monitor the samples and swabs for contamination. The RSO should monitor the samples/swabs in an area a few feet away from the patient so the audio clicks due to radiation coming from the contamination on the samples/swabs will more easily be discernible from the audio clicks due to radiation coming from the contamination on the patient. The RSO or assisting nurse should ensure proper labeling of samples and swabs and ensure detailed recording of the findings of the RSO and the physician in charge. Contaminated samples should stay in the Decon Room. At the Buffer Zone line of demarcation, the assisting nurse or RSO should place uncontaminated samples/swabs into sealable plastic bags held open by the Buffer Zone nurse, who would then close the bags and lay them aside in the Buffer Zone for further processing as needed. Even though the RSO has determined the samples/swabs are not contaminated, the samples/swabs should be monitored once more before leaving the REA. The RSO should place contaminated samples in lead containers in the Decon Room. If contamination has been introduced into the Decon Room, the radiation warning signs placed on the door(s) to the Decon Room must remain on the doors until the contamination is removed.

- If internal contamination is evident, consider procedures for decorporation of internal contamination. This may be done by using dilution, blocking, mobilzation, and chelating agents such as those shown in Table 6.4. In addition, antacids should precipitate many metals into insoluble hydroxides. Intestinal absorption of radioactive strontium may be reduced by aluminum phosphate gel. Barium sulfate may precipitate radium. Subsequent absorption of radioactive iodine into the thyroid after initial inhalation may be reduced by the administration of a saturated solution of potassium iodide. Thyroid blockage by potassium iodide is only 50% effective if administered 3-4 hours after uptake and is relatively ineffective if administered after 12 hours. Efforts to accelerate excretion of radioactive materials from the body should begin as soon as possible after uptake. The National Council on Radiation Protection and Measurements (NCRP) provided a listiing of agents for decorporating a few radioactive internal contaminants and is provided in Table 6.4

• Contaminated eyes require gentle rinsing with the irrigating fluid flowing from the nasal aspect to the temporal aspect of each eye. Monitor the eyes and rinse/washwater for contamination after each rinsing. Repeat as necessary.

• Ear canals which have become contaminated may be decontaminated by rinsing with water. As with other decon activities, the affected area and rinse/washwater should be monitored after each rinsing.

• Nostrils and the mouth which have become contaminated may be cleaned by turning the head (as the patient's condition allows) to one side or downward and rinsing with water, preventing the water from being swallowed as much as possible. If enough sufficiently hazarous radioactive material has been inhaled, bronchopulmonary lavage may be considered if the benefits outweight the risks inherent with lavage fo the lungs and if a sufficiently trained pulmonary specialist is available. Evacuation of the stomach contents by nasogastric tube may reveal ingested contamination. If stomach contamination is revealed, lavage the stomach with water and monitor until the lavage fluid is clear of contamination. Purgative measures should also be considered to acceleratve expulsion of the contaminant from the patient's gastrointestinal system.

• Skin is the most likely area of contamination. Wash with soap and water and monitor the areas washed. Repeat as necessary. Abrasive soap, hydrogen peroxide, Lava® soap, a 50% Tide®/50% cornmeal mixture, or Clorox® strength in small areas or diluted to 20% for large areas, or a 1% citric acid solution may be helpful. A betadine surgical scrub kit may also be used as a decontamination wash system. The rusty color of the betadine will aid in tracking the radiological contaminants in the decontamination wash run-off. Wherever the rusty color goes, contaminants are likely to be found until all contamination is removed and the betadine run-off is clear of contaminants. Stopping of skin decontamination should include observation of reddeing of the skin. Once skin reddening occurs, infusion of the contaminatnt into and through the skin may occur. Use the mildest wash system first.

- Contaminated hair may be decontaminated with shampooing. Monitor the rinsewater and repeat as necessary. Shaving is not indicated. Incisions in contaminated scalp may complicate or induce internal contamination. If contaminated hair persists, the hair should be clipped and retained. Head and scalp injuries which require shaving in preparation for surgery may be exceptions requiring a case-by-case evaluation by radiological experts (if immediately available). In all cases, the patient's life overrides concern about complicating the patient's internal contamination which may be aggravated by surgical procedure. The patient's life is more important than concern for internal contamination. The amount of radioactive material that could be introduced into the body by surgical procedure is relatively insignificant compared to human life.

- Contaminated wounds and surrounding skin areas should be extensively irrigated to remove the contaminants using some of the decorporating agents suggested in Table 6.4. Doctor Wald suggested that in cases of unremovable, long-lived, very hazardous radioactive wound contaminants, excision may be considered with emphasis on the benefit-versus-risk evaluation.

- Should X-rays be necessary, a portable unit may be wheeled to the edge of the demarcation between the Decon Room and the Buffer Zone and the patient placed under the X-ray arm if the decon/treatment table is on wheels. The photographic plate should be placed in a plastic bag by the Buffer Zone nurse prior to use. Once the X-ray has been taken, the assisting nurse should hold the photographic plate still inside the plastic bag so the Buffer Zone nurse can reach into the bag to retrieve the plate without touching the outside of the bag. If a plastic bag is not available to hold the film, a pillowcase will be adequate to protect the photographic plate from radiological contamination: a pillowcase is invisible to the X-rays. The plastic bag or the pillowcase, once used, stays in the Decon Room until disposed of by the RSO or the radiological health officials after monitoring for contamination. After the X-ray is taken, the X-ray unit should stay in the Buffer Zone until monitored and decontaminated as necessary.

TABLE 6.4
Decorpating Agents for Radioactive Contaminants

Method	Isotope	Agent
Dilution	^{3}H	Water
	^{32}P	Phosphorus (Neutrophos)
Blocking	^{137}Cs	Ferric ferrocyanide (Prussian blue)
	^{131}I, ^{99m}TC	KI (Lugol's solution)
	^{89}Sr, ^{85}Sr	Al-phosphate (Phosphojel)
		Al-hydroxide (Amphojel)
		Na-Alginate (Gaviscon)
Mobilization	^{86}Rb	Chlorthalidone (Hygroton)
Chelation	^{252}Cr, ^{242}Cm, ^{241}Am	DPTA
	^{239}Pu, ^{144}Ce, rare earths	
	^{143}Pm, ^{140}La, ^{90}Y, ^{65}Zn	
	^{46}Sc	
	^{210}Pb	EDTA, peniciliamine
	^{203}Hg, ^{60}Co	Peniciliamine

Patient Removal from the Decon/Treatment Room

• Once the patient's medical treatment is complete and after decontamination activities are complete, all patient areas previously identified as contaminated should be swabbed and monitored again to determine the effectiveness of decontamination. Samples, swabs, and specimens collected after decontamination should be saved as previous samples were saved but with post-decontamination labels.

• Once the patient is medically ready for discharge from the Decon Room and once the patient is confirmed as radiologically clean, the RSO should direct the clean (white) floor covering to be laid from the Buffer Zone to the decon/treatment table if the decon/treatment table is not on wheels. Personnel who have not been in the Decon Room should lay the floor covering. The personnel laying the floor covering should walk on the topside surface of the covering as it is unfolded or unrolled onto the Decon Room floor over the yellow floor covering, being careful not to touch the yellow floor covering with their hands or with the topside of the white floor covering. Do not toss the clean floor covering as a throw rug because doing so may scatter loose contamination. All personnel in the Decon Room must take great care not to step on the white floor covering.

- Once the white floor covering is in place, a clean gurney should be rolled up to the decon/treatment table (if the table is not on wheels), keeping the gurney wheels on the white floor covering. All Decon Room personnel who will be involved with handling the patient during transfer to the clean gurney should remove and outer pair of gloves or should don clean gloves before handling the patient. Also, if two or more surgical gowns are worn, an outer gown should be removed If only one gown is worn, try to keep the sleeves and face of the gown from touching the decontaminated patient. Once the patient is transferred to the clean gurney, he/she can be rolled out of the Decon Room to the Buffer Zone.

  If the decon/treatment table is on wheels, the decon/treatment table can be rolled to the line of demarcation between the Decon Room and the Buffer Zone for transfer of the patient to the clean gurney. Personnel not involved in decontamination and treatment activities should receive the patient in the Buffer Zone. The patient and clean gurney should be monitored in the Buffer Zone, ensuring that radiation coming from any removed contamination in the Decon Room does not confuse the readings of the instruments while monitoring the patient in the Buffer Zone. The final confirmatory monitoring should be done by the RSC, by radiological health officials, or by other personnel with equal qualifications, for example, nuclear power station healthp physics/radiation protection technicians.

- The Decon Team should follow the guidelines in Chapter 2, modified as necessary, to remove their PCs. The RSO and/or radiological health officials should observe removal of PCs and should then monitor all REA/Decon Room and ambulance personnel, equipment, and facilities.

FIGURE 6.1
Example Radiation Emergency Area (REA)

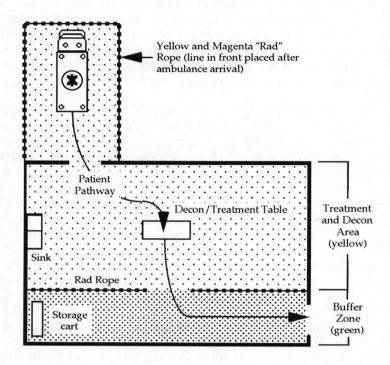

Yellow and Magenta "Rad" Rope (line in front placed after ambulance arrival)

Patient Pathway

Decon/Treatment Table

Treatment and Decon Area (yellow)

Sink

Rad Rope

Storage cart

Buffer Zone (green)

- The RSO, coordinating with radiological health officials, should ensure proper disposition of contaminated PCs, wastes, samples, and specimens and should ensure contaminated wastes, samples, and specimens are properly placarded with the trefoil (radiation symbol) prior to removal from the REA. Any equipment and materials found to be contaminated must be removed from service until decontaminated or replaced.

- The RSO should collect the dosimeters and ensure proper processing of them. The RSO should also provide notice of any follow-up measures, if any, that are required as a result of the processing of the dosimeters.

The guidelines in this Section are a distillation of the myriad of details which should be incorporated into procedures for handling and treating contaminated patients by hospital personnel. Radiation Management Consultants (RMC) in Philadelphia, Pennsylvania can help you prepare procedures for receiving contaminated patients, procedures which can be fine-tuned to your specific facility. Radiation Management Consultants can also help you prepare a Radiation Emergency Area layout such as the one shown in Figure 6.1 for your facility.

Section 4. Response to Nuclear Power Facility Incidents

The United States Nuclear Regulatory Commission (NRC) is the chief regulatory body governing the construction and operation of nuclear power facilities in the United States. On December 2, 1986, the NRC affirmed its position to all nuclear power facilities under construction and holding an operating license regarding medical services to the facilities. Inspection and Enforcement (I&E) Notice 86-98 provided clarification of the requirement that arrangements be made between nuclear power facilities and neighboring medical facilities for handling contaminated injured personnel. It is, therefore, probable that if a nuclear power facility is located or is being constructed in the locale of your medical or ambulance facility that you will be requested to enter into an agreement to provide medical support to handle contaminated injured personnel. Even if you are not located near a nuclear facility, you may be requested to provide support to providers who are so located. As Dr. Linnemann estimated, it appears that the existing mass-casualty medical response capabilities in the US may not be adequate to handle large-scale contamination and radiation injuries without a coordinated effort between multiple facilities. The capabilities of any one facility may be meager in comparison to the human needs in such an event.

The full spectrum of industrial injuries may occur at any nuclear power plant. In certain areas of a nuclear facility, the injured individual may also be contaminated with radioactive material and/or may have been exposed to ionizing radiation. Generally speaking, the classification of *contaminated injured* specifies that the victim is physically injured and/or is ill and is contaminated with radioactive materials. The US Federal Emergency Management Agency (FEMA), has published a definition which supplements the above specification of "contaminated injured." FEMA's definition states that a victim who is a contaminated injured patient is one who is

- contaminated and otherwise physically injured,
- contaminated and exposed to dangerous levels of radiation, or
- exposed to dangerous levels of radiation.

The FEMA believes radiation exposure that is a threat to life or health is in fact an injury and should be classed as such. Although "exposed to dangerous levels of radiation" does not in itself constitute a physical trauma in the traditional sense, an injury is an injury, whether by physical forces, by illness, or by radiation exposure. Although exposure to "dangerous levels of radiation" cannot contaminate the exposed individual, special radiological evaluation may be necessary to develop effective therapy for the exposed individual. "Dangerous levels of radiation" is a non-specific term since a given amount of radiation may affect some individuals differently than others. A trend is developing which seems to set the dangerous level at approximately 25 rem acute whole-body exposure.

Since a full spectrum of industrial injuries may occur at a nuclear power plant, responding to an injury at an industrial facility may require expertise in all manner of emergency medical services and extrication techniques. Although nuclear power facilities are required to maintain at least 2 qualified first-aid personnel on-shift at all times, the minimum training those individuals must have is Multi-media First Aid. Multi-media is not to be belittled, but it often does not provide the skills and knowledge that may be required for some of the bizarre, hideous trauma and extrication nightmares that may occur at any industrial site, nuclear or otherwise. You may be called upon to assist with the sometimes intense extrication needed to provide quality medical care to the patient. This Section presents the support which may be involved in providing backup medical services to a nuclear power facility.

First, the general layout of a nuclear facility is presented. Although each facility may be different, each has specific areas, usually five, in which a patient may be located.

- Owner Controlled Area   • Exclusion Area
- Protected Area   • Vital Area
- Radiological Controlled Area

Figure 6.2 is an example layout of the areas of a nuclear power station.

The Owner Controlled Area (OCA) is the area encompassed by the boundaries of the land owned by the utility. In the OCA, the utility can require a visitor to have reason and purpose to be in the OCA. The other four areas are located within the OCA.

The Exclusion Area within the Owner Controlled Area encompasses the Protected Area, the Radiation controlled Area, and the Vital Area. All land within the Exclusion Area is absolutely controlled by the Security force of the utility. Security is mandated by the NRC to control access and activities within the Exclusion Area, including denial of access and expulsion of personnel and property when necessary.

FIGURE 6.2
Example Nuclear Power Station Layout

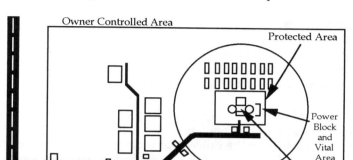

The layout of a nuclear power station in Figure 6.2 is an *example* layout and does not represent any particular nuclear facility. The perspective in Figure 6.2 serves only to portray areas to which access is or may be controlled, not to specify dimensions.

The Protected Area encompasses the Radiation Controlled Area and the Vital Area. The Protected Area is continuously patrolled by armed Security personnel. Important electrical and operational equipment are located in the Protected Area.

The Vital Area inside the Protected Area includes equipment and systems which are vital to the safe operation and shutdown of the plant. Facilities such as the Control Room and the reactor vessel(s) are located in the Vital Area. Shift operation of the reactor occurs within the Vital Area.

The Radiation Controlled Area (RCA) is an area in which special measures and controls may be necessary to control radiological contamination and exposure to radiation. The RCA is usually confined within the plant power block but may be extended due to special radiological conditions.

If an injury occurs at the plant which is beyond the capabilities of the facility to provide adequate care and treatment, the plant will request offsite medical support. This request normally originates from the plant Control Room and may be channeled through plant Security. Historically, evidence has revealed that some not-so-intelligent individuals have placed hoax calls to ambulance providers requesting an ambulance be dispatched to a nuclear plant. Therefore, if you enter an agreement with the utility to provide medical support, it may be prudent to preplan an unpublished call-back number at the plant to verify the authenticity of requests for ambulance support. The caller requesting ambulance support should provide at a minimum the following information:

- the number of patients and their names
- the extent of their injuries
- whether the patients are contaminated

If you are familiar with the layout of the plant, you should be told the best location to park the ambulance.

You should give the caller your estimated time of arrival to the plant. One of the ambulance service or hospital staff personnel or the dispatcher should make a verification call to the plant to ascertain the authenticity of the call. The verification call can be placed by a hospital official while you are enroute to the plant. Upon arrival at the plant, Security or other authorized personnel will provide direction or escort to the best location to access the patient.

If the patient is located within the Owner Controlled Area but outside the Exclusion Area, no special access authorization or outfitting of the ambulance and its personnel are normally required. Once your arrival is noted by plant Security, you will likely be permitted to proceed to the patient without an escort. If you are not familiar with the plant layout, the utility should provide an escort in order to ensure the most timely access to the patient. Some utilities have tighter restrictions regarding access within their Owner Controlled Area. If so, follow the directions of the plant personnel. Should you be unreasonably delayed, e,g., more than a minute or so, explain that you have been requested to provide medical care to a patient at the utility and that seconds may be vital to the patient's recovery: that you need to get moving *now*. In any case, don't try to force access. You are not responding to just another industrial complex incident or motor vehicle accident, you are responding to a medical emergency at a nuclear power station. The Security officers farther in the plant property (in the Protected Area) are armed and are well trained to keep unauthorized personnel out. You aren't doing the patient any good if you are detained due to unauthorized or improper access. Please do not get the wrong impression. By experience, Security personnel are more than willing and ready to help rightful medics get to the patient as rapidly as possible. Just do not try to be a jerk or a boss about getting access.

If the patient is located inside the Exclusion Area but outside the Protected Area, it may be necessary to gain access through an additional Security access control point at the Exclusion Area boundary. Simply follow the directions of the plant Security or other authorized plant personnel. An escort should be provided by the utility while inside the Exclusion Area if you are unfamiliar with the layout of the plant. No special outfitting of the ambulance or crew should be expected in this area.

If the patient is located inside the Protected Area, an armed Security officer must remain with the ambulance at all times while it is in the Protected Area. An escort for the ambulance crew must be provided by the utility and remain with the crew at all times. While an armed Security officer must remain with the ambulance at all times while inside the Protected Area, the escort for the ambulance crew may not be a Security officer. Anyone who has authorized clearance in the Protected Area may escort ambulance personnel in the Protected Area. If the patient is located inside the Radiation Controlled Area, one of the plant radiation protection or health physics personnel will accompany you to the patient. Dosimeters for the ambulance crew may be required while in the Protected Area. Required dosimeters will be provided by the utility.

If the patient is located within the Protected Area but outside any Radiation Controlled Area (RCA), no special outfitting of the ambulance or its crew except for dosimetry should be required by the utility. If the patient is located within a RCA, plant radiation protection or health physics personnel may require ambulance personnel to don special protective clothing and/or respiratory protection. Just follow their recommendations. The plant personnel will help you don the gear. However, if in your professional judgment you must get to the patient as rapidly as possible and do not have the time to don the special protective clothing, for example to treat a suspected acute myocardial infarction, request the plant radiation protection or health physics personnel to dispense with special protective clothing beyond booties and gloves. When the patient's life is at stake, it should ultimately be your call regarding how much personal protection you want. Once again, do not try to go to the patient's location on your own if the patient is in the Protected Area, let the plant personnel take you. If you do not have unescorted access[29] into the Protected Area *you must have an escort at all times while in the Protected Area.* There is no exception.

Although unlikely, you may be requested to enter an area of known or suspected contamination or elevated radiation levels. If

29. Unescorted access may be earned by attending special training provided by the plant on a periodic basis

such conditions exist, the plant medical personnel (Multi-media first aid or equivalent) may remove the patient from the area of risk. However, Multi-media training may not provide the level of extrication training that may be required for some incidents. A nuclear power facility is a bonafide industrial site with a full spectrum of possible extrication nightmares among the maze of huge piping and tanks. The utility medical personnel may not feel qualified to perform extrication and may request your support. Plant personnel will have probably removed any gross, obvious contamination, possibly by disrobing the patient. If you are requested to enter a known or suspected area of contamination or radiation, guidance and special outfitting will be provided by the plant personnel.

If the patient's injury is life-threatening and if plant personnel insist you don protective clothing beyond booties and gloves, you should make the plant personnel understand the gravity of the patient's condition. In all likelihood, the plant personnel will understand well the seriousness of the patient's condition and will request you don minimal protective clothing. Although minimal protective clothing may afford lesser protection than full protective clothing, you have the advantage of controlled actions learned herein to limit and even prevent self-contamination and the spread of contamination, the patient does not have such advantage. His/her condition may deteriorate while you protect yourself from a *possibility* of becoming contaminated: contaminated enough to maybe need no more than a good shower. Whether to don PCs and if so how much is ultimately a judgment call on your part.

Although some variations to the above access scenarios may exist at various nuclear power stations, the differences should be small. It would be wise to familiarize yourself with the site-specific access requirements of any nuclear facility, nuclear power or otherwise, to which you may provide medical support.

By observation and participation in several medical drills at nuclear power facilities, a trend of professionalism and cooperation between the utility and medical support personnel has become obvious. I have been fortunate to have had the opportunity to perform as a drill coordinator, a drill EMT/ambulance attendant, and a plant medical team member. I've assisted with the development and maintenance of Radiation Emergency Areas and have conducted the training for handling contaminated injured personnel at hospitals, for ambulance providers, and at nuclear power plants. These opportunities have convinced me of the professional, cooperative trend between local medical and utility personnel. In every case, a positive, sincere attitude was prevalent. People worked well together professionally, humbly, and intelligently.

Once at the patient site, perform necessary life support and extricate the patient to the ambulance. Except for life support activities, seek guidance from the plant personnel. They work there every day and know what they're doing, where they are, and which way to go to get the patient to the ambulance quickly.

If the patient is confirmed as contaminated or is suspected of being contaminated, plant radiation protection/health physics personnel will normally prepare your ambulance for transporting a contaminated patient. For example, they may place plastic floor and seat coverings in the ambulance. One of the plant radiation protection/health physics personnel should accompany the patient to the hospital if the patient is contaminated, not to monitor your performance, which is not his/her job, but to provide radiological guidance to you. Another plant radiation protection/health physics member may report to the medical facility in advance of patient arrival to provide radiological support directly to the emergency department staff. If not, the plant radiation protection/health Physics member which accompanies the patient to the hospital should provide the emergency department staff with radiological guidance during patient treatment.

Once you've stabilized and extricated the patient from the injury site, your escort will take you out of the area. Once at the exit from the Radiation Controlled Area, any protective equipment the utility issued may be collected, depending on your evaluation of the urgency of the patient's condition. At that time you, your equipment, and the patient may be monitored by plant personnel for radiological contamination, again depending on your evaluation of the urgency of the patient's condition. Remember that immediately life-threatening situations should take precedence over contamination concerns. In responding to a life-threatening injury, external radiological contamination should be thought of as bacterial contamination that does not multiply and can be dealt with by a good shower. Each of us must learn to deal with the potential for contracting various communicable diseases every time we work an injury: AIDS is only one of the diseases. Radioactive contamination is just one more possible risk. One benefit of radiological contamination over communicable diseases is that radiological contamination does not replicate as do viral and bacterial organisms—radiological contamination and radiation cannot "grow."

From the exit of the Radiation Controlled Area, you will be escorted to an exit from the Protected Area. There, your dosimeters may be collected and your escort will direct you out of the Owner Controlled Area to be on your way to the medical facility. It is advisable, however, for you to keep the dosimeters until you have released the patient to the medical facility and until you have been monitored by plant radiation protection/health physics personnel, the Radiation Safety Officer at the hospital, or radiological health officials. After response to the contaminated injured patient is complete, the Radiation Safety Officer should collect and return any dosimetry issued to the patient or to the ambulance personnel by the utility.

While in transit with the patient, rely on the radiological expertise of the radiation protection/health physics technician. That's why the radiation protection/health physics technician is with you. Once at the hospital, follow the guidance of the radiation protection/health physics Technician(s) until they, the Radiation Safety Officer at the hospital, or the radiological health officials have determined that you and your equipment are not contaminated. If you are contaminated, follow their recommendations regarding decontamination. They make their living knowing decontamination techniques. Also, if your equipment has become contaminated by providing medical support to a nuclear power facility, it should be the responsibility of the nuclear facility to either decontaminate or replace the equipment.

Chapter 7

DISROBING THE RADIOACTIVELY CONTAMINATED PATIENT AND RADIOLOGICAL SURVEY TECHNIQUES

PREVIEW

So far in this text, I have argued that you should pay more attention to the audio clicks of Geiger-Mueller instruments than to the meter indication. I still say for field operations when you need to get the patient to the hospital as quickly as possible, do not bother taking any meter readings, just use the audio response of the instruments to find out if radiation is present and from where it is coming. However, in the hospital prior to the arrival of professional radiological personnel, the meter indications should be noted while performing patient radiological contamination surveys.

Since most radiological contamination is likely to be found on the patient's clothing, disrobing the patient should prove effective in reducing the amount of contamination on the patient. Disrobing the patient in the ambulance will reduce the amount of contamination taken into the Radiation Emergency Area (REA) and the hospital.

In this Chapter, techniques for performing radiological surveys using radiation detection instruments and techniques for disrobing the contaminated patient are presented.

Topics herein include:

- Disrobing the contaminated patient
- Instrument selection
- Patient radiological surveys
- Contribution of natural background radiation during patient radiological surveys

Section 1. Disrobing the Radioactively Contaminated Patient

Most of the contamination on a patient is likely to be on the outside of his/her clothing. Removal of the contaminated clothing will reduce:

- the level of patient contamination,
- the chances of spreading the contamination, and
- the level of radiation exposing the patient and attendants however slight the level of contamination on the patient's clothing.

Attempts at detailed contamination surveys of the patient should wait until disrobing the patient is complete. If the patient cannot be disrobed due to his/her medical condition and you have the opportunity to perform a contamination survey in the ambulance, go ahead and survey the patient for contamination while he/she is still dressed. Delay of basic life support for serious medical conditions in favor of a radiological contamination survey or of disrobing the patient would be unwise. A natural tendency to want to at least do something about the radiological contamination should not be allowed to take priority over the patient's medical status. The Radiation Safety Officer or radiological health officials in the hospital can perform a detailed contamination survey after the doctor and the emergency department staff have disrobed the patient. Although disrobing the patient in the ambulance rather than in the hospital is desirable, disrobing the patient in the ambulance as a method of contamination control must not take precedence over the medical well-being of the seriously injured or ill patient (have I said it enough to make the point)? As removal of the patient's clothing will likely remove most of the contamination, realize that removal of the contaminated clothing will only relocate the contamination. The patient's clothing will still be contaminated and will still be a source of contamination for responding personnel and their equipment.

Disrobing a radioactively contaminated patient requires a little more attention to detail than disrobing a uncontaminated patient. Disrobing the uncontaminated patient requires attention to his/her injuries, and to preventing microorganisms on the clothing from contaminating his/her injuries or from adding to the existing microorganism contamination. In some cases, simply untying boots or shoes or slipping them off the patient's feet, pulling pants down over the feet, and feeding the patient's arms through the arm holes of a shirt or blouse is enough to remove the clothing from the non-contaminated patient, depending of course on the extent and location of the patient's injuries. However, disrobing a contaminated patient requires the same attention necessary to limiting the spread of microorganisms and to minimizing the agitation of the patient's injuries *plus* attention to the radiological contamination. The mechanics of transferring radiological contamination may be regarded the same as the mechanics of transferring microorganism contamination, the radiation exposure from the contamination notwithstanding.

If a survey for radiological contamination on the patient before reaching the hospital is feasible, the survey should wait until the patient is stabilized and placed in the ambulance. Once the patient is stabilized and in the ambulance, determine whether the patient is contaminated using a Geiger-Mueller instrument. Section 3 of this Chapter provides the details for performing a radiological survey. After the patient is stabilized, in the ambulance, and patient contamination is confirmed, disrobing of the patient should begin. There are a number of techniques for disrobing the contaminated patient's clothing: I will describe one technique which I call *flowering* the patient's clothing.

As EMTs and paramedics are taught in auto extrication classes, the patient should not be taken out of the wrecked vehicle, rather the wrecked vehicle should be taken off the patient. A similar way of thinking should be used when disrobing a contaminated patient, i.e., the contaminated clothing should be unwrapped from the patient rather than pulling the patient out of the contaminated clothing. The following technique of disrobing the patient assumes the patient is not on a backboard and is lying down, face up. When the patient is in a different position, some modification of the technique would be necessary.

While wearing at least eye protection, a surgical mask, and two or three pairs of gloves, use a pair of scissors that can be taken out of service after use to start a cutline up one of the pant legs from the cuff. Gain cutting access for the scissors by getting a pinch hold (with gloved hands) on the outside surface of the fabric, lifting the fabric away from the patient's body, then cutting from the cuff. While cutting, be careful not to touch the patient's skin and undergarments with your hands or tools or the outside surface of the clothing. Do not insert your finger under the pant cuff since your hands, gloved or not, are likely to be contaminated at this point if the patient is contaminated. If you use a contaminated finger to reach under the pant leg, you will likely introduce new contamination under the patient's clothing. Continue the pant leg cutline up to the iliac prominence, then repeat the process for the other leg. When both pant legs have been split, cut across the space between the iliac prominences to join the two pant leg cutlines, then cut up to the beltline. Do not bother unzipping zippers—just cut. Next, repeat the technique for both shirt sleeves by cutting up to the shoulder, then cut across the front of the shirt to join the two sleeve cuts. Once both sleeves are cut and the cuts are joined across the front of the shirt, cut down the chest to the bottom of the shirt. If the patient had his/her shirt tail tucked in before flowering the pants, the shirt tail will be exposed by flowering the pants and will not need to be pulled out of the patient's pants. Do not bother unbuttoning button-up shirts, just cut. Then cut up to the neckline from the cutline spanning the chest. In all your actions, avoid touching the inside of the patient's clothing since the inside of his/her clothing is not likely to be contaminated unless the contaminant is liquid.

Now you are ready to lay the patient's contaminated clothing open, i.e., "flower" the clothing. Pinch the *outside* of the fabric of the pant legs, pull the fabric away from the midline cut of the leg, and lay the fabric flat on the gurney inside out. Do the same with the other pant leg. Next, lay the fabric of the groin region against the gurney, being careful not to touch the patient with your hands or tools. The fabric between the cutline spanning the groin and the beltline should be spread out with the outside surface down as well. Flower the shirt fabric in a similar manner. Lay the shirt sleeves open with the outside of the fabric down. Flower the chest fabric by laying the fabric down against the gurney with the outside of the fabric down. The fabric around the shoulders and neck should also be spread with the outside of the fabric down.

It is unlikely that anyone can disrobe a contaminated patient in a bouncing and rocking ambulance without, in one way or another, touching the patient's skin or undergarments with contaminated hands or tools or with the outside of the contaminated clothing. However, the less you touch the patient with your hands/tools and the less contact of the patient's skin and undergarments with the outside of the clothing, the less the spread of contamination.

Now the patient's contaminated clothing is flowered. The outside of the patient's contaminated clothing is down against the gurney and the uncontaminated inside of the clothing is facing up, providing a surface which should be relatively free of contamination: a surface from which to work the patient's injuries and to monitor the patient's condition with a reduced chance of spreading radiological contamination. Remove an outer pair of gloves to provide radiologically clean hands before you work the patient's injuries and perform periodic patient assessment. Blood pressure can now be taken with much less likelihood of contaminating the BP cuff than when applying the BP cuff over the patient's shirt sleeve. You may now lay your hand on the patient's abdomen to monitor his/her breathing with less chance of contaminating the patient's skin. Listening to chest sounds with a stethoscope can now be done with less chance of contaminating the stethoscope.

Boots and shoes should be removed by cutting the shoestring or face of the boot/shoe starting at the tibia or the front of the ankle cutting down to the toes. Next, cut the backside of the boot or shoe starting at the calf or ankle cutting down to the heel. The footwear may then be removed by separating the halves. Jewelry and adornments may be removed in the usual manner, but must be treated as though contaminated. Removed metallic objects should be maintained accessible to radiological health officials since they may be able to use the metallic objects to determine if any neutron exposure has been received by the patient.

If the patient's condition permits, as another contamination control measure and if the patient's medical condition permits, consider rolling the patient on his/her side and with radiologically clean gloves place a clean sheet of plastic protective covering between the patient and his/her clothing. Placing the protective covering over the patient's contaminated clothing will sandwich the patient's clothing between the new protective covering and the protective covering previously placed to drape the gurney. After placing the protective covering between the patient and his/her contaminated clothing, recheck the patient's condition and continue life support as necessary. When the patient is transferred into the Decon/Treatment Room of the Radiation Emergency Area (REA), the patient's clothing and the protective coverings should stay on the gurney. Doing this will:

- keep the protective coverings off the decon/treatment table which will facilitate decontamination. The protective covering can become a problem when trying to wash down the patient on the decon/treatment table—some of the decon washwater would likely run down the hanging parts of the protective coverings onto the Decon Room floor.

- enclose the patient's contaminated clothing neatly to maintain positive control of the contaminated clothing for easier disposal.

The RSO or the radiological health officials at the hospital should be responsible for bagging and disposing of the "radioactive sandwich" using multiple gloves, eye protection, booties, and a gown, or any extent of PCs they wish or have time to don—the more the better. The RSO or radiological health officials should do so by rolling the new protective covering down against itself, rolling the contaminated clothing and the previously placed protective covering on the gurney inside the new protective covering, paying attention to preventing the surfaces of the protective covering and the patient's clothing from coming in contact with uncontaminated surfaces in the ambulance. Once the protective covering is rolled with the contaminated clothing and the previously placed protective covering inside, place the bundle in a large plastic bag, twist the bag opening closed, tape the twist shut, fold the twist, and tape it shut again. Carefully check the bag for holes but do not squeeze the bag to locate holes. If holes are present, tape over the holes and place the punctured bag inside another bag. When finished placing the contaminated articles in the plastic bag, remove another pair of gloves and continue with life support activities with clean gloves. Remember that if disrobing the patient in the ambulance will aggravate or jeopardize the patient's medical condition or chances of full recovery, *disregard the contamination and concentrate on medical support and get the patient to the hospital*—let the physician determine when and how the patient may be disrobed.

If a backboard is used to support the patient, or if the patient cannot be rolled, disrobing the patient in the ambulance should consist of cutting as much of the clothing away from the patient as possible without moving the patient. While cutting, be careful not to touch the inside of the garments. Handle the garments by pinching the outside of them with gloved hands. As parts of clothing are removed, they must be placed in a large plastic bag to minimize the spread of contamination. Do not wave, flip, or toss the removed clothing when placing them in the bag. Further, do not do as mother does when putting your lunch sandwich in a plastic bag: do not squeeze the air out of the bag before closing it. The Radiation Safety Officer or the radiological health officials should be responsible for final containment and disposition of the contaminated articles: you just bag the contaminated articles *if* you can without compromising quality and timely medical care to the patient.

If the disrobing the patient is performed in the ambulance, it will not have to be done in the hospital and will keep the contaminated clothing on the gurney. However, disrobing the patient can be done as easily, maybe easier in the Radiation Emergency Area

(REA) in the hospital in the same manner described above. If disrobing the patient is done in the ambulance, the patient's clothing, discarded gloves, the protective covering over the gurney, and any other item or piece of equipment used to handle and disrobe the contaminated patient should be left in the ambulance. The Radiation Safety Officer at the hospital or the radiological health officials should determine disposition of the contaminated items.

Disrobing the contaminated patient can be very complex and time-consuming as well as being a risk to the patient's injuries. Remember that radiological contamination and disrobing of the patient are *not* as important as the life and medical well-being of the patient. If you can determine from the contamination survey that only a small portion of the patient's clothing is contaminated, simply cut off the contaminated area, observing the same contamination controls for disposing of the contaminated piece(s) of clothing.

Granted, of the trauma and medical infirmities which require ambulance service, there are not many that will permit so much agitation of the patient by disrobing the patient before reaching the hospital. However, disrobing of the contaminated patient in the ambulance will lessen the possibility of spreading the contamination through the hospital, to the hospital staff, and to other patients. Just remember that the patient's life and his/her chances of full recovery from the trauma are more important than disrobing the patient.

Section 2. Instrument Selection

Emergency medical and hospital personnel should use a Geiger-Mueller type of radiological survey meter such as the CDV-700 to perform gross radiological contamination surveys of the patient. The following elements of the beta/gamma Geiger-Mueller radiation detection instrument make it ideal for gross patient contamination surveys rather than an ionization chamber radiation detection instrument such as the CDV-715:

- Geiger-Mueller survey meters have greater sensitivity than the ionization chamber instrument and will show the presence of much lower levels of radiation.

- Geiger-Mueller survey meters have audio indication of radiation where some ionization chamber instruments have no audio.

- Geiger-Mueller survey meters have a probe detector, rather than an internal detector making easier access to folds of the human body, arm pits, and groin. Also, seeing a probe passing over his/her body is less foreboding to the conscious patient than the bottom of an ionization chamber instrument.

- Geiger-Mueller survey meters have the capability to detect both beta and gamma radiations (some have alpha detection capability) where the ionization chamber type instrument may respond only to gamma radiation.

The standard CDV-700 has all of the above elements except alpha detection capability. The CDV-700 is most likely to be available to state, county, and municipal medical services and hospitals. The CDV-700 as well as any other Geiger-Mueller radiation detection instrument can be fitted with a probe for detecting alpha radiation, making it a beta/gamma/alpha detection instrument. However, an instrument fitted with an alpha probe may still be used only as a detecting instrument, not a measuring instrument unless the instrument is calibrated to the specific energy of radiation involved in the incident. An undesirable feature of the alpha probe is the probe itself. The section of the Geiger-Mueller tube which permits beta radiation to enter the enclosed gas volume, the beta window (review Figure 4.4), is a sheet of thin metal which is relatively resilient to vibration and impact. The alpha radiation window of the alpha probe, in most cases, is a thin mylar membrane which is very fragile—a sneeze can pop the membrane. Therefore, the alpha probe is likely to be unforgiving in the sometimes hostile and abusive environment of emergency rescue and extrication.

Use of the ionization chamber type instrument such as the CDV-715 is not advisable since it cannot detect beta and alpha radiation. In addition, the ionization chamber instrument requires a relatively high exposure rate to cause a readable response on the meter. It is very unlikely a radiologically contaminated trauma patient has been so contaminated that the exposure rate coming from the contamination would cause a noticeable response on the meter of the ionization chamber instrument. As the Radiation Management Consultants discovered, the highest known exposure rate coming from the contamination on an injured individual generated from a US nuclear power facility and transported to an outside medical facility up to 1991 was approximately 60 mR/hr. After disrobing the patient, the level of radiation coming from the remaining contamination was approximately 20 mR/hr (this reduction in contamination due to disrobing the patient is testimony to its effectiveness). An ionization chamber instrument such as the CDV-715 may show a small deflection of the needle in an exposure rate of 60 mR/hr and may show a flicker of the needle of the meter in 20 mR/hr. The CDV-700 Geiger-Mueller instrument would show an offscale high indication in 60 mR/hr (would peg offscale), but would well indicate the 20 mR/hr. Although an indication of 20 mR/hr on a CDV-700 would not be accurate unless the instrument has been calibrated to the energy of radiation from the contamination, the 20 mR/hr indication would provide evidence that contamination still exists on the patient and that further decontamination is indicated. The ionization chamber instrument may, in rare cases, be useful at the incident site as an exposure control aid but would not likely be useful in the hospital or ambulance as a contamination survey device.

Historical view of incidents in the United States reveals it is unlikely that emergency medical and hospital services will need an ionization chamber type radiation detection instrument while performing patient contamination surveys. The only type radiation detection instrument that will likely be needed for patient contamination surveys is the Geiger-Mueller survey meter.

The only time an ionization chamber instrument would be necessary for performing patient radiological contamination surveys is when the exposure rate coming from the contamination on the patient is gamma radiation only and is too high for the Geiger-Mueller instrument. I have *never* heard of a case where the exposure rate coming from the contamination on a disrobed patient was so high that an ionization chamber instrument could effectively be used. I suppose that an explosion forcing a large projectile of radioactive material into the patient's body could cause such a high exposure rate, but let us be realistic: even the training received to manage personnel exposures and contamination from a nuclear war uses a Geiger-Mueller survey meter (the CDV-700) for personnel contamination surveys.

When performing radiological contamination surveys on patients, the surveyor must wear dosimeters with self-reading dosimeters (SRDs) as the preferred choice. As stated earlier, the highest known exposure rate coming from the contamination on an injured patient from a nuclear power facility in the US was 60 mR/hr. The 60 mR/hr coming from the contamination injured patient from a nuclear power facility was at near-contact with the patient's skin. An attendant would have to stay intimately close to the 60 mR/hr patient for 16.7 hours to receive 1 Roentgen exposure (1000 milliRoentgen exposure), and only at the point of intimacy. High-range dosimeters are available in many ranges, e.g., zero to 1 Roentgen, zero to 5 Roentgen, zero to 25 Roentgen, zero to 100 Roentgen, and zero to 200 Roentgen. A 1-Roentgen exposure would be readable on the zero to 1 Roentgen and zero to 5 Roentgen dosimeters, and may be readable on the zero to 25 Roentgen dosimeter, but 16.7 hours of intimate patient assessment/treatment by the same individual is unrealistic. The zero to 100 Roentgen and the zero to 200 Roentgen dosimeters would not show a readable deflection for the 16.7 hour, 1-Roentgen exposure: a readable deflection that could not be confused with dosimeter drift or leakage.

The most practical dosimeter for monitoring your exposure while attending a contaminated patient is likely to be one of the low-range self-reading dosimeters, such as the CDV-138 which is zero to 200 milliRoentgen. One hour exposure to 60 mR/hr would cause enough deflection on the zero to 100 mR dosimeter to provide a credible reading, credible in that the reading could not be easily confused with dosimeter drift or leakage. Although film badges would perform as well and would provide an indication of beta exposure as well as gamma exposure, film badges do not provide the user with an immediately readable indication of his/her exposure. If you can have the "best of both worlds", use both an SRD and a film badge or thermoluminescent dosimeter (TLD) anytime you provide support to a radiation accident, as well as when performing radiological contamination surveys. If only the best is good enough, use a TLD on the outside of your PCs to determine your exposure. As mentioned earlier, the reading from a TLD is so accurate that it is acceptable as a legal record.

Several models of Geiger-Mueller, ionization chamber, and dosimetry instruments are available. Each model may provide variations of the parameters discussed in this book. Far too many models are available to permit including an example of each herein. I recommend you seek the advice of an individual experienced in radiation detection instrumentation before spending funds on any one model.

Section 3. Patient Radiological Surveys

Even if the meter indication of your radiological survey instruments may not be relied upon as accurate, the meter indication can be useful to professional radiological personnel when they know the type of radioactive material involved (Reference: Chapter 5) and the type of instrument used. So, while performing patient radiological surveys in the ambulance or the hospital with a Geiger-Mueller instrument such as the CDV-700, use the headphone to find the location(s) of the highest rate of audio clicks then take a note of the meter indication associated with the location(s). Provide those readings to the professional radiological personnel and make sure they know which instrument was used to obtain the readings. Do not try to be exact. If the needle of the meter face falls between 4.5 mR/hr and 5.0 mR/hr, just note "around 5 mR/hr." Be a little liberal about what a Geiger-Mueller instrument reads. Do not be extravagant, but do not be stingy.

The first step in performing patient contamination surveys, as well as any other activity using radiation detection instruments, is to perform an operational check on the instruments. Refer to Chapter 4 to review the operational check of the Geiger-Mueller instrument. Although Chapter 4 uses a CDV-700 to provide instructions on performing an operational check, the procedure described is adequate for most Geiger-Mueller type instruments. Refer to the vendor manual for operational check instructions specific to your instruments.

It is not advisable for ambulance and rescue personnel to take the time to perform a radiological contamination survey of the patient at the scene of the injuries or incident. As described earlier, the ambulance personnel should approach the incident site with operationally checked radiation detection instruments turned on only to determine if radiation is present and from where it is coming. In this way, the ambulance personnel will be alerted to any beta or gamma radiation at the incident site and can expect radiological contamination if radiation is present. Ambulance personnel should use the Geiger-Mueller instrument to confirm the presence and location of radiological contamination, but not exactly how much radiation is coming from the contamination. Ambulance and rescue personnel should be more concerned about the patient's medical condition than the radiological situation. If the ambulance/rescue personnel have the opportunity to perform a radiological contamination survey of the patient, they should do so in a general way. The ambulance/rescue personnel should log their findings but should leave the minute details of the contamination survey to the Radiation Safety Officer or the radiological health officials at the hospital.

Use the following suggested steps for performing a patient radiological survey

- after emergency medical services are provided,

- after the patient has been extricated and preferably disrobed,

- if the patient's medical condition permits taking time and giving attention to performing a contamination survey, and

- if the radiation detection instrument operational checks are complete.

Patient Radiological Contamination Survey
in the Ambulance

- Ensure the beta window of your Geiger-Mueller instrument is fully open.

- Place the middle beta window of the probe over the check source once again to recheck the headphone.

- Pull the probe away from the check source (and away from the contaminated patient) and take a mental note of the rate of clicks coming from background radiation.

- Pass the probe over all readily accessible surfaces of the patient at about 4 or 5 inches per second 1 to 2 inches from the patient's body and note the general area(s) giving an increase in audio clicks. If the patient's condition/injuries permit, roll the patient to monitor the posterior surface in the same way.

- Return to the area(s) giving a noticeable increase in audio clicks and recheck them with the probe at about 1/2 inch from the patient's body surface(s), but pass the probe over the patient's body at about 1 to 2 inches per second.

- Observe if the recheck reveals a definite increase in the rate of audio clicks above the rate heard in the background check. *Any increase in the rate of audio clicks above the background rate of clicks indicates radiation from contamination.*

- Note the location of the increase in clicks, not the location of the increase in meter face deflection, and record the location on an anatomical chart. Give the chart to the Radiation

Safety Officer (RSO) at the hospital. Remind the RSO that
the chart may be contaminated and that he/she should open
a plastic bag so you may put the chart in it to maximize
contamination control.

Remember that the audio response of the Geiger-Mueller
instrument is instantaneous. The survey meter needle may take a
couple seconds to stabilize and may therefore take a few seconds to
show an upscale swing due to increased radiation. If you are
watching the meter face and not listening to the audio rate, you may
conceivably pass over a spot of contamination before the meter needle
can respond. Also, if you are watching the meter face you are not
watching what you are doing with the probe and can touch the
patient with the probe. Doing so can contaminate the probe and
confuse survey indications and can contaminate the patient if the
probe is contaminated. Also be aware of the bouncing every
ambulance in motion suffers while transporting a patient. Trying to
keep the probe (or yourself) from touching the patient while
performing a radiological contamination survey while the ambulance
is in motion is nearly impossible. Again the medic in the back of the
ambulance is between a rock and a hard place. You cannot determine
whether the patient is contaminated unless you perform a
radiological survey. If you perform a radiological survey while
transporting the patient in the bouncing ambulance, you likely will
not be able to do so without touching the patient with the probe or
with parts of your own body. Whatever you chose, to survey or not
to survey, put the patient first.

Patient Radiological Contamination Survey
at the Hospital

Using the anatomical chart provided by the ambulance
personnel, the Radiation Safety Officer at the hospital should gleen
the information from it and prepare a fresh, uncontaminated chart,
then resurvey the patient as follows, annotating his/her findings on
the fresh chart:

- After patient transfer to the decon/treatment table, instruct
  the ambulance attendants to standby in the ambulance until
  monitored for radiological contamination.

- Note the locations of contamination on the patient found by
  the ambulance personnel. While the patient is handled

during transfer to the decon/treatment table, use the information on the chart provided by the ambulance personnel to inform the attendants who perform patient transfer of the contaminated areas and request they not handle those areas, if possible. Handling the patient during transfer can be as significant to recovery as the treatment of injuries. So, do not demand the attendants not handle the contaminated areas if they need to do so to provide quality patient handling. The attendants transferring the patient must also wear PCs, at least booties, gloves, eye protection, surgical masks, and gowns. If the attendants must handle contaminated areas of the patient, they may do so with confidence that the contamination will stay on the PCs. Once the hospital attendants have completed transfer of the patient to the Decontamination/Treatment Room (Decon Room), they should standby in the REA until monitored for contamination.

The RSO should realize that, by now, the ambulance attendants *and* the personnel who transferred the patient from the ambulance are standing by, wondering if they are radioactively contaminated. The RSO should consider training additional personnel in the use of radiation detection instruments so the additional personnel may survey the ambulance and assisting personnel while the RSO and radiological health officials are busy with patient services.

- If the physician-in-charge concurs that the patient's condition permits performing a radiological survey for contamination prior to beginning medical treatment, begin the radiological contamination survey using an operationally checked Geiger-Mueller instrument with the headphone attached. If medical treatment must begin immediately, monitor the patient as much as possible without interfering with medical procedure.

- Pass the probe over every surface of the patient's body at about 1 to 2 inches per second and about 1/2 inch from the patient's body, showing special attention to the locations of contamination found by the ambulance personnel and to the folds of the body, the hands, the feet, the shoulders, the buttocks, and the head/face. Avoid allowing contact between the probe and any surface of the patient's body. Placing the probe in a plastic bag will help prevent the probe from becoming contaminated and will not significantly affect the efficiency of the probe to detect radiation. Realize that if the plastic bag (or probe) becomes contaminated, the instrument will show an indication of the radiation coming from the contamination on the plastic bag or probe. The radiation coming from contamination on the plastic bag or probe will add to the radiation coming from the contamination on the patient, confusing the findings of the survey.

• When an area of contamination is found, hold the probe at about 1/2 inch from the contaminated surface for four or five seconds and observe the survey meter reading. Record the meter reading on the anatomical chart. As stated at the beginning of this Section, do not try to be exact. If the Geiger-Mueller instrument indicates somewhere between 4.5 mR/hr and 5.0 mR/hr, the notation on the anatomical chart should read "Approximately 5 mR/hr." Inform the physician-in-charge as survey results are revealed.

• Begin decontamination when the physician-in-charge indicates decontamination may begin, either general decontamination or local decontamination. Follow the directions of the physician-in-charge when performing patient decontamination, or assist him/her using the decontamination guidelines provided in Chapter 6.

Section 4. The Contribution of Natural Background Radiation During Patient Radiological Surveys

When responding to an incident involving radioactive materials, it is important to get a "feel" for sound of the background radiation rate in your area on an operationally checked Geiger-Mueller instrument because *any* credible increase in the rate of clicks above the natural background rate will be due to radiation from the radioactive material, whether from the source or from contamination on the patient. Absorb the previous statement boldly; *using an operationally checked instrument, any credible increase in the rate of clicks above the natural background rate will be due to radiation from the radioactive material.* This statement means exactly what it says.

Natural background radiation can contribute to the survey findings during a radiological contamination survey, but not to a great degree. In particular, exposure rates are instrumentally additive. For example, the response of a radiation detection instrument to the exposure rate coming from two sources of the same amount will be more than the exposure rate coming from only one of the sources. The importance of this statement is that when you use a survey meter to detect radiation, the survey meter does not care about from where the radiation is coming. The radiation the instrument is detecting may be coming from the contamination on the patient, from the contamination spread to the ambulance or other areas, or from the major source of radiation. Likewise, the survey meter does not know or care whether the radiation is coming from contamination on the patient or on the probe. Therefore, it is important for the surveyor to determine the background rate of exposure in the area he/she is performing the survey. Once the background radiation level in the area of the contamination survey is known, the background rate needs to be taken into account if the area background rate is more than the normal background rate. Radiological health experts can make use of this information you can provide from a patient radiological contamination survey.

American Medical Association. A guide to the hospital management of injuries arising from exposure to or involving ionizing radiation. Chicago: A.M.A; 1984.

American National Standards Institute. Guide for hospital emergency departments on handling radiation accident patients. Project N13.28. New York: ANSI; 1985.

Andrews. G. A. The medical management of accidental total-body irradiation. In: Hubner, K. F. ; Fry, S. A., eds. The Medical Basis for Radiation Accident Preparedness. New York: Elsevier/North Holland; 1980: 297-310.

Annals of the ICRP. The Principles and General Procedures for Handling Emergency and Accidental Exposures of Workers. Pergamon Press Vol. 2, No. 1, 1978.

Anno, G. H.; Baum, S. J.; Withers, H. R.; Young, R. W. Symptomatology of acute radiation effects on humans after exposure to doses of 0.5 Gy-30 Gy. Health Phys. 56: 821; 1989.

Arena, V. Ionizing Radiation and Life. C. V. Mosby, St. Louis, 1971.

Baranov, A. E.; Gale, R. P.; Guskova, A.; Piatkin, E.; Selidovkin, G.; Muravyova, I.; Champlin, R. E.; Danilova, N.; Yevsccva, L.; Patrosyan, L.; Pushkareva, S.; Konchalovski, M.; Gordceva, A.; Protasova, T.; Reisner, Y.; Mickey. M. R.; Terasaki, P. I. Bone marrow transplantation after the Chernobyl accident. N. Eng. J. Med. 321: 205-212; 1989.

Baranov, A. E.; Guskova, A. K. Acute radiation disease in Chernobyl accident victims. In: Ricks, R. C.: Fry, S. A., eds. The medical basis for radiation accident preparedness II. Clinical experience and follow-up since 1979. New York, NY: Elsevier; 1990: 79-87.

Bayler, R.; Carothers, A.; Chen, X.; Farrow, S.; Gordon, J.;Ji, L.; PIper, J.; Rutovit, D.;Stark, M.; Wald, N. Radiation dosimetry by automatic image analysis of dicentric chromosomes, Mutat. Res., In press, 1991.

Bond, V. P.; Fliedner, T. M.; Archambeau, J. O. Mammalian radiation lethality. New York: Academic Press; 1965.

Browne, D.; Weiss, J. F.; MacVittie, T. J.; Pillai, M. V. eds; Treatment of radiation injuries. New York, NY; Plenum Press, 1990.

Butturini, A. ; DeSousa, P. C.; Gale, R. P.; Cordiero, J. M.; Lopes, D. M.; Neto, C.; Cunha, C. B.; DeSousa, C. E. P.; Ho, W. G.; Tabak, D. G.; Sanpai, J. M.; Buria, A. Use of recombinant granulocyte-macrophage colony stimulating factor in the Brazil radiation accident. Lancet ii: 471-475; 1988.

Conklin, J. J.; Walker, R. I.. Military radiobiology. Orlando, FL; Academic Press, 1987. Finch, S. C. Acute radiation syndrome. J.A.M.A. 258: 664-667; 1987.

Dorland's Illustrated Medical Dictionary, 24th edition, W. B. Saunders Company, Philadelphia and London.

Drum, D. E. Managing the Medical Aspects. (unknown).

Federal Emergency Management Agency Guidance Memorandum MS-1. Medical Services. November 18, 1986.

Fliedner, T. M.; Nothdurf, W.; Heit, H. Biological factors affecting the occurrence of radiation syndromes. In: Broerse, J. J.; MacVittie, T. J., eds. Response of Different Species to Total Body Irradiation. Boston, MA: Martinus Nijhoff Publishers, 1984: 209-219.

Fliedner, T. M. Hematological indicators to predict patient recovery after whole-body irradiation as a basis for clinical management. In: Ricks, R. C.; Fry, S. A., eds. The medical basis for radiation accident preparedness-clinical experience and followup since 1979. New York, NY: Elsevier 1990: 445-460.

Gale, R. P.; Butturini, A.; Bortin, M. M. What does total body irradiation do in bone marrow transplants for leukemia? Int. J. Radiation Oncology Biol. Phys. 20: 631-634; 1991.

Gale, R. P.; Reisner, Y. The role of bone marrow transplants after nuclear accidents. Lancet i: 923-926; 1988.

Gerstner, H. B. Acute clinical effects of penetrating nuclear radiation. J.A.M.A. 168: 381-388; 1958.

Gilberti, M. V.; Wald, N. The Pittsburg radiation accident: twenty-three year follow-up of clinical and psychological aspects. In: Berger, M. E., ed. The medical basis for radiation accident preparedness III: psychological perspectives. Oak Ridge, TN: Oak Ridge Associated Universities, In press, 1991.

Medvedev, G. The Truth About Chernobyl. Basic Books, NY, 1991.

Gale, R. P.; Butturini, A. A use of hematopoietic growth factors in radiation accidents. Int. J. Radiation Oncology Biol. Phys. 19:1291-1295; 1990.

Guskova, A. G.; Baranov, A. E. Treatment of acute radiation disease (ARD)-Experience from Chernobyl. In: Berzelius Symposium XV, Umed; 1988: 157-185.

Cember, H. Introduction to Health Physics. Pergamon Press, 1969.

Hubner, K. F.; Fry, S. A., eds. The medical basis for radiation accident preparedness. New York, NY: Elsevier/North Holland; 1980.

Illesh, A. Chernobyl. Richardson and Steinman, Inc., New York, 1987.

International Commission on Radiological Protection. The principles and general procedures for handling emergency and accidental exposures of workers. Publication No. 28. New York: Pergamon; 1977.

Indiana State Board of Health. Guidelines for the Care of Radiation Accident Patients; 1980.

International Atomic Energy Agency. Environmental Monitoring for Medical and Allied Health Personnel; 1966.

International Atomic Energy Agency. Evaluation of Radiation Emergencies and Accidents. Technical Report Series No 152; 1974.

International Atomic energy Agency. Manual on early medical treatment of possible radiation injury. Vienna: IAEA Safety Series 47; 1978.

International Atomic Energy Agency. The radiological accident in San Salvador. Vienna; 1980.

Shapiro, J. Radiation Protection - A guide for Scientists and Physicians. Harvard University Press; 1972.

Jammet, H.; Mathe, G.; Pendie, B.; Duplan, J.-F.; Maupin, B.; Latarjet, R.; Kalie, D.; Schwarzenberg, L.; Djukie, Z.; Vigne, J. Etude de six cas d'irradiation totale aigue acidentelle. Rev. Franc. Etudes Clin. et Biol. IV: 210-225, 1959.

Keller, P. D. A clinical syndrome following exposure to atomic bomb explosions. J.A.M.A. 131: 504-506; 1946.

Leonard, R. B.; Ricks, R. C. Emergency department radiation accident protocol. Ann. Emerg. Med. 9: 462-470; 1980.

Linnemann, R. E. A systems approach to the initial management of radiation injuries. In: Boyd, D.; Edlich, R. F.; Micik, S., eds. Systems Approach to Emergency Medcial Care. Norwalk: Appleton-Century-Crofts, Norwalk; 1983: 341-369.

Linnemann, R. E. Soviet Medical Response to the Chernobyl Nuclear Accident. From the Department of Radiation Therapy, University of Pennsylvania School of Medicine, and Radiation Management Consultants, Philadelphia. JAMA ; 258: 637-643; 1987.

Lloyd, D. C.; Purrott, R. J. National Radiological Protection Board. Chromosome Aberration Analysis in Radiological Protection Dosimetry. Radiation Protection Dosimetry, Vol. 1, No. 1; 19-28.

Luthra, Y. K.; Mattson. J. L.; Yochmowitz, M. G. Inhibition of radioemesis by catecholamines in dogs. Radiation Research 85: 583-591; 1981.

Mathe, G.; Jammet, H.; Pendie, B.; Schwartzenberg, L.; Duplan, J.-F.; Maupin, B.; Latarjet, R.; Larrieu, M.-J.; Kalie, D.; Djukie, Z. Transgusions et greffes do moelle osscuse homologue chez des humains irradies a haute dose accidentellment. Rev. Franc. Etudes Clin. et Biol. IV: 226-238; 1959.

Medvedev, G. The truth about Chernobyl. New York, NY. Basic Books; 1991.

Medvedev, Z. A. The Legacy of Chernobyl. Norton, New York, 1990.

Metcalf, D. The granulocyte-macrophage colony stimulating factors. Science 229: 16-22; 1985.

Mettler, F. A.; Kelsey, C. A.; Ricks, R. C. Medical management of radiation accidents. Boca Raton, FL: CRC Press; 1990.

National Council of Radiation Protection and Measurement. Mangement of persons accidentally contaminated with radionuclides. NCRP Report No. 65.; 1980.

National Council on Radiation Protection and Measurements. NCRP Report No. 48. Radiation Protection for Medical and Allied Health Personnel; August 1, 1976.

National Council on Radiation Protection and Measurements. NCRP Report No. 65. Management of Persons Accidentally Contaminated with Radionuclides; April 15, 1980.

Nienhuis, A. W. Hematopoietic growth factors. N. Eng. J. Med. 318: 916-918; 1988.

Perman, V.; Cronkite, E. P.; Bond, V. P.; Sorensen, D. K.. The regenerative ability of hemopoietic tissue following lethal X-irradiation in dogs. Blood 19: 724-737; 1962.

Response to Radioactive Materials Transport Accidents. Radiation Emergency Assistance Center/Training Site (REAC/TS), Oak Ridge Associated Universities DOT/RSPA/MTB-79/8. US Department of Transportation, Office of Hazardous Materials Regulation, Washington, D.C.

Ricks, R. C.; Berger, M. E. and O'Hara, F. eds. The medical basis for radiation accident preparedness III: psychological perspective. New York, NY: Elsevier; In press, 1991.

Ricks, R. C.; Fry, S. A. eds. The medical basis for radiation accident preparedness II-clinical experience and follow-up since 1979. New York, NY: Elsevier; 1990.

Ricks, R. C.; Hubner, K. F.; Fry, S. A., eds. REAC/TS: Its role as a Specialty Referral Center and Training Site, Proceedings of the Conference - Medical Basis for Radiation Accident Preparedness. Elsevier/North Holland, Inc:.291-296; 1989.

Rippon, S.; Blake, E. M.; Payne, J; staff. Chernobyl: The Soviet Report. Nuclear News; October 1986.

Rosen, J. C.; Gur, D.; Pan, S. F.; Wald, N. Long-term removal of [241]Am using Ca-DTPA. Health Physics 39: 601-609; 1980.

Rothman, S.; Lichter, S. R. The nuclear energy debate: scientists, the media and the public. Public Opinion Aug/Sept: 47-52; 1982.

Sachs, L. The molecular control of blood cell develpoment. Science 238: 1374-1379; 1987.

Saenger, E. L. The nuclear physicians role in planning for and handling radiation accidents. In Freeman, L. M.; Weissman, II. W., eds. Nuclear medicine annual 1984. New York, NY; Raven Press; 1984; 1-22.

Saenger, E. L.; Andrews, G. A.; Linnemann, R. E.; Wald, N. Radiation accident preparedness - medical and managerial aspects. An Audio-Visual Self-Instruction Course. New York: Science-thru-media; 1982.

Saenger, E. L.; Keriakes, J. G.; Wald. N; Thoma, G. E. Clinical courses and dosimetry of acute hand injuries to inductrial radiographer from multicurie sealed sources. In: Hubner, K. F.; Fry, S. A., eds. The Medical Basis for Radiation Accident Preparedness. New York: Elsevier/North Holland: 327-333; 1980.

Schenk, R.; Gilberti, M. V. Four extremity radiation necrosis. Arch Surg. 100: 729-734; 1970.

Schleien, B. Preparedness and response in radiation accidents. Rockville, MD: National Center for Devices and Radiological Health, U.S. Public Health Service; 1983.

Stovie, P.; Fishcoff, B.; Lichtenstein, S. Rating the risks. Environment 21: 14-20 36-39; 1979.

Thoma, G. E.; Wald, N. The diagnosis and management of accidental radiation injury. Jour. Occup. Med. 1: 421-447; 1959.

Thomas, E. D.; Rudolph, R. H.; Fefer, A.; Storb, R.; Slichter, S. Buckner C. D. Isogenic marrow grafting in man, Exper. Hematol. 21: 16-17; 1971.

Thomas, E. D.; Storb, R,; Clift, R. A.; Fefer, A.; Johnson, F. L.; Neiman, P. E.; Lerner, K. G; Glucksberg, H.; BUchner, C. D. Bone Marrow Transplantation. N. Eng. J. Med. 292: 832-843; 843; 1975

Thomas, E. D. The role of bone marrow grafts in irradiation accidents. Int. J. Radiation Oncology Biol. Phys. 19: 1289-1290; 1990.

U.S. Nuclear Regulatory Commission. Health effects models for nuclear power plant accident consequence analysis. Low LET radiation. Part II: Scientific bases for health effects models. Albuqurque, NM: Sandia National Laboratory; NUREG/CD-4214 (SANDS85-7185), Rev. 1, Part II, 1989.

U.S. Nuclear Regulatory Commission. Reactor safety study: an assessment of accident risks in U.S. commercial nuclear power plants, Appendix VI. Springfield, VA; National Technical Information Service; WASH-1400 (NUREG-75/014); 1975.

United Nations Scientific Committee on the Effects of Atomic Radiation. 1988 Report to the General Assembly. Annex G. Early effects in man of high doses of radiation. New York, NY; United Nations; 1988; 545-647.

U.S. Nuclear Regulatory Commission Inspection and Enforcement Notice No. 86-98: Offsite Medical Services. December 2, 1988.

U.S.S.R. State Committee on the Utilization of Atomic Energy. The accident at the Chernobyl nuclear power plant and its consequences. In: IAEA Experts Meeting report, 25-29 August 1986, Part II, Annexes 2,7. Vienna: 1986: 1-36.

Van Dyk, J.; Keane, T. J.; Kan, S.; Rider, W. O.; Fryer, C. J. Radiation pneumonitis following large single dose irradiation: a reevaluation based on absolute dose to lung. Int. J. Radiat. Oncol. Biol. Physics. 7: 461-467; 1981.

Vriesendorp, H. M.; van Bekkum, D. W. Susceptibility to total body irradiation. In: Broerse, J. J.; MacVittie, T. J., eds. Response of different species to total-body irradiation. Boston, MA; Martinus Nijhoff Publishers; 1984: 43-57.

Wald, N.; Pan, S.; Thomas, E. D. Cytogenetic observations in accidental human radiation injury treated by bone marrow transplantation. 12th International Congress of the International Sociey of Hematology, Boston, MA; Abstract A-7: 4; 1986.

Wald, N.; Watson, J. A. Medical modification of human acute radiation injury. In: Proceedings of IVth International Congress of International Radiation Protection Association; 24-30 April 1977; Paris. IRPA, 1977: 1183-1190.

Wald, N. Diagnosis and therapy of radiation injuries. Bul. N.Y. Acad. Med. 59: 1129-1138; 1983

Wald, N. Hematological parameters after acute radiation injury. In: Manual on radiation hematology. Vienna: International Atomic Energy Agency, 1971; 253-264.

Wald, N. Radiation accidents and their emergency management. In: Manni, C.; Magalini, S. L., eds. Emergency and Disaster Medicine. Proceedings of the Third World Congress, Rome, 1983. New York: Springer-Verlag; 1985: 61-70.

Wald, N. Radiation Injury. In: Wyngaarden J. S.; Smith, L. H., eds. Cecil Textbook of Medicine, 16th ed. Philadelphia: Saunders; 1982: 2228-2234.

Young, R. W. Acute radiation syndrome. In: Conklin, J. J.; Walker, R. I., eds. Military Radiobiology: Orlando, FL: Academic Press; 1987: 165-190.

The definitions in this Glossary are provided as applicable to the terms and phrases used in this book. The definitions herein are not intended to be legal definitions.

• A •

α - alpha

Activity - The amount of radioactive material, either in the source or contained in the package.

Acute exposure - Exposure to radiation received in a short period of time, i.e., a one-time or single-event exposure.

Activated water - Water which has been exposed to ionizing radiation which shows an increase chemical reactivity.

ALARA - Stands for As Low As Reasonably Achievable, meaning using any activity, technique, or device to minimize exposure to ionizing radiation.

Alpha radiation/alpha particle - Two protons and two neutrons ejected as a bundle from the nucleus of a radioactive atom. The Alpha particle may be considered the nucleus of a Helium atom. An Alpha particle can capture two free electrons and become a Helium atom.

amu - Atomic mass unit

Atom - The smallest particle an element can be divided into and still be that element.

Atomic mass number - more commonly known as just atomic mass. The mass of an atom as a unit. The sum total mass of all subatomic particles in the nucleus of an atom. The atomic mass of an atom is symbolized as a number superscripted in the upper left corner of the element symbol.

Atomic mass unit (amu) - a unit for measuring the mass of atoms and subatomic particles. One amu is equal to $1/12$ of a carbon-12 atom.

Atomic number - the atomic number of an element is the sum of the protons in the nucleus. The atomic number of an atom is symbolized as a number subscripted in the lower left corner of the element symbol.

Atomic weight - atomic mass.

• B •

β - Beta radiation

Beta Radiation - An electron ejected from the nucleus of a radioactive atom. Neutron decay can generate Beta radiation.

Beta Shield - A device or substance which stops Beta radiation.

Beta Window - An area of a radiation detector or beta shield which is transparent to Beta radiation.

Bootie - As used in htis text, a protective waterproof shoe cover to aid in radiological contamination control.

• C •

Cataract - An opacity of the crystalline eye lens or of its capsule [Dorland's Illustrated Medical Dictionary, 24th ed].

CEDE - Committed Effective Dose Equivalent.

Centi - A prefix meaning $1/100$th. Abbreviated c.

CDE - Committed Dose Equivalent.

Chemical Affinity - The property of an element or compound to seek another element or compound due to chemical compatibility.

Chief Determining Organ - The main organ of system in which a radiation sickness syndrome would manifest itself.

Chronic (protracted) exposure - Exposure to radiation received over a long period of time. Also called Protracted Exposure.

Ci - curie. Defined as 3.7×10^{10} (37,000,000,000) disintegrations (rays or particles) per second).

Committed Dose Equivalent (CDE) - Specific internal dose received by an individual organ.

Committed Effective Dose Equivalent (CEDE) - The Committed Dose Equivalent multiplied by a Weighting Factor (W_f) for the subject organ. $CEDE = (W_f)(CDE)$.

Compound - Two or more elements chemically combined as a unit.

Contamination (radiological/radioactive) - Radioactive material anywhere it is not wanted.

Contents, Package - For the purposes of packaging of radioactive material, the type of material contained in the package.

Coulombic law of charges - The law which states opposite charges attract and like charges repel.

Covalent electron - An electron shared between two atoms in chemical bonding.

cps - Cycle per second.

Curie [Ci] - 37,000,000,000 disintegrations per second.

Cycle - The point-to-point distance between the crests of waves, either physical (mechanical) waves or electromagnetic waves.

• **D** •

DDE - Deep Dose Equivalent.

Decon - Decontaminate or decontamination.

Decontamination - The act of removing radioactive material.

Deep Dose Equivalent (DDE) - External whole-body exposure measured by dosimeters.

Delayed somatic effects - The effects of radiation exposure observed in the exposed individual long after exposure (chronic somatic effects).

DOE - [US] Department of Energy.

Dose - The amount of radiation absorbed by human tissues.

• E •

Electron-volt (eV) - The unit of energy used to express electromagnetic radiation energy.

Electron - A subatomic particle that orbits the nucleus of an atom. The electron possesses approximately 1/1840 atomic mass unit and a negative electrical charge exactly equal to but opposite in polarity of the proton.

Electron configuration - The arrangement of electrons in orbit about a nucleus.

Electron excitation - Absorption of energy by an electron causing the electron to jump to the next higher energy shell.

Electron shell - An energy level about the nucleus of an atom which electrons may occupy. There are five possible shells.

Electrostatic units (esu) - A unit of electrical charge to express the charge of a proton (+) or electron (-).

Element symbol - The one of two letter designator for an element, usually the first letter or first two letters of the name of the element.

Element - The form of a substance that cannot be reduced into a simpler substance without involving the nucleus.

Exposure - The amount of radiation received, or the act of being bombarded by radiation.

Extremity exposure - Exposure to ionizing radiation of the arms from the elbows to the tips of the fingers and the legs from the knees to the tips of the toes. After Jnauary 1, 1994, the elbows and knees will be part of the whole-body.

EDE - Eye Dose Equivalent.

Eye Dose Equivalent (EDE) - The actual dose the eye receives taking into account any eye protection worn by the patient.

· F ·

FEMA - Federal Emergency Management Agency.

Flea (radioactive) - A small particle of highly radioactive material as a contaminant.

Frequency - The rate or number of waves passing a point is an given period of time, usually associated with electromagnetic radiation.

Free radical - An atom or molecule with an unpaired electron and extra energy.

· G ·

γ - Gamma radiation.

Gamma radiation - Electromagnetic (energy only) radiation from the nucleus of a radioactive atom.

Genetic effects - The effects of radiation exposure which may appear in new generations.

Geotropic - As it relates to a self-reading dosimter, the property of the viewfield hairline to shift position due to the effects fo gravity.

Gray - 100 Rad.

Ground level - The normal or home energy shell of an electron.

· H ·

Half-life - The length of time needed for an amount of radioactive material to reduce to one-half the original amount.

Hertz - One cycle per second.

· I ·

Inverse square law - Double the distance from the source of radiation and the exposure rate will quarter.

Ionization - The loss of one or more electrons from a parent atom, causing an imbalance in electrical charge distribution in a previously neutral atom or molecule.

Ionizing radiation - Radiation with the capability to ionize atoms: to disassociate an electron from its parent atom.

Ion pair - A pair of particles resulting from ionization. One member of the pair possesses a negative charge, normally an electron, and the other possesses a positive charge, normally the parent atom minus one or more of its electrons.

Isotope - A form of an element that has the same number of protons in the nucleus as the original form of the element but contains a different number of neutrons.

• J •

• K •

KeV - One thousand electron volts.

Kilo - A prefix meaning 1000. Abbreviated k.

• L •

Latent period - The period of time between cessation or abating of prodromal symptoms of radiation injury and the manifest of radiation injury.

Law of charges (Coulombic) - The law which states opposite charges attract and like charges repel.

Leukemia - A fatal disease of the blood-forming rgans, cahracterized by a marked increase in the number of leukocyte precursors in the blood, together with enlargement and proliferation of the lymphoid tissues of the spleen, lymphatic glands, and bone marrow: attended with progressive anemia, internal hemorhage (as into the retina, etc.), and increasing exhaustion [Dorland's Illustrated Medical Dictionary, 24th ed].

LD - Lethal dose

$LD_{50/60}$ - The level of radiation dose which should cause death to 50% of the exposed population within 60 days.

Localized exposure - Radiation exposure received at a particular location or locations.

• M •

Mass - The relationship of weight to volume of an object or material. The greater the weight of a given object or material per given volume, the greater the mass.

Matter - Anything that occupies space and has weight.

MeV - One million (mega) electron volts.

Micro - A prefix meaning $1/1,000,000$th. Abbreviated μ.

Milli - A prefix meaning $1/1000$th. Abbreviated m.

Molecule - The smallest particle a compound can be divided into and still be that compound.

• N •

Neutral - A body or collection of bodies with an overall electrical charge of zero. The neutron is neutral. An atom with equal numbers of protons and electrons is neutral.

Neutron-to-proton ratio - The ratio of neutrons to protons in the nucleus of an atom. The neutron-to-proton ratio can be responsible for a nucleus being radioactive.

Neutron - A subatomic particle in the nucleus of an atom. The neutron has no electrical charge but possesses approximately one unit of atomic mass. The neutron can be considered a proton and electron held together by the Coulombic law of charges.

Neutron cross section - The apparent size of a target to a projectile neutron.

Neutron decay - A neutron breaking apart into its proton, electron, and energy components. Neutron decay can result in nuclear radiation.

Neutron transformation - Neutron decay.

Non-nuclear radiation - Radiation which does not come from the nucleus of a radioactive atom.

Non-stochastic effects - The effects of radiation exposure experienced by the patient when he/she recieves a specific amount of radiation dose at or above a given threshold.

NRC - [US] Nuclear Regulatory Commission.

Nuclear radiation - Radiation from the nucleus of a radioactive atom.

Nucleus - The center or core of an atom. The nucleus contains protons and neutrons, except for the nucleus of Hydrogen which contains no neutrons.

• O •

Operational check - A system of checks which determines the operability of an instrument.

Owner Controlled Area (OCA) - At a nuclear power station, the Owner Controlled Area is the area around the plant which is owned by the utility.

• P •

Package contents - For the purposes of packaging of radioactive material, the type of material contained in the package.

Particulate radiation - Material (matter) radiation ejected from the nucleus of a radioactive atom. Examples of particulate radiation are Alpha and Beta radiation.

PCs - Protective clothing.

Prompt somatic effects - The effects of radiation exposure observed in the exposed individual soon after the exposure (acute somatic effects).

Protected Area - An area at a nuclear power station which is continuously patrolled by armed security officers in which access is denied except to authorized personnel.

Protective clothing (PCs) - Garb donned to protect the wearer from radioactive material contamination.

Proton - A subatomic particle in the nucleus of an atom. The proton possesses approximately one atomic mass unit and a positive electrical charge exactly equal to but opposite in polarity of the electron.

Prodromal period - a period after initial exposure to ionizing radiation in which symptoms of radiation injury may appear clinically, typically two days or less.

Protracted exposure - Exposure to radiation received over a long period of time. Also called Chronic Exposure.

• Q •

• R •

Radiation Controlled Area (RCA) - At a nuclear power station, the Radiation Controlled Area is an area in which access is controlled for the purposes of controlling exposure to radiation and to radioactive contamination.

Radiation - Rays or particles emanating from a source, diverging as the rays or particles proceed from the source.

Radioactive contamination - Radioactive material anywhere it is not wanted.

Radioactive material - For the purposes of transportation, radioactive material is defined as any material having a specific activity of 0.002 μCi per gram of material.

Radioactivity - Nuclear instability resulting in the emanation of radiation from the radioactive source. Radioactivity is the process: radiation is the product of radioactivity. Radioactivity is not a nuclear chain reaction.

Radiological survey - A survey using instrumentation to determine the presence of ionizing radiation or radioactive contamination.

Radiosensitivity - The sensitivity of individuals or tissues to radiation exposure. Radiosensitivity is related in part to the rate of reproduction of cells: the higher the rate of reproduction of cells, the higher the radiosensitivity.

rad - Radiation Absorbed Dose.

REACT/TS - Radiation Emergency Assistance Center/Training Site.

rem - Roentgen Equivalent Man.

Roentgen - A unit of exposure in air to X- or Gamma radiation.

RSO - Radiation Safety Officer.

• S •

SDE - Shallow Dose Equivalent.

Shallow Dose Equivalent (SDE) - Replaces skin dose as a term after January 1, 1994. Involves the skin of the entire body.

Sievert - 100 rem.

Skin dose - Radiation dose to the skin of the patient.

Somatic effects - The effects of radiation exposure observed in the exposed individual.

SRD - Self-reading dosimeter.

Stay time - The length of time the individual spends in the exposure field.

Stochastic effects - The effects of radiation exposure which have no specific threshold dose.

Subatomic particles - The building blocks of an atom, specifically, the neutron, the proton, and the electron.

Syndrome Symptoms - The level of exposure (dose) at which a radiation syndrome should appear in most individuals.

• T •

TEDE - Total Effective Dose Equivalent.

Teratogenic effects - The effects of radiation exposure observed in children exposed while in utero as an embryo or fetus.

TLD - Thermoluminescent dosimeter.

TODE - Total Organ Dose Equivalent.

Total Effective Dose Equivalent (TEDE) - Summation of the Deep Dose Equivalent for the whole-body and the Committed Dose Equivalent (CDE) for each organ to determine the effective whole-body dose. $TEDE = DDE + \Sigma[(W_f)(CDE_{for\ each\ organ}]$ or $TEDE = DDE + \Sigma CEDE_{for\ each\ organ}$.

Total Organ Dose Equivalent (TODE) - Algebraically combines the Deep Dose Equivalent (DDE) and the Committed Dose Equivalent (CDE). $TODE = DDE + CDE$.

Transport Index - In the shipment of radioactive materials, the Transport Index is the total of exposure rates at one meter from each package containing radioactive materials.

• U •

• V •

Valence electron - An electron in the outermost orbit of an atom which is responsible for chemical bonding between atoms.

Viewfield - The area of view through a self-reading dosimeter.

Vital Area - At a nuclear power station, the Vital Area is the area in which equipment and structures vital to the safe operation of the plant are located.

• W •

Wavelength - The point-to-point distance between the tops of waves, usually associated with electromagnetic radiation.

Weight (atomic) - Atomic Mass.

Weighting Factor (W_f) - A value to multiply times the Committed Dose Equivalent (CDE) to determine the Committed Effective Dose Equivalent (CEDE) for a particular organ

Whole-body exposure - Exposure to ionizing radiation of the head, neck, trunk of the body, lens of the eye, arms above the elbows, and legs above the knees.. After Jnauary 1, 1994, the elbows and knees will be part of the whole-body.

• X •

X-radiation - Electromagnetic ionizing radiation generated by excitation of electrons. X-radiation is *not* nuclear radiation.

• Y •

• Z •

Numeric

• A •

• B •

• C •

• F •

• G •

• H •

• I •

• J •

• K •

• L •

• M •

• N •

• S •

• X •

• Y •

• Z •

• Symbol •